"Entangling Alliances with None"

Also by Robert H. Elias
Theodore Dreiser: Apostle of Nature

Editor:
Letters of Theodore Dreiser
Chapters of Erie, *by Charles Francis Adams, Jr.,*
and Henry Adams

"Entangling Alliances with None"

*An Essay on the Individual in
the American Twenties*

ROBERT H. ELIAS

*W · W · Norton & Company · Inc ·
New York*

FIRST EDITION

Library of Congress Cataloging in Publication Data
Elias, Robert Henry, 1914–
    "Entangling alliances with none."
    Includes bibliographical references.
    1. United States—Civilization—1918–1945.
2. United States—Intellectual life.   I. Title.
E169.1.E54   917.3'03'91   72–10403
ISBN 0-393-01097-X

1 2 3 4 5 6 7 8 9 0

For Jay, Abby, Sadie, and Eben

Contents

Je commence à croire qu'on ne peut jamais rien prouver. Ce sont des hypothèses honnêtes et qui rendent compte des faits : mais je sens si bien qu'elles viennent de moi, qu'elles sont tout simplement une manière d'unifier mes connaissances. . . . Lents, paresseux, maussades, les faits s'accommodent à la rigueur de l'ordre que je veux leur donner mais il leur reste extérieur. J'ai l'impression de faire un travail de pure imagination.

ANTOINE ROQUENTIN IN *La Nausée*

Preface

WHAT DISTINGUISHES the historical is what changes the meaning of the facts, and if one believes that history is basically an account of how the individual progressively clarifies his own meaning—his freedom or scope or limit—then a necessary concern of the historian is the concept of the individual that undergoes redefinition. That is the concept that must provide a denominator common to all, or most, of those aspects of a period—or even an era—that have significance for later times. How did the individual see himself? What did he assume he was? To what did he aspire when he used the first person singular? Did he recognize any limits? Did he regard encounters as necessary for enabling him to know what he stood for and who he was, or as simply obstacles to self-realization?

No period or place, of course, is completely isolated. What is common or shared in one decade or country usually has origins in another and consequences for still another. Yet, on occasion, a sufficient number of ideas or attitudes converge with enough force and intensity to confer on a particular fragment of space and time a mark sufficiently distinctive to invite interpretation and that search for the common denominator that will give the fragment historical significance. Such convergence occurs, I am convinced, in the American twenties.

The purpose of the present study is to suggest a way of defining the concept of the individual that gives those years their special character. The search begins with a study of children and the family and moves outward. What man was to be fathered by the child? What image of the individual—of the eventual adult—can be inferred from theories of child care, from changes in the institution of marriage, from shifting loyalties within the family? How was such an individual to be educated? Why did Progressive Education flourish—or, at least, what was it in Progressive Education that attracted disciples and generated enthusiasm? Was there a common conception?

As the individual went to work, he confronted the problem of whether he could express himself in his work, or had to work in order to express himself elsewhere. Was he wanting to be self-employed, an absentee owner, a laborer, a manager? What did his position mean to him, whatever that position was?

The problem of struggling to earn a living was obviously related to the problem of governing the country in which everyone was struggling, and the approach to governance provides another indication of what the individual was. This is particularly evident in the presidency, the office that comes closest to embodying the national will. How did the president conceive of his presidential obligations? What role did he believe was a proper one for him? Was he to be an umpire or a leader, a spokesman for a national purpose or a man elected to protect everyone else's opportunity to speak? Did he contribute to a sense of individual self-indulgence and social indifference, or did he press for self-sacrifice for subordinating the individual to the society? Did members of different political parties disagree with his assumptions, or did they, even while disagreeing about legislation, share those assumptions? How did policies, domestic and foreign, reflect conceptions of individual fulfilment?

Here there is a link to assumptions about and among ethnic minorities and radicals, illustrated by attitudes toward Prohibition and Al Capone and toward social protest and the plight of Sacco and Vanzetti. Here, too, is a link to the history of black nationalism: What was Marcus

Garvey's appeal and wherein did it fail? How is that failure related to the concurrent Harlem Awakening?

The novelists and poets who became important in the twenties—represented by such writers as Sinclair Lewis, Ernest Hemingway, and T. S. Eliot, Langston Hughes, Jean Toomer, and those others who participated in the Harlem Awakening—provide further clarification of the meaning of social issues and the relation of the individual to his society. What was their conception of the good life? Was there, moreover, a radical difference in what white and black writers said? Did they agree or disagree about their art or about the social role of their art? If many of them expressed alienation, was it of the same sort? In addition, did literary developments bear a relationship to developments in the plastic arts? What, in fact, did experiments by painters with abstraction signify for the arts generally? Did the individual gain in dignity when rendered in new formal patterns, or was he somehow dehumanized?

Finally, of course, one faces the moral issue. Was the individual redefining himself in an atomistic way or in a unifying way? What were the effects of scientific skepticism, the implications of moral relativism?

It would be pretentious as well as foolish to suppose that all questions could be answered with the mere uncovering of a single concept. Yet if one undertakes to say what is historical about a period in which behaviorists, Freudians, and followers of John Dewey flourish, in which Andrew Mellon is thought to be the greatest secretary of the treasury since Alexander Hamilton, in which Calvin Coolidge is the representative president and Charles A. Lindbergh the ultimate hero, in which at the same time Sinclair Lewis, Hemingway, and Eliot establish themselves as important writers, one must find some links. To put it simply, one must find out what John B. Watson, Coolidge, and Hemingway shared.

I have been selective but I hope not entirely arbitrary in the examples I have focused on. In the attempt to demonstrate the possibilities of my approach I have favored the implicit and the diverse, and sometimes the discrete, over the explicit and the more closely related that would, I have felt, but multiply redundant instances of what I had established. It should, therefore, not be difficult for others to supply connections with what I have omitted. In the light of my comments about the arts, the meaning of urban architecture—the pigeonhole existence fostered by skyscrapers—should be clear. In the light of what I point out about the poets, especially the Harlem poets, the important developments in music—the composers' search for an indigenous style—should have a place. And in the light of what I say about specific writers and their works, other specific writers and works should be easy to incorporate: for example, Hart Crane's vain struggle with communicable coherence, Robinson Jeffers's celebration of his roan stallion, Wallace Stevens's insistence on the private eye, Willa Cather's lament for the lost Marian Forrester, James Branch Cabell's symptomatic cold-cream-jar cover, the difference between the William Faulkner of the twenties and the William Faulkner of the thirties, Eugene O'Neill's need for masks and other devices to overcome the stage realism that he found inadequate. Even the historians' and biographers' debunking of the social importance of the individual person, together with their discovery of value in such seemingly alienated individuals as Herman Melville and Henry Adams, assume a clearly relevant place.

Since I am interested in defining what is shared in the twenties, I think I do not beg the question by also neglecting what any decade contains: the seeds of the next. Likewise I leave for others the elaboration of parallels between the twenties and our own time. After reading about the changes in marital relations and the arguments about education in the earlier decade, one looks at those of the sixties and seventies with a feeling of *déjà vu*. After immersing oneself in the feeling of political withdrawal that the earlier Republicans expressed, one wonders whether nowadays an old story is simply being retold. And after scrutinizing the achievements of the surrealists and Dadaists, one wonders whether there is anything new. But apart from the fact that history cannot repeat itself, there are differences that affect the meaning of the parallels. Where there was self-satisfaction, there is dissatisfaction; where private interests were pursued, such interests are now widely called into question; where virtue was peculiarly American, what is American is often now equated with vice. To understand that—to understand what we are now about—requires once again the identification of the common denominator. I hope that I have set forth a way of proceeding.

Whatever the value of my presentation may be, it has been immeasurably enhanced by suggestions I have received from others. My teacher in philosophy at Williams College, John William Miller, whose influence his students continue to acknowledge through the years, first posed the questions that have led me to a concern with the nature of history. My colleagues in American Studies and related fields at Cornell University, ready to provide bibliographical guidance, to participate in seminars, or to comment on numerous pages of manuscript have given me encouragement and direction when I have most required them. In particular, Douglas Dowd, Paul W. Gates, Walter LaFeber, Harry Levin, Saunders Redding, Clinton Rossiter, Gordon F. Streib, and Robin M. Williams, Jr., together with my friends George P. Brockway and Edward A. Hoyt, have extended my range, saved me from inaccuracies, and compelled me in a variety of ways to sharpen my thinking and my writing. And my students on whom I have tried out my ideas term after term—most often in seminars concentrating on the 1920's—have said so many good things in discussions, asked so many difficult questions, written so many challenging papers that I really should name more than a score of them if so long a list did not seem to diminish the individual contribution of each. A few I have quoted, and acknowledged in my notes; but whether named or not, they all have put something valuable of their own into my work.

I must also mention help of a seemingly more mechanical but actually no less critical nature that I have received in preparing the book for publication. The extraordinarily skillful members of the reference department of the John M. Olin Library at Cornell have consistently enabled me to locate and consult elusive materials held elsewhere that I otherwise would have to cite secondhand with a consequent loss of authority. Margaret R. McGavran, despite her need to complete her doctoral dissertation on schedule, has laid aside her own writing in order to check my quotations and verify my sources, and done so with a commitment and devotion that most of us lavish on only our own enterprises. Anne L. Carver, with the sharpest of eyes, has contributed a final check that will, I hope (perhaps vainly), catch all the remaining instances of imperfect typing and copy reading. And the editorial experts of W. W. Norton have expended astonishing care on the innumerable details that give format a communicative function. In this connection George Brockway, by assuming responsibility as the book's chief editor, has gone beyond the early role of critical friend to combine his invaluable understanding of authorial intent with his publisher's acute awareness of readers' responses, and thereby led me to provide clarity and force in passages that were most in want.

Finally, I cannot simply allude in the conventional fashion to the moral support I have had from my wife. For at every stage, with every draft, she has also been obliged to provide the response of the ultimate critical reader.

"Entangling Alliances with None"

Chapter One

The Individual and His Family

The Child is father of the Man . . .

WILLIAM WORDSWORTH

WHEN JOHN B. WATSON, behaviorism's foremost exponent, published his *Psychological Care of Infant and Child* in 1928, he dedicated it to "the first Mother Who Brings Up a Happy Child." His dedication was not cynical or ironic, not sardonic or even wistful. Rather, it embodied hope, confidence, and in addition to the optimistic expectations of the behaviorists, a conception of individuality and freedom shared to a significant degree by many unlike-minded contemporaries, among them Freudians and proponents of companionate marriage. Dr. L. Emmett Holt, whose *The Care and Feeding of Children* had been widely read since its first appearance in 1894, had successfully dealt with physiological care. Now, certainly, was the time to deal with a matter of even greater importance and urgency: psychological care. A child's health impaired by a bad diet or illness could be restored with a few days' proper treatment, but "once a child's character has been spoiled by bad handling, which can be done in a few days, who can say that the damage is ever repaired?"[1] Watson proposed, in terms of an appealing social ideal, to help parents systematically prevent further damage.

Watson did not minimize the extent of the problem or the ubiquity of the danger. Everywhere he went he heard children whining, saw them clinging to maternal necks, discovered that they were afraid of the dark, and learned that they dawdled unconscionably long on the toilet. In "the majority of American homes," he could say, there was "invalidism in the making":

Here is a picture of a child over-conditioned in love. The child is alone putting his blocks together, doing something with his hands, learning how to control his environment. The mother comes in. Constructive play ceases. The child crawls its way or runs to the mother, takes hold of her, climbs into her lap, puts its arms around her neck. The mother, nothing loath, fondles her child, kisses it, hugs it. I have seen this go on for a two-hour period. If the mother who has so conditioned her child attempts to put it down, a heartbroken wail ensues. Blocks and the rest of the world have lost their pulling power. If the mother attempts to leave the room or house, a still more heartbroken cry ensues. Many mothers often sneak away from their homes the back way in order to avoid a tearful wailing parting.[2]

On another occasion, during a two-hour ride in an automobile with "two boys, aged four and two, their mother, grandmother and nurse," Watson calculated that "one of the children was kissed thirty-two times—four by his mother, eight by the nurse and twenty times by the grandmother."[3] It was precisely such treatment of children that he called "bad handling." "Mothers just don't know," he wrote, "when they kiss their children and pick them up and rock them, caress them and jiggle them upon their knee, that they are slowly building up a human being totally unable to cope with the world it must later live in."[4]

Watson's criticism followed logically enough from behaviorism's premises. In 1912 the behaviorists had sought to transform psychology into what they conceived to be a scientific discipline. They challenged "all medieval conceptions," as Watson called them, and undertook to purge from the vocabulary of science "all subjective terms such as sensation, perception, image, desire, purpose and even thinking and emotion as they were originally defined." "Consciousness" did not exist; the introspective method provided no control; instincts and inherent traits were fictions.[5] The approach to the human organism was a simple experimental one, and only what could be seen was relevant:

> The rule, or measuring rod, which the Behaviorist puts in front of him always is: Can I describe this bit of behavior I see in terms of "stimulus and response"? By stimulus we mean any object in the general environment or any change in the physiological condition of the animal, such as the change we get when we keep an animal from sex activity, when we keep it from feeding, when we keep it from building a nest. By response we mean that system of organized activity that we see emphasized anywhere in any kind of an animal, as building a skyscraper, drawing plans, having babies, writing books, and the like.[6]

If other psychologists, such as William MacDougall, insisted that Watson's view was impractical because it would exclude "incentive," "responsibility," and "goal" from man's life and thus paralyze effort in business, law, and society generally, Watson could always reply that they misunderstood the nature of thought. "Thinking," he pointed out, "is merely talking, but talking with concealed musculature." And words themselves "are . . . the conditioned . . . substitutes for our world of objects and acts," the regulators of all behavior.[7] Whether behaviorism's interpretation was itself simply a "system of organized activity" did not concern Watson. He looked ahead to the time when, if there were a sufficient concentration of "energies and resources," "we could grow men in test tubes." "Life" was in his view "an organic machine that takes in food and lets out waste products, that can grow and form habits and repair waste. . . ."[8] Children, then, were little organic machines, or—in terms with greater metaphoric appeal—little clocks. A fourteen-year-old child, according to Watson, should be brought up to "know" himself as he knew his clock and thus become "behavioristically self-correcting —just as now the body unaided (unless too pronounced an infection sets in) heals its own wounds."[9] Parents, therefore, who rocked and hugged their children knew nothing about the care of organic machines, or even what animal psychology had taught in the wake of Pavlov's experiments:

> If you expected a dog to grow up and be useful as a watch dog, a bird dog, a fox hound, useful for anything except a lap dog, you wouldn't dare treat it the way you treat your child. When I hear a mother say "Bless its little heart" when it falls down, or stubs its toe, or suffers some other ill, I usually have to walk a block or two to let off steam.[10]

Watson could not expect the individual home to disappear at once, much as he would have liked to promote "more scientific ways of bringing up . . . finer and happier children."[11] But he could hope to persuade parents that it was possible even within the existing family structure "to create a problem-solving child."[12] He could assure them that there were no mysteries: "If you start with a healthy body, the right number of fingers and toes, eyes, and the few elementary movements that are present at birth, you do not need anything else in the way of raw material to make a man, be that man a genius, a cultured gentleman, a rowdy or a thug."[13] Watson asserted on more than one occasion that he could take any healthy infant "at random and train him to become any type of specialist I might select—doctor, lawyer, artist, merchant-chief and, yes, even beggar-man and thief, regardless of his talents, penchants, tendencies, abilities, vocations, and race of his ancestors."[14] The training would be based on the knowledge that a child at birth exhibited only two "natural" fears: a fear of loud, sharp noises and a fear of falling or lack of support. Watson had established the reality of those fears to his satisfaction by striking bars loudly beside infants' ears and eliciting screams and by jerking blankets suddenly from quiet, supine infants and again eliciting screams. A father's powerful "Don't" could thus build on the fear of noise to affect behavior, and other negative responses could similarly be "built in" to train a child to get along in a group.[15]

It is, in fact, in the image Watson projected of the individual in relation to the group that the most significant implication of his treatise lies. The image emerges from Watson's description of "a sensible way of treating children":

Treat them as though they were young adults. Dress them, bathe them with care and circumspection. Let your behavior always be objective and kindly firm. Never hug and kiss them, never let them sit in your lap. If you must, kiss them once on the forehead when they say goodnight. Shake hands with them in the morning. Give them a pat on the head if they have made an extraordinarily good job of a difficult task. Try it out. In a week's time you will find how easy it is to be perfectly objective with your child and at the same time kindly. You will be utterly ashamed of the mawkish, sentimental way you have been handling it.[16]

The critical phrase is "to be perfectly objective." Handled without sentimentality, the child rapidly becomes self-sufficient in taking care of material needs. At six to eight months, with hunger the stimulus, the child yearning for the missing bottle accepts a cup; by the time he is a year and a half, he manages the cup himself; and by the time he is three, he uses a knife and fork competently and butters his own bread. In the bathroom he becomes just as proficient: at nine months he confronts the toilet in solitude; at the age of three, if he is a boy, he succeeds in using the facility standing up; and within another six months he and his sister manage to reach the adult seat and perch on it without disaster. At twenty months he blows his own nose; at twenty-one months he brushes his own teeth. Somewhere between three and four years he can be relied on to use a flashlight to take care of his midnight toilet calls, can be entrusted with the job of bathing himself, and can be left to dress himself in every particular except, perhaps, for the tying of shoelaces. A child who is thus able is a child ready for society. "Until the child is two he belongs to the home," Watson explained. "At two he goes out under his own power to see the world. To get along in this new world he must enter it prepared."[17]

What is arresting here is that preparation consists primarily in the acceptance of routine and of objectivity. The child will encounter other children, but parents must carefully guard against friction among them. "No mother has a right to have a child who cannot give it a room to itself for the first two years of infancy," Watson declared. "I would make this a *conditio sine qua non*."[18] And no mother should permit a serious quarrel over toys between, say, brothers close in age:

> If she is a wise mother, she will have prepared herself in advance for just such a scene. When her children are so near together in age, she will have purchased identical toys for both boys. When a scene occurs she will go quietly and get the mate of the toy in question, take both the toys in her hands, show them and when crying stops offer them to the young hopefuls.[19]

As in a kennel, into which only a mischief-maker would toss but a single bone, the individual becomes accustomed to satisfying his needs and wants without frustration. In his world there are in effect no other persons, no desires conflicting with his. The child is

> a child who never cries unless actually stuck by a pin, illustratively speaking—who loses himself in work and play—who quickly learns to overcome the small difficulties in his environment without running to mother, father, nurse or other adult—who soon builds up a wealth of habits that tide him over dark and rainy days—who puts on such habits of politeness and neatness and cleanliness that adults are willing to be around him at least part of the day; a child who is willing to be around adults without fighting incessantly for notice—who eats what is set before him and "asks no questions for conscience sake"—who sleeps and rests when put to bed for sleep and rest—who puts away 2 year old habits when the third year has to be faced—who passes into adolescence so well equipped that adolescence is just a stretch of fertile years—and who finally enters manhood so bulwarked with stable work and emotional habits that no adversity can quite overwhelm him.[20]

In the world of others he does not really exist either. In Watson's own words this is "a child as free as possible of sensitivities to people and one who, almost from birth, is relatively independent of the family situation."[21] Watson might have added that this child is to become equally independent of the social situation. For in becoming adjusted to the demands of the adult world the child must not be

denied a duplicate of his brother's toy—must not be ha-
bituated to denial, defeat, and despair. Watson seems to
have envisaged a society in which each individual is absolutely autonomous and all individuals remain collectively
harmonious. No paths cross. No commitments clash. No
limits affront feelings or the will. Individual fulfilment consists in freedom from engagement, in insulation from
adversity. George Santayana succinctly defined the implications of the Watsonian dream:

> I foresee a behaviorist millenium; countless millions of walk-
> ing automatons, each armed with his radio, will cross and recross
> a universal telephone exchange, all jabbering as they have been
> trained to jabber, never interfering with one another, always
> smiling, with their glands all functioning perfectly (which *is*
> happiness) and all living to a sunny old age, when instead of
> vocal behavior before one another, or sub-vocal arithmetic at
> a desk, they will separately indulge in pedal behavior before a
> pianola, or will typewrite, at the vertiginous rate of life-long
> experts, pages and pages of short lines (which *are* poetry). Truly
> a wonderful exhibition, which for all I know might last forever.
> But alas! I was never brought up to behave, and when I *think* of
> that exhibition, my ill-regulated language-habit leads me sub-
> vocally to add these two syllables: what for?[22]

Watson was doing nothing less than warning, like the country's First Parents, against all entangling alliances.

If Watson's ideas about child care were at a later time
to seem both socially ominous and psychologically simple,
they provided, for the twenties at least, scientific guidance
where guidance had been generally wanting.[23] His words
were spread across the supplements of the Sunday papers;
his articles appeared in *Parents' Magazine, Collier's, Harper's*; he showed movies, he lectured, he conducted a cor-
respondence course, and frequently, as one scholar has
shown, "was called in to pronounce on many matters" by
magazines like *The Nation*. His major premises were even
embodied in the United States Department of Labor's
twenty-five-cent booklet *Infant and Child Care*, which, re-

search reveals, reached and still "reaches an audience greater than any other government publication."[24]

There was a substantial growth of parent education during this period. Not only had the federal government become active, but also some seventy-five major organizations were by the end of the decade conducting programs directed toward informing parents how to rear their children.[25] Watson's influence on these programs and on the literature issued was far greater than that of anyone else, including Freud, whose account of the unconscious Watson regarded as meaningless.[26] Yet, whatever the explanation for Watson's greater popularity—Freud was, perhaps, more difficult to understand and apply—the conceptions of individuality and freedom held by Freud's followers were strikingly compatible with those of the behaviorists. J. C. Flügel's *The Psycho-Analytic Study of the Family* makes clear the extent.

Flügel, senior lecturer at University College, London, and honorary secretary of the International Psycho-Analytical Association, was one who could propose an authoritative application of the Freudian view in terms that what has been called "the lay intelligentsia" could welcome.[27] The principal concern of his discussion of the child's relation to the family was to show that excessive parental influence may incapacitate children for life in the adult world. Children may be the victims of driving and dominating parents and thereby become lazy adults, unable to help themselves physically or guide themselves morally, passive, dependent, wholly wanting in "personal initiative." Or they may be the victims of enervated and indecisive parents, and thus lack precepts and examples to follow. Children may, in short, identify themselves with their parents and be very much like them; or they may react against their parents and become their opposites. Although this range of alternatives includes the possibility for children to develop into desirable adults, Flügel emphasized primarily the potential disasters.[28] The role of sexual drives and taboos, and the way infantile tendencies may prefigure adult relationships, of course mattered to Flügel as they must to any Freudian. But what is relevant in the present context is the kind of freedom and individuality that Flügel thought desirable—the nature of the disasters he wished to prevent.

For Flügel, as for Watson, organization, institutional structures (family or community), constituted potentially frustrating forces. Both Watson and Flügel posited a larger world where what is institutionalized constitutes a primarily hostile opponent, but where no overriding interest exists. Authority here is felt as something other than necessary limit. Flügel equated it with parents first and with "far-reaching and complex state organization" second, each menacing "the full development of individuality" and threatening to provoke violent, even criminal, responses.[29] When individuality's development is so conceived, one must then naturally beware of all ties that constrain or bind—not only the filial ones but all personal ones generally. Domination seems to be peculiar to parents; it comes to be associated in some degree with the effect one person may have upon another. Although behaviorists and Freudians differed in their accounts of love and self-assertion, they were linked in their insistence that the individual becomes himself in the degree to which he is unencumbered by other selves, impregnable against the assault of other personalities, secure from the press of finitude. A society of such individuals can then be no other than one in which all interests harmonize—one whose largest interest is the maintenance of a condition of universal adjustment to whatever interest already prevails: what radical challenges may occur must, in consequence, impinge on no one. Therefore, it is the parents' task to remove as early as possible the causes and occasions of disharmony. Children have to grow up to understand that they will fulfill themselves not in their encounter with physical and moral limits but in their ability to live without such encounters, or at least to feel that harsh demands made on them are not really demands at all.[30]

It is not surprising that such should have been the linking conceptions. Although they had not been explicitly formulated, they were implicitly embodied in changes that were taking place at the same time in the nature of family relations generally—especially in the United States—and in attempts to reform the marital relation in particular. Historians have repeatedly documented the effects of industrialism and urbanization on the patterns of family life and the experiences of both married and unmarried women from Middletown to Megalopolis. Everyone has read about the way the rise of industrial centers and the abandonment of the farms led to the disintegration of neighborhoods, the diminution of a sense of locality, the decline of family enterprises. Wage earners, usually men, worked far from their homes, which became simple living spaces in place of focal points for collective endeavor. The economic concerns of householders along any single street might coincide or they might not; generally, they were discrete. Communities began to lose distinctive qualities and stood as points marked on a road map. When children came home from school, they did not do so to pick up their portion of the burden of gaining a livelihood but only to recuperate sufficiently to return to their teachers next morning or, on weekends, to borrow the car and get away from home on a date. The husband abandoned the world of his affairs at 4:30 or 5:00 PM and likewise returned to refuel himself. The wife and mother, largely deserted when no preschool children remained— and this occurred earlier than it used to because families were smaller—either reconciled herself to maintaining general headquarters for the others in the family or sought to include in her day social pastimes that, now and then, might be marked by civic concern—or secured a job herself. Whatever was done, fulfilment for the individual was more likely to lie outside the family or home than within it. Each member of the family had his own circle of friends, and these circles seldom intersected. Moreover, as the range of activities outside the home and community increased, and as atomicity of purposes came to characterize family life, its organization more and more resembled a federated structure. It is little wonder that Watson could question the value of the family in terms isolated from all considerations except those related to the bringing up of children.

More significant than the patterns of family life themselves, though, are the attitudes and preoccupations that the patterns disclose. As the family's functions and the ways of fulfilling those functions changed, the lives of the individual members became increasingly autonomous. The patriarchal family developed into a more democratic one; husbands and wives participated equally in decision-making; children as they grew up expected to contribute on an equal footing to the achievement of an acceptable consensus.[31] With increased knowledge of contraception and a growing belief in scientific approaches to problems, parents by controlling family size more adequately than they had in the past could give more attention to each individual child than they could have given to more children.[32] In short, a multiplicity of interests supplanted the common interest; the welfare of each member became more important than the collective welfare. Moreover, like the mothers with a shortened span of maternal responsibility, children with fewer siblings could concern themselves more with their own immediate or future careers than with shared domestic obligations: just as they were to be freed by the behaviorists from parental overkissing and by the Freudians from parental dominance, so were they to be able as soon as possible to be freed from home to go their own way.[33] As Miriam Van Waters, referee of the Juvenile Court of Los Angeles, remarked: "We call them good citizens if they take care of themselves." In turn, children as they became adults expected their parents even when old to be as independent.[34] Numerous other students of family life, many of them contemporary, discovered in the loosening of ties and commitments a fostering of "the attitude that personal comfort is the end of life"[35] and, in addition, evidence of a general belief, not confined to the urban centers, that a family is successful in the degree to which it enables children to leave it.[36] If children had a definable function, that function was closer to one of parental self-expression than to one of communal security.[37]

No relationship better illustrates the contracted locus of loyalties than the marital one. Although many wives assumed the task of providing their husbands with a secure social position, and consequently had to devote increasing attention to clothes and appearance,[38] they generally rejected the older view that their lives and interests should be submerged in those of their husbands or children. Clothes and appearance, after all, could serve the women as well as their spouses. The development of individuality, the pursuit of personal happiness, the subordination of a sense of domestic responsibility to a search for private satisfaction characterized the attitudes of more and more wives until it was possible to assert that for both men and women the psychology of marriage had changed.[39] Anyone who recalls the era of silent films can confirm that marriage was the culmination of romantic aspiration and the guarantor of its realization—it would provide the widest scope for individual fulfilment.[40] "Modern man, especially in America," Denis de Rougemont has noted, "simply does not conceive of any other reason for marriage except romance." In Rougemont's view the logical outcome of romantic marriage must be divorce.[41]

Rougemont's logic is essentially correct. Even before the end of the nineteenth century proponents of what was called the "new hedonism" said, "Self-development is greater than self-sacrifice."[42] And throughout the Progressive Era the divorce rate rose, at least statistically (recorded data reflect only what was legally permissible, not necessarily what happened in people's lives);[43] and by the middle of the twenties the number of childless couples increased,[44] and college women were coming to shun marriage as incompatible with the maintenance of "the sense of personal worth, personal possibilities of achievement, and a conviction of the right of every human being to conditions of life in which he or she may thrive, develop his abilities and be happy," an attitude even more characteristic of the men.[45] George Jean Nathan, declaring that monogamic marriage could flourish only in the nation's drab and otherwise "uneventful" provinces,[46] described the condition in which he found the home during the decade:

> . . . the average American home is no longer a harbor and a haven but rather a mere place of debarkation. The married man, his wife and his children no longer see their home as a retreat and a safeguard from the world, but as a dressing-room in which to make up for the show on the outer stage. And even where they do not so see it, they see it as a place not of peace and rest and homely quiet but as one to be made indistinguishable from a sideshow.[47]

And the diversions could become disastrous:

> The man whose home, when his day's work is over, is—even though it be of his own making—a radio lecture bureau and jazz factory is not a man with tranquillity in his heart. A woman with a telephone constantly at her ear is a woman first and a wife and mother second. Show me an American home with a radio called upon to entertain it, with children abandoning their playing of "The Beautiful Blue Danube" on the piano to do the Black Bottom in front of the phonograph, with pictures of Pola Negri and John Gilbert above the kitchen sink, with the telephone ringing and with a Ford at the front door, and I'll show you a family that is heading rapidly for trouble.[48]

Philippe Ariès has, to be sure, seen in the increasing emphasis on individual fulfilment a strengthening rather than a weakening of the family as an institution: the family has become a value, has evolved the private home, has created conditions for treating the children equally and for fostering greater intimacy between children and parents. For Ariès the home after the nineteenth century provides the predominant moral setting for molding the emerging members of the family, the growth of neighborhood schools in preference to boarding schools testifying to the importance of making sure that children return to their parents' influence each day.[49] Yet, when that moral setting is itself one in which individual autonomy approximates an absolute good, the significant fact is less that private homes have flourished than that private purposes have pervaded them.

Of course, it is also proper to place the familial and marital relations of the twenties in a context that extends backward beyond the decade, beyond the Progressive Era or the twentieth century, beyond even the time when John Milton argued that incompatibility is valid ground for divorce. In *The Law of Civilization and Decay* Brooks Adams many years ago pointed out:

> As the pressure of economic competition intensifies with social consolidation, the family regularly disintegrates, the children rejecting the parental authority at a steadily decreasing age; until, finally, the population fuses into a compact mass, in which all individuals are equal before the law, and all are forced to compete with each other for the means of subsistence. When at length wealth has accumulated sufficiently to find vent through capitalistic methods of farming and manufacture, children lose all value, for then hiring labor is always cheaper than breeding. Thenceforward, among the more extravagant races, the family dwindles, as in ancient Rome or modern France, and marriage, having become a luxury, decreases. Moreover, the economic instinct impels parents to reduce the number of possible inheritors of their property, that its bulk may not shrink.
>
> Upon women the effects of these changed conditions is prodigious. Their whole relation to society is altered. From a religious sacrament marriage is metamorphosed into a civil contract, dissoluble, like other contracts, by mutual consent; and, as the obligations of maternity diminish, the relation of husband and wife resolves itself into a sort of business partnership, tending always to become more ephemeral. Frequent as divorce now is, it was even more so under the Antonines.[50]

But again here, instructive as it is to emphasize that families disintegrated and marriages became ephemeral at other times, what matters more for an understanding of the twenties specifically is not simply that families were in trouble again, but rather that their troubles at that particular time manifested values peculiarly congenial to the society generally.

Judge Ben B. Lindsey, having presided some twenty-seven years over the Juvenile and Family Court of Denver, both recognized those values and, in attempting to mitigate the distress that he had seen those values produce, advanced a proposal, in the air since before the turn of the century, that actually reaffirmed them: the companionate marriage. "Companionate Marriage," he explained, "is legal marriage, with legalized Birth Control, and with the right to divorce by mutual consent for childless couples, usually without payment of alimony."[51] He knew that in practice such marriages had long existed and such divorces frequently occurred; he knew, too, that in the absence of legal sanction only hypocritical collusion made them possible. He hoped to eliminate the hypocrisy by legalizing the practice. More important, he hoped that by securing formal acceptance of companionate marriages he could contribute to the salvaging of the marital institution itself. Why should couples be bound forever when they found themselves agonizingly mismatched in one way or another? Why should they consider it a disgrace if they found new partners preferable or additional partners zestful? Why should chastity be enthroned, monogamy revered, or adultery cruelly damned? Why should religious tradition produce consciousness of sin because of actions that in the modern world simply satisfied physiological or psychological needs? Was there not evidence in facts themselves to indicate "that triangular relationships in marriage make *some* persons happy, and that such relationships, when the parties mutually consent to them, have put many a marriage on a psychologically stable basis"?[52] If marriage as an institution was to be saved, it must be made to serve those who entered into it. Whatever his critics might charge, Lindsey insisted that "modern marriage is no longer to be either fixed or judged by its CEREMONY":

The marriage is to be judged by its practices and customs. The customs of marriage are determined by what the majority do. Since no one in his right senses seriously disputes that the great majority of married couples indulge in a sex relationship which definitely and intentionally avoids the begetting of more than a chosen number of children, or if they so desire, none at all, it must be conceded that, as judged by its customs, modern marriage IS companionate marriage.[53]

If marriage still retained a social function, that was subsumed by its primary function of satisfying the personal—perhaps private—needs of the two partners.

Narrowly conceived, those needs could be dismissed as merely romantic expectations of satisfying "a highly idealized desire for response,"[54] by their very nature likely to be incompatible with expectations of the long shared life that marriage should inaugurate.[55] Lindsey meant nothing so narrow, however; marriage was not to be undertaken so lightly—the whole person was involved in the intimacy he envisaged. He was not proposing "divorce the moment the flame of romantic passion begins to cool";[56] he wanted simply to acknowledge that marriage entailed a risk. He was not advocating the trial marriage; he did not want to presume failure. He was not even providing implicit support for premarital tests like those that would require an engaged couple to live under the scrutiny of the girl's mother to establish the prospective husband's domestic proficiency, or that would assure a girl of a chance to observe her beloved asleep, on the ground that "no girl ought to marry until she has seen her husband asleep and finds out whether he snores and sleeps with his mouth open."[57] His conception of personal satisfaction was more complex than any implied by simple precautions or remedies. But whether simple or complex, it was personal satisfaction and nothing larger that emerged as the modern criterion of marital success. In the words of a contemporary scholar, birth control had reduced the social significance of marriage and left it "a private matter of concern only to those persons forming an alliance."[58]

Beyond that, whether one of those forming that alliance maintained it or not was also a private matter, of concern only to him—at least, if no children had to be taken into account (and children were a limitation only because no other means for their disposal had been developed). For if there was no purpose other than personal satisfaction, there was no reason to endure its diminution or destruction. Compatibility must be the issue, satisfaction the standard. Lindsey did not discount the possibility of marital disagreements and serious quarrels. But if he agreed with Felix Adler's thesis "that wherever there is friction the conflict of impulses and desires can only be overcome by pointing to some over-arching super-eminent end, some commanding purpose which the persons concerned alike recognize,"[59] he would have had to define that purpose as finally the maintenance of a relationship without friction. In turn, each of the two members of the alliance would then have to find the marriage a success in the measure to which the other member did not gainsay him. As among the children reared by the behaviorists and the Freudians, the self was to be regarded as free when it was undominated and ultimately secure from contingency. In the writings of Watson, the Freudians, and Lindsey there is, despite alluring affirmations of individuality's social value, the pervasive implication that the realization of a true individual requires a person to be in radical ways wholly separate.

Chapter Two

The Individual and His School

*All great ideals are exposed to the danger of strangu-
lation by the very institutions and practices which they
themselves have created. In the course of time these institutions and practices tend to impose themselves as
ends instead of means, and they begin to demand a
blind half-superstitious reverence.*

BOYD H. BODE[1]

No ONE could have objected more vigorously to associating
Progressive Education with the separation of individuals
from social conflicts than those who in the twenties promoted educational experiment and reform in the primary
and secondary schools. Whether they were followers of
Herbert Spencer, Edward L. Thorndike, John Dewey, or
someone else, most of them began by seeking to relate education to "life," to make it relevant to the child's future
role in his community, to provide "early . . . training for
individual usefulness."[2] Traditional education had become
stultifying, abstract, elitist, even private; the public, who
had to support the schools with taxes, had begun to demand
something different, something more appropriate to its
various needs, and between 1852, when Massachusetts
passed the first state-wide law requiring compulsory school
attendance, and 1918, when Mississippi passed the last,
that public had made clear that it was to the schools that it
looked for satisfaction.[3] At the same time, however, since

the public will was forcing into the schools pupils with widely divergent goals and varying aptitudes,[4] the educators had
to concern themselves as much with methods and techniques
for interesting and motivating the children as with society's
larger expectations. In 1894, for example, as a consequence
of New York's first compulsory education law, all New York
City's children from ten through twelve had been required to
attend school, with conditional working papers available
to them thereafter. The law had soon been extended to include children seven through fourteen, and by 1924 children
not only had to wait until the age of fifteen to secure working
papers if they had not already graduated, but were further
required to attend continuation school until eighteen as well.
That meant, as concerned educators pointed out, that during the first quarter of the twentieth century "the compulsory school life of the New York child [was] almost
doubled" and the schools' responsibilities were made more
complicated.[5]

Necessarily, once the schools were compelled to accept
all children whose age and health alone made them eligible,
the classroom was bound to become a place of dutiful futility
for teachers whose habits were rigidly authoritarian and
whose syllabi were designed, not for groups characterized
by heterogeneity of background and multiplicity of purpose,
but for homogeneous classes of the intellectually and economically privileged. One can link the democratizing of
education in the United States to the rise of scientific thinking and the emphasis on "tested thought,"[6] to the efflores-
cence of the egalitarian spirit and its distrust of favor,
faction, and radical singularity,[7] to the growth of business
enterprise and industry's need for workers adjusted to urban
conditions, the English language, and American mores.[8] One
can, further, cite the development of courses in citizenship,
in vocational skills, and in subjects like health and hygiene
to illustrate in what ways after the Civil War the schools
were expected more and more to prepare children for self-
reliance in the workaday world and to teach what parents

either no longer could or no longer wished to teach at home.[9] But one cannot define the meaning of that democratizing until one sees that, even while the educational goal was in theory a social one, the fulfilment of their social responsibilities obliged the schools—at least the experimental ones, which were designed as models for the rest—to focus increasingly intense pedagogical attention upon the individual child and in so doing to foster a concept of the individual that implied separateness from the very conflicts that the reformers of the twenties wanted the schools to prepare the child to confront.

The arguments of the reformers constituted variations or qualifications of what Herbert Spencer had said in the late 1850's, in *Education: Intellectual, Moral, and Physical.* The function of education was, he had written, "to prepare us for complete living": it should teach one how to remain healthy, how to gain a livelihood, how to bring up children, how to develop orderly "social and political relations," and how to gratify one's "tastes and feelings"—in that descending order of importance.[10] The conquest of the forces of nature was primary; the filling of the residual spare time was secondary; and all courses of instruction, or subjects of study, were to be judged in terms of those distinctions. The study of physiology would contribute to bodily preservation. The knowledge of the sciences (at that time largely ignored in the schools) would contribute to the development of efficient methods for producing, preparing, and distributing commodities: mathematics was thus useful "for all the higher arts of construction"; chemistry, for bleaching, dyeing, and printing textiles, and for smelting ores; biology, for the improvement of agriculture.[11] Instruction in child care would contribute to additional understanding of the preservation of life;[12] even more abstract studies such as those in history and the arts would return the student to the practical world: history should be "the natural history of society," or "Descriptive Sociology," designed to yield practical understanding of "the ultimate laws to which social phenomena conform";[13] the study of painting must inevitably lead to an understanding of the laws of appearance;[14] the appreciation of poetry must culminate in respect for "those laws of nervous action which excited speech obeys."[15] Science was the foundation of the arts; it excited poetry rather than extinguished it;[16] it was superior to language "as a means of discipline" because "it cultivates judgment."[17]

The commitment to what science could assert carried with it a commitment to the methods that science employed, or to what Spencer viewed as the necessary direction of "intellectual progress": "from the concrete to the abstract."[18] For educators this meant "the substitution of principles for rules, and the necessarily co-ordinate practice of leaving abstractions untaught until the mind [had] been familiarized with the facts from which they [were] abstracted." The "most important" educational activity was then to be "the systematic culture of the powers of observation,"[19] and since the inductive method required the successful retention of what was observed and since retention was dependent upon the extent to which observations were pleasurable or interesting, the child's tastes and interests would determine what the schools must do. "Unless we are to return to an ascetic morality," Spencer had remarked, "the maintenance of youthful happiness must be considered as in itself a worthy aim. . . . [For] a pleasurable state of feeling is far more favourable to intellectual action than one of indifference or disgust."[20] In consequence, he had approved of contemporary concern for the pupils' responses:

. . . of all the changes taking place, the most significant is the growing desire to make the acquirement of knowledge pleasurable rather than painful—a desire based on the more or less distinct perception that at each age the intellectual action which a child likes is a healthful one for it; and conversely. There is a spreading opinion that the rise of an appetite for any kind of knowledge implies that the unfolding mind has become fit to assimilate it, and needs it for the purposes of growth; and that on the other hand, the disgust felt toward any kind of knowledge is a sign either that it is prematurely presented, or that it is presented in an indigestible form. Hence the efforts to make early education amusing, and all education interesting. Hence the lectures on the value of play. Hence the defence of nursery rhymes, and fairy tales. Daily we more and more conform our plans to juvenile opinion.[21]

Hence, too, his own concluding proposal: *"The subject which involves all other subjects, and therefore the subject in which the education of every one should culminate, is the Theory and Practice of Education."* [22] He had meant, of course, without begging the question, the study of what was "conformity to the methods of nature";[23] but he had not meant to advocate such study for its own sake; it, too, must have practical consequences beyond the enhancing of the school day:

Bear constantly in mind the truth that the aim of your discipline should be to produce a *self-governing* being; not to produce a being *governed by others.* Were your children fated to pass their lives as slaves, you could not too much accustom them to slavery during their childhood; but as they are by-and-by to be free men, with no one to control their daily conduct, you cannot too much accustom them to self-control while they are still under your eye. This it is which makes the system of discipline by natural consequences, so especially appropriate to the social state which we in England have now reached. . . . Now that the citizen has little to fear from any one—now that the good or evil which he experiences throughout life is mainly that which in the nature of things results from his own conduct, it is desirable that from his first years he should begin to learn, experimentally, the good or evil consequences which naturally follow this or that conduct.[24]

Thus the purpose of education was to enable children to become free adults, and the procedure was to teach subjects and adopt methods that the interpreters of nature found appropriate.[25]

Nowhere was the criterion of appropriateness more congenial than in the United States, where economic interests that sought the services of workers trained to the limit of their abilities were implicitly supported by psychologists and social theorists who argued that democratic values would be best strengthened if education were tailored to individual differences. In a broad sense the receptive attitude of American reformers was represented early by that of Liberty Hyde Bailey, who had become Cornell University's first professor of horticulture in 1888, later the College of Agriculture's dean, and who regarded country life with its closeness to earth as the foundation of the nation's physical and moral health. It was not, however, in his promotion of agriculture or development of nature-study clubs that he was significantly representative; it was in his belief that what education must do was to relate young people to their communities. Although his own interest was agriculture, and he was convinced that the rural life could best bring individuals into close touch with the Creation, his approach was in principle applicable anywhere: children must learn about the life around them whatever their community; they must leave the confinement of the traditional schoolroom to learn in the shops and the fields; they must cease to be passive and must become active; local problems must provide a focal point of the curriculum in even the primary grades. Ultimately, not only did some state laws require the introduction of agriculture into the primary schools, but also some city school systems promoted the development of school gardens in the slums.[26] The child was to be educated in terms of where he was, geographically, mentally.

It was from a point of view such as this that Abraham Flexner, as a teacher in a Louisville high school in 1890, established a separate school for boys who had failed. Relying on his own enthusiasm, cleverness, good humor, patience, and an ability to stimulate competition, he "treated these boys as individuals. . . . I let each go at his own pace."[27] It was also from this point of view that twenty-five years later he, with the encouragement of Charles W. Eliot of Harvard, formulated a plan for a model school that became the famous Lincoln School.[28] Eliot at the time was arguing for "more hand, ear, and eye work," to be provided in activities ranging from drawing, carpentry, and sewing to music, cooking, and natural science;[29] the want of an ability to use the senses, of an ability to use instruments of precision, of an ability to sing, draw, or play a musical instrument among "many highly educated American ministers, lawyers, and teachers" was lamentable.[30] The need for perfecting skills in a mechanized age was as great as training in war, hunting, and manual skills—fostered by quick observation—had been in feudal times.[31] Flexner agreed. Traditional education had concerned itself only with training "the mind." Flexner wanted pupils to develop "a firm grasp of the physical world . . . [and] of the social world."[32] He wanted them to read, not in order to learn literary history, but in order to develop interest. He argued that the study of foreign languages had no intrinsic value; but since one might travel, engage in foreign trade, study, or otherwise find some enjoyment in knowledge of another language, he favored the teaching of living languages. He wanted to overcome the effects of teaching mathematics as a mental discipline and to link it with science, industry, civics. He advocated physical education. Every subject to be taught must "[serve] a purpose that [the teacher] knows and can state."[33] Everyone must, as James Earl Russell, dean of Teachers College, was saying, be educated for something.[34]

Teachers College itself, beginning with Russell's leadership in 1897, embodied the clearest of institutional commitments to develop that sort of education, becoming the nation's leading professional school of education. Numerous names, familiar and unfamiliar, can be associated with that enterprise. The influence of none, however, either before World War I or during the decade following, was so important as that of Edward L. Thorndike in educational psychology and of John Dewey, through his disciple William Heard Kilpatrick, in educational philosophy. Together these men provided a rationale that, when applied by their followers, made the term "Progressive Education" synonymous with a singular combination of scientific methods, pluralistic values, democratic ideals, and self-defeating practices.

Thorndike, under the influence of William James at Harvard, had become interested in the laboratory study of animal "intelligence" and the way specific responses to specific stimuli could be developed through physiological bonds in the neural system. Human beings, he believed, could "learn" in analogous ways: teachers would simply have to identify mental traits or tendencies and manipulate them for desired ends.[35] Identification could be undertaken systematically; for mental traits were as distinguishable, as measurable, as weight, height, or age—only, because of the multiplicity of traits and the infinite variations among individuals, a good deal more complicated to classify. In three individuals, for example, five traits could (but need not) produce some three thousand varieties of combinations.[36] "In practice it means," Thorndike said, "that each individual must be considered by himself."[37] It also meant, in practice, that there would have to be a good deal of mental testing to determine traits and capacities. The proliferation of intelligence and aptitude tests during and after World War I cannot, of course, be attributed to Thorndike alone. Testing had been undertaken by Francis Galton and by James McKeen Cattell in the United States in the last quarter of the nineteenth century and by Alfred Binet and Théodore Simon in France in the first decade of the twentieth.[38] But Thorndike's approach and its influence contributed to a climate favorable both to such tests and, more important, to the acceptance of relative norms. For the recognition of basic differences among individuals was bound to make the application of uniform standards seem unjust. In fact, if schools were to be organized in terms of a need for relativity, they would in principle have to become tutorial centers; if they were not to become such centers, pupils would at least have to be grouped, and the teacher's methods, materials, and judgments be adjusted to the kinds of pupils he was teaching: his standards would, in short, have to be made appropriate to the group before him.[39]

Thorndike, in his promotion of the scientific calculation

of ability and in his sanctioning of the relativism it led to, recalled a good deal that Herbert Spencer had said. At the same time, although he argued that "the teacher must educate pupils by means of their own activities," he did not wish to imply "that what a pupil does of his own accord is right."[40] He even insisted that there were "right habits of thought and action."[41] But he was unable to go beyond general statements about the primacy of "practical ability" in comparison with "culture of the semi-selfish sort,"[42] and finally left it to the teacher to decide when a pupil's interests were desirable enough to constitute "right" ends and when they should simply remain means. "Good teaching decides what is to be learned by an appeal not to interest, but to the general aim of education," he explained.[43] The general aim, however, was phrased in terms that presupposed more precision than Thorndike was prepared to provide:

Education as a whole should make human beings wish each other well, should increase the sum of human energy and happiness and decrease the sum of discomfort of the human beings that are or will be, and should foster the higher, impersonal pleasures. These aims of education in general—good-will to men, useful and happy lives, and noble enjoyment—are the ultimate aims of school education in particular. Its proximate aims are to give boys and girls health in body and mind, information about the world of nature and men, worthy interests in knowledge and action, a multitude of habits of thought, feeling and behavior and ideals of efficiency, honor, duty, love and service.[44]

A teacher's determination of whether he was a good teacher had, then, to depend either on his intuition or on his observation of a class's responses. He was finally left in a position to conclude that whatever succeeded in holding his class's attention might in itself, on the pupils' level, well be a contribution to "higher, impersonal pleasures" and "worthy interests" and hence its own justification. As one student of the subject has reported, "the person to be educated [decided] in part what the proximate aims of education [were] to be."[45] Thorndike could not have agreed with such a simplification, but he could substitute for guidance nothing other than "masters, models, facts, creeds and ideals . . . impartially chosen in the light of pure reason as the best for the nation's welfare" with the hope that "the conflicting wants of [society's] members" would be harmonized by a "rational" state.[46] Whether one stressed differences or consensus, one educated for harmony, trusting that differences would not become radical and that uniformity would not be stifling. Unless there was a formula for detecting pure reason, each pupil would, necessarily, in part decide his own aims, defining what was appropriate, and if every aim was because of its appropriateness consequently acceptable—and if concomitantly no standards were imposed by others—then, indeed, educators might discover conditions as harmonious as those Santayana associated with the behavioristic millennium.[47]

John Dewey did not share Thorndike's approach to testing; he opposed "classification and quantitative comparisons" and argued for moral equality, or "aristocracy made universal," by which he did not mean "submergence of individuality in mass [or any other] ideals and creeds" but rather conditions of "unique opportunities and differential manifestation; superiority in finding a specific work to do. . . ."[48] He had begun his intellectual career as something of a Hegelian; then in the 1880's, sensitive to new ideas, he had become interested in applied psychology, and when he had read William James's *Principles of Psychology*, he had found authority for elevating objective-psychology theory above metaphysics and for abandoning absolutism in favor of experimentalism. Observing the social changes produced by American industrialism, temperamentally sympathetic to a Jeffersonian view of democracy, and aware that the schools were increasingly expected to supplant the home and the community in building character, in providing initial vocational training, and in generally preparing children for later life, he had addressed himself to the social function of education and the educational problems that needed solution. But although he wanted schools to be

embryonic communities in which children would learn
how to become members of the adult society, where he believed values would be shared, he became so concerned with
the ways of making the learning possible and the importance of preserving individuality as the value to be shared
that he concluded by strengthening those educational experiments that, like Thorndike's efforts, both greatly mag-
nified the role of the pupil in defining the proximate aims
of education and left unexamined the character of the society he was in fact tending to create.[49]

What Dewey intensely wished was that education should
enable each individual to pursue his own aims, with whatever capabilities he could be trained to use; for he was confident that all activities were equally valid, equally worthy,
and that a democratic society flourished in the extent to
which everyone could contribute something particularly
his own—in the extent, that is, to which self-expression
and social service became one. As early as 1897, in his
"pedagogic creed," Dewey had suggested not only what he
wished education to do but also the means that education
must employ to do it. He had written in part:

I Believe that

—all education proceeds by the participation of the individual
in the social consciousness of the race. This process begins
unconsciously almost at birth, and is continually shaping the
individual's powers. . . .

—the only true education comes through the stimulation of the
child's powers by the demands of the social situations in
which he finds himself. Through these demands he is stimulated to act as a member of a unity, to emerge from his original narrowness of action and feeling, and to conceive of
himself from the standpoint of the welfare of the group to
which he belongs. . . .

I Believe that

—the school is primarily a social institution. Education being
a social process, the school is simply that form of community
life in which all those agencies are concentrated that will be
most effective in bringing the child to share in the inherited

resources of the race, and to use his own powers for social ends.

—education, therefore, is a process of living and not a preparation for future living.

—the school must represent present life—life as real and vital to the child as that which he carries on in the home, in the neighborhood, or on the playground.

—that education which does not occur through forms of life, forms that are worth living for their own sake, is always a poor substitute for the genuine reality, and tends to cramp and to deaden.

—the school, as an institution, should simplify existing social life. . . .

—as such simplified social life, the school should grow gradually out of the home life. . . .

—this is a psychological necessity, because it is the only way of securing continuity in the child's growth. . . .

—it is also a social necessity because the home is the form of social life in which the child has been nurtured and in connection with which he has had his moral training. It is the business of the school to deepen and extend his sense of the values bound up in his home life. . . .

—the child should be stimulated and controlled in his work through the life of the community. . . .

—the discipline of the school should proceed from the life of the school as a whole and not directly from the teacher.[50]

The teacher should but study the child's interests to discover what the child "is ready for."[51]

Difficulties were inescapable. On the one hand, the school was to be a society in itself, not necessarily a preparation for the larger existing society. On the other hand, it was to represent and extend that other society, particularly by extending whatever values the child had found in his own home. The school was thus to be both autonomous and dependent: its life must be as "real" as the one lived outside the school (and the reality of that outside life was surely autonomous); yet it must in no way violate the moral training experienced elsewhere. The teacher must wait upon the child's interests, but he also must have a fixed objective in terms of which he could determine readiness. There was, perhaps, an assumption that all individuals if left to themselves would in the natural course of events create discipline. Yet if that was true, then it required a belief that nature was essentially social and that individuals naturally would engage in social endeavor. If, though, the teacher was expected to provide control, discipline, or direction *in*directly, then Dewey was apparently authorizing manipulation that could contradict the idea of letting education occur through "forms of life . . . worth living for their own sake." The teacher was to be an illusionist. Did one learn what one pleased, or did one expect the teacher to make one pleased with what one learned?

For Dewey, who was at the outset primarily engaged in confronting the inadequacies of traditional education and who was confident that the natural and the social would coincide, there could as yet be no contradictions. The interests of the child and the requirements of the adult society did not necessarily conflict. As Lawrence A. Cremin has stated:

[Dewey's] initial hypotheses . . . were that life itself, especially those occupations and associations that serve man's social needs, should furnish the ground experience of education; that learning can be in large measure a by-product of social activity; that the main test of learning is the ability of individuals to meet new social situations with habits of considered action; and that schooling committed to cooperative effort on the one hand and scientific methods on the other can be a beneficial influence on the course of social progress.[52]

Between 1896 and 1904, when Dewey as director and his wife as principal ran an experimental school in Chicago, Dewey put his ideas to the test and became convinced of their validity, although he recognized a need for their refinement. In general, the school program sought both to honor the nature of children and to remain a socializing institution. For the four- and five-year-olds home life was simply extended. There were conversations about food, clothing, and the house; there were opportunities to measure sugar and berries and make jelly, to build a "wholesale house" and play grocery store, where both the jelly and the ingredients for it could be sold; there were visits to orchards and farms. Fundamentally, the home life was extended in ways that would make visible the home's connection with other parts of the society—the agricultural, industrial, and intellectual—and the value of exact knowledge and clear communication. As the children grew older they constructed model farms, planted seeds and watched for results, studied inventions and the methods of scientific observation, and learned about how what they saw had come to be. They studied American history, Chicago history, European backgrounds. With interest in other times and places awakened, they developed a wish to know foreign languages and an ability to read stories about life in other societies. By the time they were thirteen they could undertake cooperative projects as well as independent work. In Dewey's words, "we see a movement away from direct personal and social interest to its indirect and remote forms."[53] Since the indirect and remote forms were those on which civilized societies depended for sustenance, the movement fostered by the school enabled the children naturally to benefit the society in whose homes they lived.

By 1915 many others were experimenting in similar ways, putting into practice, as Dewey and his daughter Evelyn reported in *Schools of Tomorrow*, "some of the theories that have been pointed to as the soundest and best ever since Plato, to be then laid politely away as precious portions of our 'intellectual heritage.' "[54] Whether the schools were following the precepts of Rousseau, of Froebel, of Pestalozzi, or of Madame Montessori, or whether they were play schools, microcosmic settlements, or small workshops designed to prepare pupils for urban occupations, what most mattered was their common assumption and their common direction. The child's natural growth consistently provided the pattern for the educational programs—one school

was even referred to as the Organic School.[55] Where conventional schools concerned themselves with adult expectations, the experimental ones concerned themselves with "the
present needs of the child; the fact that he is living a full
life each year and hour, not waiting to live in some period
defined by his elders, when school is a thing of the past."[56]
Like Rousseau, who found "sacrificing the present to the
remote and uncertain future" a "cruel" method,[57] Dewey
revered childhood and, by extension, "the needs and opportunities of growth."[58] Children when young needed to move
about, play, shift attention from one object to another;
they could not yet concentrate for long periods and work
with fine details—in fact, they were often to be prevented
from reading at too early an age[59] and, instead, to be given
an opportunity to develop their senses, as Madame Montessori had recommended,[60] and their ideals. Bad habits fixed in
daily living were to be overcome in school through the sort
of play that usually took place out of school. "Children who
play house and similar games in school, and have toys to
play with and the material to make the things they need in
their play, will," the Deweys explained, "play house at
home the way they played it in school."[61]

The educators' trust in natural development was accompanied by a trust in natural curiosity: if taken on a
nature walk, children would ask questions about the trees
and the flowers;[62] if given a chance to perform some useful
tasks, they would want to know how to do them better.[63]
Such curiosity would be awakened not by the mechanical
study of the properties of squares and rectangles, for example, but by having to use materials which made the
knowledge of such properties useful.[64] Moreover, if the
school was a country school, nature walks were appropriate; but if it was an urban school, the study of nature would
be "like one of the fine arts . . . aesthetic rather than directly
practical," and so the experimental play-school teacher in
the city took her charges through the streets to watch new
construction, the hoisting of mortar and bricks, the activity

of the brick-laden barges on the river, the transfer of coal from barge to truck, "facts . . . more closely related to them than the things of country life."[65] For the older children this appeal to personal meaning often proved rewarding enough to discredit the more authoritarian approach. The Deweys cited the experience of a geography class that could not understand the purpose or workings of the Panama Canal. The teacher, a resourceful experimentalist, then asked them to pretend that the United States was at war with Japan and that they, the class, constituted the United States Government. Immediately the pupils perceived the need for such a canal, the difficulties of overcoming the obstacle of a mountain range, the principle of locks; they made models, consulted maps, and understood all that had remained opaque in the textbook.[66] The circumstances had been made familiar; their natural curiosity had been awakened; their age had made it possible for them then to use the materials available.

Not all pupils would have been ready for such responses at that age, but the experimental teacher would have known to treat each pupil as an individual. None was ever to be forced to undertake any tasks for which he was not prepared; in the experimental schools there were no failures, no mistakes, no compulsions. Pupils were either ready or unready. They might be ready in one subject area, not ready in another. They proceeded at their own pace, free not so much to do as they pleased but to do as they pleased with what was given them.[67] Experience generated learning, and learning, even when it was devoted to subjects as conventional as arithmetic, geography, or foreign languages, was never abstract, because it was consistently offered in conjunction with experiences to which such learning would be relevant. During their formative period, the experimental schools encouraged a range of activities, but not "mere" activities: the activities had to be "directed toward some end," with "some educative content";[68] the schools did not try "to make all the child's tasks interesting to him, but to select work on the basis of the natural appeal it [made] to the child,"[69] so that the end would always carry him through the occasional drudgery of the means.[70] There was, in short, education by experience, "learning by doing,"[71] "an education in which learning and social application, ideas and practice, work and recognition of the meaning of what [was] done" would be common to all and thus strengthen the "spirit of a democracy" by helping to unite instead of tending to separate individuals with different economic and social destinations.[72]

The specific ends were perhaps traditional enough; Dewey and his contemporaries scorned neither the three R's nor the need to know geography, history, and science. The practical value had only to be stressed. But the techniques were innovative. So many children had either left school or remained to learn nothing that it had become a question of how to teach the old subjects better. And increasingly the new schools emphasized the development of techniques until these themselves became substantive ends. By the 1920's a sufficient number of other experimental schools were in existence to constitute a movement. On April 4, 1919, the Progressive Education Association was formally established, with Charles W. Eliot as honorary president, and five years later the journal *Progressive Education* was founded. Although many of the schools were in existence just before or during the war, they flourished primarily after the peace, and it was only then that they gave American education the special character associated with the term "Progressive Education."

Agnes de Lima, who spent "many years" visiting both traditional and experimental schools in the early twenties and who wrote about her findings in *The New Republic* and *The Nation*, articles finally collected in *Our Enemy the Child* (1926), distinguished three kinds of reformers: those who wanted to improve the methods of teaching the accepted body of knowledge; those who wanted to change the curriculum to make its offerings more relevant to the 1920's; and "those who view[ed] education as an organic process which changes and develops as the child himself changes and grows."[73] Yet these categories were not discrete. For all their differences in emphasis, the various reformers during the twenties shared the belief that the appeal must be made to the child himself. Whether he played store, visited a nearby construction pit, learned French instead of Latin and hygiene instead of botany, or moved gradually from the handling of blocks to the planning and construction of model cities requiring the knowledge of geometric and physical properties, the child's interests and capabilities crowded out of the educator's mind the claims made on the present by the future. The child's needs, not adult society's, must be met so long as the child remained a child. Miss Mabel R. Goodlander, who in 1916 had begun an experimental elementary class that grew into the Ethical Culture School, stated the new wisdom succinctly: "We must learn to appreciate more sympathetically each child's point of view, and we should be willing to accept his judgment in many things frankly and sincerely even when it differs from our own."[74]

Neither Miss Goodlander nor others who were engaged in the experimental enterprise felt a need to address themselves to the question of imposing limits. When and how did childhood end? Did the teacher simply trust that the demands of the outside world would provide those consequences that would teach the child his adult social role? How could that outside world itself ever be called into question? What, in fine, were to be the standards if they were not only whatever was generated by the child's point of view? The irrelevance of such questions was unwittingly implied in *Progressive Education* itself, to which Isador H. Coriat, a physician, psychiatrist, and former president of the American Psycho-Analytical Association, contributed "The Psycho-Analytic Approach to Education." "The object of all pedagogic influence is," he wrote, "to train the pupil along the lines of sublimation which produce a minimum of conflict, to permanently substitute for the ego-ideal of the individual, the group-ideal of society."[75] Although Miss Goodlander stressed the value of subordinating adult demands to the child's, and Dr. Coriat emphasized the value of adjusting the child to an ideal defined by adult consensus, both significantly tried to minimize conflict. When conflict was to be minimized, the purposes of individuals would have to be such that the occasions for conflict would also be minimized; anxieties, disappointments, frustrations, and failures would become anachronisms; and educational methods themselves would have to reflect abhorrence of conflict by shunning imposition and fixed requirements, arbitrary by definition. Indeed, as the work of numerous experimental schools makes clear, what marked the character of Progressive Education in a lasting way was precisely the notion that the individual was free to be himself insofar as no other self claimed priority.

The attractions of the experimental schools were difficult to resist, as Agnes de Lima discovered in her visits, especially when the alternatives were traditional schools. In the traditional classroom she found a teacher named Miss Perkins, who *commanded* forty-six boys, fixed them with her eye "until the last child was frozen into immobility," and gave the signal for forty-six arithmetic books to appear. The atmosphere was one of tension, strain, and uniformity.

> The teacher's voice was hard and metallic and her face lined with a multitude of little seams of nervous irritation. Police duty is hard work, when it means keeping forty-six children caged and immovable in a tiny room five hours a day, five days a week for ten months a year.

The room was small; two of the walls were filled by blackboards; on the teacher's desk three peonies drooped. The discipline was all negative. Poems, recitations, songs were repeated day after day, dully. The children, the most noticeable of whom was "thin and undersized . . . [and] misshapen," were "doomed by law to spend the sunniest hours of their lives there." At the end of the day they "burst out into the free air of the streets like so many exploding shells." In the experimental classroom the teacher was not a spinster. Her name was Mrs. Spencer, and she "was warm and human. She loved her work, she loved the children." In her room nothing drooped. There were flowering plants in the window boxes; cut-outs on the windowpanes and the closet. The motto on the wall, "Self Control," was alluded to from time to time by the teacher and class in half-humorous chorus. The children were always encouraged; their worries dissolved into smiles. When they were singled out it was for help, not for suffering. The day's lesson was lively, diverting, consisting, for example, of a "review" of Europe, Asia's coastline, Corot's greatness—"He leaves something to your imagination," a pupil explained. "Right!" Mrs. Spencer replied—followed in rapid sequence by arithmetic, writing, spelling, reading, and a drama ("The Mad Tea Party").[76] In place of "a barren waste of desks and blackboards, and materials confined to paper, pencils and books," the children in the newer classrooms "even up to the highest grades [were] surrounded with a great variety of things to do with—blocks, paints, crayons, weaving, clay, sand, lumber, boats, printing presses, typewriters, science apparatus, stage sets, sewing machines, electrical appliances, every manner of musical instrument. . . ."[77]

If there seems to have been lack of design in the new curriculum, it is because the curriculum had only to suit the children's nature and to deal with what children considered realities—not necessarily books, that is; children were to be "learning through living."[78] As Dewey's foremost disciple, William Heard Kilpatrick, wrote in 1926: "This new curriculum consists of experiences. It uses subject-matter, but it does not consist of subject-matter."[79] The effort was to put into practice what came to be known as "The Principles of Progressive Education":

1. Freedom to Develop Naturally.

    The conduct of the pupil should be governed by himself according to the social needs of his community, rather than by arbitrary laws. Full opportunity for initiative and self-expression should be provided. . . .

2. Interest, the Motive of All Work.

    Interest should be satisfied and developed through: 1) Direct and indirect contact with the world and its activities, and use of the experience thus gained. 2) Application of knowledge gained, and correlation between different subjects. 3) The consciousness of achievement.

3. The Teacher a Guide, Not a Task-Master.

    . . . Progressive teachers will encourage the use of all the senses, training the pupils in both observation and judgment; and instead of hearing recitations only, will spend most of the time teaching how to use various sources of information, including life activities as well as books. . . . [Small classes were essential for this purpose.]

4. Scientific Study of Pupil Development.

    [The focus should be on this] rather than on simply teaching subject matter.

5. Greater Attention to All that Affects the Child's Physical Development.

    [This means that light, air, ventilation, and playgrounds were necessary.] . . . make abounding health the first objective of childhood.

6. Co-operation Between School and Home to Meet the Needs of Child-Life. . . .

7. The Progressive School a Leader in Education Movements. . . .[80]

The emphasis in the practice varied according to the ages of the pupils with which the schools were experimenting. The approaches, however, coincided to a remarkable degree and reflected a basic difficulty: the teacher should have a vital role in defining direction, but should do nothing that might seriously impede a child's moving in a direction he himself had set. The need as described by one prominent educator was "to hold the balance between true standards of workmanship and personal expression by means of discipline that is positive but not inhibitory. . . . Especially since the best of the teachers in the new schools are still reacting against their own over-formal training."[81]

On the most elementary level the focus was on "the educational possibilities of children's play."[82] Caroline Pratt, whose Play School, founded in 1913, was portrayed in the Deweys' *Schools of Tomorrow* and became the City and Country School soon after, elucidated her school's approach in the mid-twenties.[83] The teacher should be like the great artist who "is an instrument that plays itself whether consciously or unconsciously"—"an artist in pedagogical composition."[84] Yet he was not to be wholly passive; play among the four-year-olds was expected to stimulate questions;[85] teachers were to "keep in mind future programs, and there is always a conscious preparation for what is to come."[86] At the same time, children were to carry out their own purposes, not the teacher's, however disguised: the school should serve the present, not the future.[87] Miss Pratt particularly valued the child's present moment.

Among classes for children a little older there was more attention to the future, but it was never formalized; children were supposed to become adult almost as a matter of painless course. In 1905 Teachers College had established the Speyer School for children of kindergarten and first-grade ages (four to six years old). There the plan had been one of subtle manipulation:

. . . choices and decisions were turned over to the children whenever possible to do so without waste of time and effort. A conscious attempt was also made to work out a technique of teaching, built upon a new conception of the teacher as a guide rather than as a dictator. The teacher was conceived of as the mature member of a social group of immature beings, in which her wider experience, wiser judgment, greater knowledge and technique were to be at the disposal of the children, when she or they felt the need of adult direction.

The interest in the experiment had been slight, but ten years later, with the creation of Horace Mann as Teachers College's "demonstration school," interest in such educational programs had increased markedly and by the mid-twenties was well established. The teachers at Horace Mann sought a "medium in which habits of self-direction and social co-operation could be established" so that the school could serve "as a laboratory of democracy."[88] Habits were inventoried; supervisors and classroom teachers strove to produce "desirable changes in thought and feeling, or in conduct"; and conduct was regarded "as a happy means of solving individual or group problems."[89] The children formulated their own rules, and usually heeded them,[90] but what constituted true solutions to problems could not be concretely stated. Did the children succeed if they heeded rules that bore no resemblance to the rules of the larger society? Was it simply a matter of majority rule or individual accommodation? Did discontented individuals have any choice other than between conforming or withdrawing? Happily, amid the activity and enthusiasm the question seems not to have been raised. For the teachers could count on their pupils' naturally finding pleasure "in imitation of grown-up activity."[91] Accordingly, they recommended for promotion those children who could work intelligently, cooperate with both spontaneous and organized groups, and assume responsibility.[92] The attitude throughout was characterized by a concern with childhood and a "reverence for the dawning mental life."[93]

The extent to which the mental life could actually dawn and could foster intellectual activity was made explicit in 1924 by Elisabeth Irwin, a psychologist who was a member of the Public Education Association, after she had experimented for six years in one of New York City's public schools (PS 64) "to create a school environment in which the child himself could feel that he belonged."[94] Although her specific concern had been to reorganize and administer a large public school in ways that would take account of "wide variation in the physical and psychological constitution of children of the same chronological age,"[95] her general approach, developed further in PS 61 in 1923, had been and continued to be to create a child's world and then accommodate that world to individual differences:

> The environment of the modern school is one in which the child functions. The setting is not framed for the potential adult but for the child, today, tomorrow and the next day. This granted, the conception of education as being of the intellect soon fades into the background. First of all a child functions physically, then emotionally, and then intellectually. In the traditional school this order is reversed and therefore the child does not function at all. He is educated in the passive voice.

To enable the child to function properly, then, the environment had to be one in which the child could gain a "feeling of power and control." Chairs should be small enough for him to move; crayons should be within reach; the room should be filled with light and decorated with gay curtains; the stories read should be free of didacticism.

> If the first few years of children's lives are devoted to self-initiated activities, to free use of their hands, their bodies, and their imaginations without much regard to what they learn or to the actual quality or finish of what they make, it automatically happens that their standard of performance goes up. Their intellectual curiosity awakes and they themselves begin to wish to be taught the technique of the work they are doing and demand the information that the traditional school is so eager to give them.[96]

In such an environment the children's peculiar interests "initiate and guide the activities within and without the school." One group of underweight children, for example, studied nutrition and bought, cooked, and ate their own lunches; another group studied "transportation in the streets and from the docks nearby"; many liked to improvise plays and discover and use each other's "talents"; one boy who had gone to a department store with his class to see the Christmas displays and had wandered by chance into the art gallery played truant the next day because of an interest in drawing and a desire to visit the gallery again. The day after that he was copying the "Holy Family," and soon his classmates were copying their favorite pictures and even sketching portraits of each other.[97]

For activities like these to be contagious, the pupils had to some degree to be carefully grouped. Miss Irwin found that at least broad categories were necessary: the bright, the normal, and the dull. The gifted studied the Indians; the normal played store; the dull—or sometimes neurotic—created a circus.[98] Yet the grouping was never viewed as limiting or arbitrary; the implication was not meant to be that there were latent standards of achievement or other norms. The function of the categories was only to enable the teachers to suit the means of education to the children and thus "individualize" them.[99] Moreover, individualization carried no danger of anarchy in Miss Irwin's mind; social sanctions were bound to operate within any group—after all, not everyone could use the typewriter at the same moment.[100] If there happened to be a child for whom the sanctions were meaningless, or ineffective, doubtless he would have been thought simply misplaced. For every child had the capacity to awaken to something and the desire to be part of some group.

Margaret Naumburg's experience in the Walden School she had founded and directed was, according to Agnes de Lima, similar to Miss Irwin's:

During 1924 and 1925, for example, the twelve years old group studied anthropology with the help of Dr. A. A. Goldenweiser of the New School for Social Research. The course developed from an initial visit to wholesale markets and observation of immigrant peoples in them. This led to a discussion of races and their cultures and various experts were invited by the children to address them on these subjects. Dr. Goldenweiser's material on the Iroquois Indians so interested them that they asked him to return and the course thus gradually developed. The stenographic notes of the sessions show an amazing intellectual acumen and range of knowledge on the part of the students. They discussed such topics as primitive cultures, taboos, superstition, religion, morality, inheritance of acquired characteristics, and toward the end of the first term outlined a text on anthropology for children, since no satisfactory one exists.[101]

With careful planning, all children could have intellectual experiences of that kind. But social experiences were more difficult to prescribe, and there continued to be discussion about the degree of emphasis that group activity and group adjustment should receive. In Helen Parkhurst's Dalton School, the classroom system with its recitations was abolished in order to eliminate the use of averages as standards.[102] In Mabel Goodlander's Ethical Culture School both the teachers and the children moved about, sitting where they pleased and talking as they wished, restrained simply by the understanding that they not annoy others: the discipline of peers limited capriciousness and selfishness.[103] In Carleton W. Washburne's Winnetka, Illinois, schools, nothing beyond the three R's was theoretically required of all children: each child would develop at his own pace, and although each would have to know that 7 plus 8 equaled 15, only a select few would ever have use for the determining of square root and only those few needed to learn that. So, according to Washburne, each child had to know essentials, have "an opportunity to express his own individuality," and "be made to realize that he [was] part of the social organism."[104] The importance of the social requirement, however, resisted definitions. Although Margaret Naumburg was aware of the need to create "positive" discipline and maintain "true standards of workmanship," she wanted in no way to inhibit "personal expression,"[105] and was deeply worried lest social responsibility be equated with "Americanization" or with the inculcation of faith in all that existed, resulting in the "extinction of individuality."[106] In fact, it was the extinction of the child that she and others during the twenties were most worried about.

Nothing makes the dominance of that feeling clearer than the titles of some of the books of the decade dedicated to Progressive Educational reform: *The Child-Centered*

School, Our Enemy the Child, Creative Youth, Shackled Youth, Fitting the School to the Child. And in no school at that time was the feeling more pervasive than in the Lincoln School, which Abraham Flexner had been encouraged by Charles W. Eliot to found and which James S. Tippett, Hughes Mearns, Harold Rugg, Ann Shumaker, and Gertrude Hartman enthusiastically described on the basis of their participation in the work of the school during the twenties. At the outset the teacher was expected to occupy a central position. "The work of the classroom, as the life of the school, does not proceed of its own momentum," the curriculum-makers stated. "The great responsibility for the success of the classroom as an integral part of the life of the school rests upon the teacher. What she does is all-important."[107] At the same time, the curriculum itself was conceived in ways that encouraged the teacher to be primarily catalytic rather than directive in what she did. Among grades and within grades units were planned to reflect the individual child's natural curiosity, and teachers had but skillfully to stimulate it. Concrete experiences were used to generate interest that would lead to work in basic skills and promote the acquisition of increasingly general knowledge and the posing of even abstract questions.

First-graders, for example, studied the farm. They visited farms and kept recollections fresh by making clay animals, dolls, shelters, trees. They cooked foods and fruits and learned some science in so doing. They read "The Singing Farmer" in "manuscript" and appropriate pages in their primer, and developed one of the three R's. They wrote down names and sent short letters to their parents and absent classmates, and learned some writing in the course of that. They went to the station to see apples being freighted, walked through a market to observe how farm produce was sold, made a map out of blocks locating farms, homes, and the city, and gained an understanding of economic, geographic, and social relationships. They put on little plays ("Corn Play," "Christmas Eve on the Farm"), wrote rhythms for plays, drew and painted, and learned at least twenty-five farm songs, and so began to express themselves in the arts.[108]

Third-graders studied boats. Many had had summer experiences with boats that could be discussed. They cut pieces of wood to resemble boats. The teacher prepared a bulletin about boats. The class went to see the *Half-Moon* and boat models. The children began to ask questions: What made boats "go"? Why were they of many different shapes? How were they used? Who used them? What kept them afloat? With such questions before them, the children studied problems of construction (industrial arts, arithmetic, science), read about early explorations and the countries from which seagoers sailed (reading, history), made maps to show routes taken by the Vikings, Phoenicians, Egyptians, and early Mediterranean peoples (geography), painted pictures of models (fine arts), and sang boatmen's songs (music). Thus they performed work that could be associated with the traditional categories, improved their manual skills, became more precise in the use of words and numbers, came to appreciate the value of writing, acquired awareness of the past and of change, and added specific information to their knowledge—all culminating in a desire to learn about other matters, such as world geography and travel, what clothing the Vikings wore, how the modern alphabet had evolved from that of the Egyptians and Phoenicians, the weight and casting of metals, and the construction of modern buildings, involving a comparison of Solomon's Temple with the Lincoln School.[109]

By the time they were in the sixth grade, the children could begin with the topic "How Man Has Made Records" and after visits to museums, libraries, and a paper factory publish a magazine, make a book out of wood, experiment with wax tablets, design linoleum blocks for Christmas cards and magazine covers, marble end sheets, and compile a bibliography. In the course of their work on the unit they wrote reports and contributed to the school magazine, acquired an understanding of the way both the fine arts and the industrial arts entered into book-making, and learned about the evolution of the book and methods of reproduction in ancient and modern cultures.[110]

During the last six years, an integrated program enabled them to study "man and his environment," the impact of technological development on culture, "ancient and modern cultures," and "living in contemporary America."[111] "The constant effort," Tippett and his colleagues noted, was "to broaden interests as well as tastes."[112] Each unit was to "be kept near to present needs, and . . . be thought worth while by the child."[113]

Those who worked in the creative arts found the emphasis on personal expression and the child's own judgments especially satisfying; for they regarded "self-expression as a means of growth" and not as something to be measured by aesthetic standards.[114] They believed in the "cultivation of the creative spirit . . . [as a] recipe for distinction":

The story of the leaders of the race is the story of those who cultivated the creative spirit in spite of the schools. . . . The masters of men have ever refused formal education, or they have revolted, or they have evaded instruction, or have cleverly turned it to their own uses. But these are the strong of will who have fought their way to the right to be free. The mass has not been strong of will. . . . The newer education is learning the uses of the mysterious forces of the spirit through which one may literally educate oneself for all the important needs of living.[115]

They viewed the adult or social presence as distracting or destructive:

An unhampered child is always self-active and creative. He is absorbed in his own interests and is therefore reluctant to receive suggestion or direction from the outside.[116]

. . . in the young child painting is play for him and he is better off with almost no teaching. The creative fantasy must be respected and allowed free play a long time before any laws of art can be brought to the child without harm. The expression of feeling or the representation of objects as they appear to the comprehension of the child are essential to the building of an inner honesty and a faith in his own powers.[117]

Not only outside suggestion but also outside conceptualization or formalization was a threat to growth. Although the encouragement of untrammeled expression had in recent times accompanied activity in the primary grades of many schools of all levels, the Lincoln staff were concerned because such expression subsided in the final school years. Hughes Mearns, who taught writing to those who were in their last five years, undertook to keep the spirit of the early years alive to the end. His interest was

in the swirl of wild and often incoherent imaginings that roared continuously in the conscious undercurrent of the mind. Impersonations of grandeur; stories, lived throughout months and never really ended; fictitious debates with authority; daydreams of power, love, and hate; inventions that defied all the laws of everything; practical plans for the next contest in the school yard; phrases of incomparable beauty and often of no meaning at all; this was the sort of mind stuff that I had specialized in.

And it was the sort of mind stuff that he wished to nourish. In the child's mind he found a reason purer than anything that existed in the adult world of "tradition, prejudice, or arbitrary authority."[118] His classroom attitude was essentially to shrug off or deprecate whatever implied outside organization. When one of the girls in a class of his asked, almost menacingly: "Are we going to have grammar?" he quickly established rapport not by declaring: *"If in my judgment this class needs grammar, this class will have grammar!"* but by gazing out the window and meditatively replying: "Grammar? I don't know . . . I never use it myself."[119] He had no sympathy with "sticklers for the rules" who did not "trust their own individual sense of appreciation." He was uninterested in "abnormalities in script, in punctuation, spelling, verse form, and particularly in grammar." The intimate and the self-revealing were what mattered—the "exquisite child quality," as he described it. *"The creative school cares not how inept and slovenly a*

*lad may be this whole term if it sees something personal
and fine taking slow possession of him."* "Children's art
at its best is always in the nature of a confession; it admits
one instantly into the privacy of personal thinking and
feeling."[120]

Mearns did, to be sure, contrive to exert some influence.
He did more than simply ration paper and pencils. To friends
who wished to know how he succeeded in eliciting from his
classes work of higher grade than they could elicit from
their classes, he revealed:

> . . . I so manage the controls that the highest approval goes
> solely to that work which bears the mark of original invention. To
> be sure, one must perform this office so adroitly as never to be sus-
> pected of controlling at all. No matter how crude the product,
> judged by the usual standards of adult perfection, the work with
> the individual touch is given the place of distinction; and there
> it is kept for all to see. Not that other contributors are neglected
> or made needlessly to feel their lack; there are many easy de-
> vices for the encouragement of those who have not yet found
> their native tones. Experience with the better brings, not con-
> tempt, as the proverb foolishly avers, but affection; and a real
> knowledge of the good will always drive out a taste for the
> inferior.

He favored, in effect, "distinguishing the good and ignoring
the conventional."[121] In so doing, however, he created—at
least in print—a sharp dichotomy between conventions and
formal discipline on the one hand and excellence on the
other. What partook of the conventional was doomed to be
"imitative" and to "obstruct . . . clear and beautiful thinking." Excellence was certain to be rooted in "untutored
speech," and "the real child" was the one rescued from
"nagging [social] pressure."[122] In fact, Mearns's tactic of
reassuring children uncertain about grammar, spelling, and
punctuation became almost a prescription for securing his
encouragement:

> When they write for me, these who are "poor in English,"
> I do not "correct" their papers. I figure that they have had enough
> of that ritual in the past, and obviously it has not led to grace.

Instead, I look for the idea, thought, picture, feeling, argument which they are seeking to convey, and whatever it is, I try to admire it. And usually I can admire it, for, a strange thing at which I have never ceased to wonder, the "poor in English" have often the most alluring things to say. As a rule they are unconventional in their thinking, and often they have a natural gift of invention and an instinctive feeling for art values. Perhaps it is because their earliest teachers, in their proselytizing zeal for conformity, tried to kill that originality with "corrections"; and so these unique youths had learned to scuttle out of sight, thus losing all chance of training. Or it might be that this loss of training was their real gain! Blessed are the poor in English, I am often constrained to say, for they shall see with their own eyes.[123]

The contradictions did not become a problem, because circumstances kept them concealed, enabling Mearns to ignore what might have compelled him to face the most disturbing implications of his position. For the supposedly "native language" produced by the untutored minds he so cherished already consisted of a vocabulary that must have originated either in books or among adults who had themselves read books:

> I shall be coming back to you
> From seas, rivers, sunny meadows,
>   glens that hold secrets:
> I shall come back with my hands full
> Of light and flowers.
> Brooks braided in with sunbeams
> Will hang from my fingers. . . .[124]

> My grandmother
> Is like an apple:
> With all the joy
> Of the autumn of life.[125]

> Rain comes steadily down;
>   The streets are all ashine;
> A limousine glides past. . . .
>   Two high school girls
> With name-besmeared slickers
>   Are crossing the street. . . .

> My soul with soft music
> Quivering;
> My heart groping
> In the twilight—
> Unquiet.[126]

Moreover, Mearns himself observed, "Reading . . . is one of the important foods of the creative life. . . . creative youth is well-read youth. . . . Nearly all the high-school poets are great readers."[127] Inasmuch as the pupils in the Lincoln School came from homes that were "above the average" and had enjoyed "cultural contacts" that could be called "broad,"[128] Mearns did not in practice have to confront the limitations of his precepts. The conventions that the culturally starved might have considered arbitrary were simply part of the daily experience of the Lincoln School's pupils. Had they not come from an environment rich in opportunity and the kind of experience that could contribute to self-expression, self-assertion, and speculative and abstract thinking, then surely at some moment Mearns, or teachers in earlier grades, would have had to address themselves to insisting on at least those conventions necessary to even untutored communication, unless they were prepared to dispense with verbal expression entirely. This Mearns certainly did not have to do.

In principle, insistence on any particular activity for which a particular child might lack a bent was wrong. The school must fit the child; the child was the center. Any means of self-expression would be theoretically acceptable. Harold Rugg and Ann Shumaker, in *The Child-Centered School* (1928), gave currency to that notion in their contrast between traditional and experimental schools:

> [The traditionalists'] criteria of education were discipline, logical thinking, power of sustained intellectual effort, the retention of classified knowledge. They coveted better scholarship, logic, grasp of the continuity of racial development. Almost never have they had clearly in the forefront of their thought the active growth of the pupil through dynamic self-expression.
> Conversely, the proponents of freedom in education, under

the revolutionary leadership of John Dewey, have focused attention upon the continuous growth of the child, upon freedom, initiative, spontaneity, vivid self-expression.[129]

Unlike the schools that provided "systematized lessons, rigorous examinations, set practice exercises, and recitations," the child-centered schools "visualize[d] the curriculum as a continuing stream of child activities, unbroken by systematic subjects, and springing from the interests and personally felt needs of the child. . . . The aims of education increasingly centered on the development of his individuality."[130] Rugg and Shumaker might have offered the old ideals as at least valid ends, with self-expression as the best means of achieving them; but instead, they implied that self-expression without let or hindrance was the ultimate end. They posed "understanding, . . . independent thinking, . . . [and] critical judgment" as the simple alternatives to "repetition and memorization," and "the development of the power to think" as the alternative to "the storing up of facts";[131] but they could not propose any standard by which some kinds of understanding, some subjects about which to think, some matters requiring judgment might be ranked as more desirable or important than others. The child would decide. Although the authors of *The Child-Centered School* might, along with other educators, invoke the name of John Dewey, their emphasis was significantly different. As Cremin has remarked:

... whereas the Deweys [John and Evelyn in *Schools of Tomorrow*] had seen the crux of progressive education in its connection with social reformism, Rugg and Shumaker found their insight in its tie with the historic battle of the artist against the superficiality and commercialism of industrial civilization. The key to the modern creative revolution, they argued, was the triumph of self-expression, in education as well as in art; hence in creative self-expression they found the quintessential meaning of the progressive education movement.[132]

Of course, social adjustment was important: the school was to provide an "environment by which each child can learn to live with others and yet retain his personal identity."[133] Yet who would have to adjust to whom remained obscure. At best, the acceptance of the reality of others appeared to be a matter of strategy. Mearns was explicit on this point:

> My greatest fear has always been that I might stir up a power in youth that would defeat him in the only life he is able to live. . . .
>
> Most of all I feared that those youths would be accused of presumption, which is the name the adult often employs to designate the use of judgment in the young. We knew, therefore, that we must teach them some of the rigorous and unchanging customs of the world: that one must defer and keep silent in the presence of most elders; that one must learn diplomacy in expressing views of any sort that differ from the prevailing run; that college sophomores resent even the possession of common sense by freshmen. . . . It must be drilled into them that the greatest danger of strong youth is a vain sacrifice in needless martyrdom: it is almost always folly to begin a lone fight with authority or with social groups or with any established organization. Finally, they should be convinced that while it is possible for youth to be wiser at times than its elder overlords, . . . that youth is not wise who announces the fact or even hints that such might ever be.
>
> This is nothing more or less, in short, than the possession of decent public manners. . . .[134]

The public world was, then, a world to circumvent rather than a world to seek. What had begun as a movement to educate pupils in relevant subjects "for individual usefulness" was become a movement to enable children to enjoy childhood longer and more fully. Dewey supposed that one of the child's native impulses was a social one[135] and that to release the child—to free him—was to promote the welfare of a society in which each individual could occupy a satisfying and satisfactory place.[136] But Progressive Education's apostles in the twenties, when undertaking to free the child, cared more about the freeing of the impulses than about the socializing consequence; they did not take for granted all that Dewey did, and so it is no wonder that they wrote about whether curricula should reflect "the *actual activities of mankind,*[137] with the teacher laying out educational routes as engineers laid out railroads,[138] whether interest was to be aroused primarily as a *"driving force,"*[139] and whether pedagogical success was measured by the degree to which "the present child life" of the pupil was enhanced,[140] and their activities were purposeful.[141] Collectively, as their writings everywhere indicate, these educators valued hard work, disciplined thinking, and a society characterized by the tolerance of acknowledged differences; but they devoted a preponderant amount of their attention to finding ways of making the work seem less hard, thinking seem less in need of discipline's melancholy connotations, and personal relations seem less a matter of affirming the risks of offensive self-assertion than of finding the mode that would render the sense of differences inconsequential.

Harold Rugg and Ann Shumaker urged the proponents of "the theory of self-expression" not "to minimize the other, equally important, goal of education: tolerant understanding of themselves and of the outstanding characteristics of modern civilization";[142] but in enlarging on what they meant they, in the light of their own preoccupations, could simply prescribe combining a "willingness to listen" with critical judgment: a teacher would be exhibiting an ideal response if he said to a pupil: "Fred, your point is well taken, but what is your authority?"[143] No more than any of their contemporaries could they define the criteria or say when the listening should stop—or even what authority was authoritative. At worst this pluralism was deceptive, concealing conceptions of a fixed society as rigid as the traditional ones, enabling David Snedden of Teachers College to ask, as a sociologist: "But why should girls study algebra?"[144] and to warn against inducing too many to study the Greek classics because that was "luxury at the expense of taxpayers and endowments."[145] At best it was sufficiently unsettling to lead a professor of education such as Boyd H. Bode, at Ohio State, to point out: "Some aims are good and some are bad. . . . What is needed is some principle or standard for selection."[146] But insofar as a premise of the reformers was that the natural was what should be acknowledged and cultivated, and insofar as nature worked in ways that were as various as they were mysterious, no educator could become a partisan of any particular manifestation or be confident that his standard of selection had objective validity. If then he appealed to the interests and purposes of the children as ultimate, he tended to make them absolute, systematically divorced from the maintenance and perpetuation of an order within which individuals continually clashed and resolved disagreements.

Dewey himself, who was by then, as George P. Brockway once remarked, "a great leader who was misled by his followers,"[147] was unhappy about what had happened. "Progressive schools," he told the Progressive Education Association in 1928, "set store by individuality, and sometimes it seems to be thought that orderly organization of subject-matter is hostile to the needs of students in their individual character. But individuality is something developing and to be continuously attained, not something given all at once and ready-made."[148] As much as their fellow-reformers who were attempting to improve child care and marital relations, the devotees of Progressive Education regarded institutionalized structures as inherently hostile to individual freedom rather than as necessary for its continuous realization. It is in this sense that they suggested that the individual fulfilled himself in the degree to which no one impinged on his will.

Chapter Three

The Individual and His Livelihood

*The free man does what he likes in his working time
and in his spare time what is required of him.
The slave does what he is obliged to do in his working time
and what he likes to do only when he is not at work.*

ERIC GILL[1]

OUTSIDE THE home and the school, freedom, individuality, and fulfilment required disengagement from the ultimate risks of selfhood just as much as they did within the home and the school. Adults who stood on the General Motors assembly line, who worked for the local A & P, who sold life insurance policies for Equitable, who managed the steel plants in Pittsburgh—even the owners whose stake in their businesses and industries enabled them to enjoy long vacations on the beaches of Florida or France—felt free and affirmed themselves apart from those activities that gave them their living rather than in terms of them. Whatever their responsibilities for what they did, or produced, they were most themselves when they were spending the money that compensated them for what they termed their work. The laborer who screwed bolts in the Buick scarcely expressed himself in that Buick: he had no say in its design, its quality, its price—he could express himself only when he bought one. The local manager, concerned with the efficient movement of the assembly line, could scarcely care whether

it was a Buick or a Dodge that he was hired to oversee;
only efficiency was important. The owner, often an absentee one, was interested in trademark, design, and price only
insofar as they contributed to profits or gain: money was
the measure of his productive contribution. The Buick was
fundamentally nobody's car; it was the product of a coalition maintained to enable the members of the coalition to
earn money enough to be themselves after the whistle blew.
"When better automobiles are built, Buick will build them,"
advertisements once stated; but what dictated standards
was less a conception of the mechanically or aesthetically
ideal car than a calculation of what would be a more profitable one. The commitments were to the ledger. Insofar as
money must be figuratively regarded as the language of the
economy, it was as though the commitments of poets were
to words in themselves—as though they wrote villanelles
to increase their vocabulary, and what they did with the
language did not particularly matter. Ends and means had
been inverted.

The inversion can be described and accounted for in a
variety of ways, and even viewed as ancient. The confusion
of what was Caesar's with what was God's, the preoccupation with the things of this world, the depravity of the
avaricious, the flourishing of usury were not phenomena
peculiar to the twenties, the twentieth century, or even the
period following the development of the steam engine.
From the Scriptures to Richard Henry Tawney the role of
material wealth in maintaining power and in posing ethical
questions is a matter of record. Moreover, the historical
process itself seems to have linked the present to the past
with a chain that defies distinctions. The growth of national
feeling as an economic force out of the corporate feeling
associated with the fourteenth-century cities, the rapid expansion of trade and concentration of wealth during the
Renaissance, the very criticism of contemporary practices
voiced by Martin Luther during the Reformation appear to

be part of the inflexible logic attending the rise of capitalism and the strengthening of the corporate structures that capitalism demanded. In fact, the continually increasing importance of finance, the advantage of standardizing products, the need to distribute goods widely at the lowest possible cost—all those characteristics commonly associated with the consequences of the industrial revolution—constitute invitations to distinguish modern from Elizabethan times simply in terms of degree rather than of radical difference. Yet, insofar as the difference is in fact one that is deeply imbedded in the changed locus of loyalties and commitments that one finds everywhere in the economic life of the twenties, that difference is more than simply one of degree.

Portents of this change had been manifest to perceptive observers for almost a century. In 1834 Ralph Waldo Emerson had noted: "In a former age men of might were men of will; now they are men of wealth."[2] But social awareness of it was still sufficiently new in 1913 for Woodrow Wilson, with all his historical consciousness, to call attention at that time to conditions American society would have to confront:

We have come upon an age when we do not do business in the way in which we used to do business. . . . There is a sense in which in our day the individual has been submerged. In most parts of our country men work, not for themselves, not as partners in the old way in which they used to work, but generally as employees,—in a higher or lower grade,—of great corporations. . . . [Most] men are the servants of corporations.

You know what happens when you are the servant of a corporation. You have in no instance access to the men who are really determining the policy of the corporation. . . . Your individuality is swallowed up in the individuality and purpose of a great organization.[3]

. . . Many a workingman to-day never saw the body of men who are conducting the industry in which he is employed. And they never saw him. . . . The truth is, we are all caught in a great economic system which is heartless. The modern corporation is not engaged in business as an individual. When we deal with it, we deal with an impersonal element, an immaterial piece of society.[4]

What he could see was that for most men the purposes that defined their individual lives had become divorced from the way they earned their livelihood. What Emerson had referred to as might was measured by money earned rather than by products created—it expressed itself in the possession of the means of power rather than in the exercise of power for purposes beyond the acquisition of its instruments—and those without might maintained themselves without connection with the policies that affected them or that they affected. In 1919, in a cable to a special session of Congress, Wilson stated a need for a "genuine democratization of industry" and a "cooperation and partnership based upon a real community of interest and participation in control";[5] but after the war even democratization and cooperation could ordinarily only serve what Wilson implicitly deplored—the submergence of the individual in corporate anonymity. Garet Garrett, a popular writer about finance who believed that a "reckless, egoistic, experimental spirit" governed Americans and that a "passion for power" motivated business,[6] perhaps best defined the postwar condition when in 1922 he was compelled to say that business was "not conducted by men. It is conducted by corporations." And the corporation was "both a perfect instrument for the impersonal ends of business and a cave of refuge for the conscience. . . . A corporation does many things which no one of its directors would do as an individual. . . . Nobody is personally responsible."[7] Garrett did not mean, of course, that no conception of responsibility remained in the realm of the economy. Quite the contrary. He was pointing out that in the realm of the economy responsibility existed, but it existed separated from the individual—it was in no sense a function of his identity or character: in business the person was without moral meaning. It was this change in the individual's status—this violation of wholeness—that made the inversion of ends and means more than a mere matter of degree.

Actual working conditions favored the cleavage. There was often physical distance between individuals and what they did. In Middletown, for example, the Lynds found that three of the presidents of the seven largest industrial plants lived in other states and that two of those three plants were controlled by directors few of whom had ever been to Middletown.[8] The situation could be duplicated in towns and cities throughout the country. There was also structural distance. As George E. Roberts, vice-president of the National City Bank in New York, observed: "Employers and employes no longer worked shoulder to shoulder or met frequently in the course of their work."[9] There had, therefore, developed throughout industry a need for so-called "channels of authority and communication."[10] Yet, these conditions were scarcely self-created or self-perpetuating; they did not exist apart from the beliefs they embodied, any more than the decade's great and virtually unique pyramiding of holding companies and speculation in securities and real estate could occur in a vacuum.[11] If it can be said that in the twenties the last vestiges of self-help ideology were obliterated by what one scholar has alluded to as "the realities of bureaucratic life,"[12] it must also be said that those realities depended upon widespread acceptance of the value of commitment to business's impersonal ends.

Evidence of acceptance appeared in both defense and criticism of business and industry. On the surface some of the statements appeared to contradict the notion that ends were impersonal. Charles N. Fay, vice-president of the National Association of Manufacturers and a former public utility executive, wrote in 1926: ". . . history shows that the prime motive of capitalism—namely, *selfishness,*—merely reflects the conviction, *inborn in every living creature,* that *it is his natural right to keep, own and control whatever he himself has made, saved, thought out, bought or fought for. . . ."*[13] Professor Gus W. Dyer, a professional spokesman for the NAM, declared: "There is but one way to produce a man, and that is to pitch him out and give him the reins and let him make himself."[14] According to Dyer, that was the American way; for the Founding Fathers

believed that every man with one single drop of Anglo-Saxon blood in his veins was able to take care of himself, that he did not need to have somebody stand for him and they sent him out with this commission: "Go forth! Everything in this country that belongs to anybody is for you. Find your place, make your own fight, accept your own responsibility. To whine, to complain is to acknowledge defeat and confess yourself less than an American citizen."[15]

In the words of William Feather, a publishing executive, "Birth was given to the American idea the year the steam engine was invented";[16] it was Feather's opinion that the "John D. Rockefeller who gives away millions is not a hero, but the Rockefeller who made a billion dollars out of oil is a hero. The Carnegie who made steel and millions of dollars was a hero, but the Carnegie who gave medals to heroes and built libraries was just a sweet old lady."[17] Eden Phillpotts put it more simply in Nation's Business: "A man is worth the wages he can earn."[18] Yet, devoted to self-centeredness as the declarations might seem, the kind of selfishness celebrated by Fay was not incompatible with impersonality; when Nation's Business in 1925 carried an editorial entitled "Dare To Be a Babbitt!" and argued that the world would be better with more Babbitts than with more of those who jeered,[19] it demonstrated that a desire for private profit, gain, money would not individualize anyone. It would only assure that the man of might would be regarded as a man of wealth rather than of will.

It has, to be sure, long been customary to distinguish business from industry. Charles Wesley Wood, a free-lance journalist, reiterated the usual wisdom in 1927 in writing: "Industry is the application of power to the job of supplying human wants. Business is just trade."[20] But where the individual's relationship to his work was to be defined, the spokesman for industry primarily refined the arguments of businessmen without posing any fundamental challenge to assumptions. Indeed, they revealed how pervasive their commitment to business values was, the extent to which the form of industrial organization finally dictated industrial purposes. It was what Thorstein Veblen emphasized by saying that "the corporation is always a business concern, not an industrial appliance. It is a means of making money, not of making goods."[21] Although some businessmen talked of "service" as though they were public benefactors, the more thoughtful of them left no doubt that whatever service they performed was really nothing more than to extend the opportunity for private profit.[22] They talked of "a new point of view" among the "best upper class men in business" and equated it with a desire to honor the public interest;[23] they wrote about "mutual service" and about earning the trust of consumers;[24] they formulated codes of ethics and advocated a professional approach to management.[25] But, whether they spoke through Edward A. Filene, Walter S. Gifford, Owen D. Young, or Gerard Swope, they made it clear that business or industrial leadership was whatever managerial talent made it, and that managerial talent comprised primarily an ability to recognize and satisfy the claims of a range of interest groups for which management was finally the steward or trustee.[26] This, in turn, meant that management was inevitably preoccupied with the maintenance of harmonious relationships with all interest groups, with good public and employer-employee relations, with fair dealing generally, in order not to jeopardize enterprises whose ultimate end was the making of money.

Indeed, it was the making of money that the various groups necessarily shared as an interest sufficiently compelling to constitute an objective to which special claims should be subordinated. The managers, as a distinguishable category of experts, were charged to perpetuate conditions in which no interest other than profit could dominate. Concerning profit-making they knew best. Charles M. Schwab of Bethlehem Steel, even while recognizing his employees'

need to have a voice in the regulation of their working conditions, said in 1928: "I will not permit myself to be in a
position of having labor dictate to management."[27] The
implicit distinction was important. Working conditions were
not matters of fundamental policy; whatever adjustments
had to be made by management would plainly be to allevi-
ate discontent in order to enable employees to implement
policy formulated above. Yet the formulation of that policy
was based on premises that no individuals, even above, were
at liberty to modify. No one made this more obvious than
Judge Elbert H. Gary, the president of U.S. Steel, when
in his statement to the Annual Meeting of Stockholders,
April 18, 1921, he declared: ". . . any plan which seeks to
deprive the investor of the control of his property and
business is inimical to the fundamental ideas of our country
and to the public welfare. . . . It is a fair and wise conclusion that anyone claiming the right to a voice in the
management of the property of a corporation should do
so through a stockholding interest, and thus share responsibility and liability and profits with all other stockholders."[28] The right to control was limited to investors, and
investment was generally by definition intended for monetary gain.

In one sense, this right to control was an aspect of
"the right of private economic enterprise" that Carl Becker
has shown to be "one of the essential liberties associated
with the liberal-democratic revolution."[29] But the liberal-
democratic revolution had sought to free individuals to
develop their distinctive capacities and in the exercise of
their wills to distinguish themselves as persons. Insofar as
their freedom was equated with the control that stockholders
could enjoy, their development could express itself in only
quantitative terms. A man was indeed worth the wages he
could earn. Just before the outbreak of the First World War
there were few corporation heads who had ever sought to
found companies of their own; they had become managerial

leaders through training as engineers or lawyers—in fact, leadership could best be attained not through pioneering or creating but through managing organizations in ways that would produce wealth.[30] By the time the war was over, it was generally understood among executives that such wealth was the primary objective, to be used *"to give many weaker men the certainty of self support in honorable toil."*[31]

The "weaker men" themselves certainly concurred. Mass production and the assembly line did not compel workers to seek a share in actually formulating company policy. Large-scale processes simply left them feeling increasingly removed from the industries for which they worked. Their jobs, as one personnel manager told the Lynds, were "endlessly monotonous," deadening. A bench molder explained that now that he had got the hang of his tasks, "there isn't twenty-five per cent of me paying attention to the job."[32] The involvement of workers like that was so slight that they lacked pride in their product, and if they were ambitious at all, could think in terms of only more pay rather than more say. Even the unions in their attempt to improve working conditions were unable to persuade workers to involve themselves sufficiently in unions to make collective action effective.[33] No more than the average executive did the average worker regard a worker's labor as a form of investment; there wasn't twenty-five per cent of himself involved. Throughout industry the sole consideration was "revenue." A French observer, André Siegfried, struck by the absence of all other considerations, noted the consequence for the worker: "During the day the worker may only be a cog in the machine, they say; but in the evening at any rate he becomes a man once more."[34] Siegfried, like most Frenchmen, could see how much personal meaning had departed from labor in which the individual artisan no longer had any role—in which processes could as in Middletown sometimes be completed "without the intervention of the human hand."[35] For the American worker devoted no thought at all to the finished product.[36] His distance from the product, however, was similar to the executive's. In 1933, testifying before a United States Senate Committee, Charles Schwab stated that during the prosperous years of the preceding decade "I was not engaged in making steel. I was making money!"[37] It was to that he had been devoting more than 75 per cent of his attention.

John D. Rockefeller, Jr., both during and after the war, and especially as a consequence of the Colorado Fuel and Iron Company's Ludlow Massacre, spoke of the desirability of bridging distances, ending clashes between capital and labor, and providing common ground for a partnership of all interests. He deplored the joylessness of labor and its "sense of isolation and detachment." With plans that were being proposed in England before him, and with advice that he had solicited from W. C. Mackenzie King, he argued for a council of representatives in industry, where labor, capital, management, and the community would each have a voice, and hoped that all would thereby accept the interests of business as their own. It was evident, however, that Rockefeller's idea was only that of welfare capitalism at its most generous. Communications would be improved; a variety of points of view would be heard; understanding would be increased; workers could hope for neat houses, green lawns, and white fences, and for better working conditions. But nowhere in his proposal did Rockefeller consider what Veblen called "the instinct of workmanship" and the satisfactions it demanded. Nowhere did he distinguish between the effective use of resources as a fulfilment for individuals and the profits made from others' use of resources.[38] He appeared to be troubled primarily lest workers not be and feel well cared for. Like Myron Taylor, who believed that "no steel worker or his dependents should lack the essentials of life," he regarded the conditions of work rather than the functions of work as the central issue. And doubtless like Taylor, he must have felt that assurance of favorable conditions was more difficult for a corporation than for individuals because of "responsibilities to stockholders."[39]

Structurally, perhaps, corporations and businesses really belonged to the stockholders. To them management was theoretically responsible; to them were to be attributed the policies that all other groups implemented. If anyone wished a say in policy-making, he should own stock and take the risks of investment. Numerous stock-sharing plans were evolved for the purpose of enabling workers to acquire a stake in the welfare of their enterprise, supposedly with a share in its control. Yet the very nature of stockholding meant precisely the contrary to control. Shares were widely distributed; the small shareholder did not attend meetings, and if he had attended could have had no significant voice; if he voted, he most likely consigned his vote to the directors as his proxies, and frequently, without his attention being called to the implications, was relieved of one set of securities in exchange for those of another corporation that carried no voting privileges at all. He shared in no liability incurred by management; he did not have any part in determining how profits were distributed; at the most, he could hope for sufficient attention from salaried executives to be mailed periodic reports and illustrated brochures about the operation of the company. Moreover, even though management referred to its responsibility to stockholders, the fact remained that the salaries of executives were so high, and so independent of the dividends earned by the company's securities, that the managers in practice were responsible to no one other than to what was commonly a small group that either directly or indirectly through holding companies owned a controlling percentage of shares.[40] The ordinary stockholder was actually so detached from what his investment financed that he knew or cared even less than the worker about the product, and was so much more interested in diversifying his holdings that he could scarcely view any one company as his or any specific kind of industrial activity as representing his will. In every way he was as much an absentee as the directors who had never visited Middletown. His decision-making was, in consequence, restricted to whether or not he should sell his shares.

It was this separation from significant personal decisions and personal responsibility that deeply troubled some of the decade's more searching social critics. The most distinctive group, the Southern agrarians, were moved to propose an alternative to industrial society generally. Somewhat in the spirit of Henry Charles Carey of the preceding century, who regarded man as other than *"a mere instrument to be used by capital* to enable its owner to obtain compensation for its use,"[41] they rejected—at least for their region—"the American or prevailing way" of life, with its industrial ideal of "Progress," and advocated "a Southern way," with its agrarian ideal of the "imaginatively balanced life."[42] "The modern man has lost his sense of vocation," they stated.[43] Engaged in labor that he presumed to be evil, he searched for laborsaving machinery in order to have time for what was really good: consumption. He overproduced, he lost his job, he did not receive a just share of the wealth, he became the victim of the accelerating tempo of industrial demands; without a satisfying relationship to his labor, and with no contact with the mysteries of nature, he was left aimless in a world where religion, the arts, and traditional amenities had no place. What the Southerners hoped was that they could point out the way to recovering the modern man's lost sense and thus help him reintegrate his life.

Their thinking, published in 1930 as a collection of statements entitled *I'll Take My Stand,* was as much a clarification of the decade that was concluding as it was a program for the decade that was beginning, and in particular it was a clarification of the role of the individual in the economy during the twenties. Insofar as the saving of labor was widely viewed as "pure gain," labor itself was implicitly separated from personal fulfilment; it was "mercenary and

servile." Insofar as labor was "practiced solely for its rewards," the acceptance of the "act of labor as one of the
happy functions of human life [had] been in effect abandoned."[44] The Southerners affirmed the priority of "private
dignity and happiness" over what they regarded as industrialism's "abstract social ideal . . . the hypothetical [ma-
terial] welfare of some fabulous creature called society."[45]
One's vocation should take the form of labor that could be
pursued with "intelligence" and "leisure" and indifference
to "the volume of . . . material production."[46] As John
Crowe Ransom explained it: "The good life depends on
leisure, but leisure depends on an establishment, and the
establishment depends on a prevailing magnanimity which
scorns personal advancement at the expense of the free
activity of the mind."[47] In the view shared by Ransom
and his collaborators, "the culture of the soil is the best and
most sensitive of vocations."[48]

That did not mean that they supported agriculture in all
its forms or espoused a national back-to-the-land movement.
Agriculture could be—and often was—as industrialized as
a textile or steel mill; a national return to the land, if motivated primarily by a desire for financial gain, would be
spiritually just as brutalizing as the deadening routine of
the bench molder. In fact, the Southerners warned against
exactly such a misconception of what they believed:

A man can contemplate and explore, respect and love, an object
as substantial as a farm or a native province. But he cannot contemplate nor explore, respect nor love, a mere turnover, such as
an assemblage of "natural resources," a pile of money, a volume
of produce, a market, or a credit system. It is into precisely these
intangibles that industrialism would translate the farmer's farm.
It means the dehumanization of his life.[49]

Industrialism implied the values of the factory system, cheap
labor, the chaining of effort to the wheel of Progress,[50]
change, instability, the separation of man from his environment, the dissolution of the shared values on which all culture rested. Agrarianism implied the religious "sense of na-

ture as something mysterious and contingent," the "free and disinterested observation of nature that occurs only in leisure," the cultivation of "such practices as manners, conversation, hospitality, sympathy, family life, romantic love— in the social exchanges which reveal and develop sensibility in human affairs."[51] In industrial life man and his vocation were separated; in the life projected by the agrarians man and his vocation were unified. It was, the Southerners believed, this unity that was historically characteristic of their region. Therefore they urged, in Ransom's words, a revival of "the sectional feeling of the South to its highest pitch of excitement in defense of all the old ways that are threatened":

The attitude that needs artificial respiration is the attitude of resistance on the part of the natives to the salesmen of industrialism. It will be the fiercest and most effective if industrialism is represented to the Southern people as—what it undoubtedly is for the most part—a foreign invasion of Southern soil, which is capable of doing more devastation than was wrought when Sherman marched to the sea. . . . It will be in order to proclaim to Southerners that the carpet-baggers are again in their midst. And it will be well to seize upon and advertise certain Northern industrial communities as horrible examples of a way of life we detest—not failing to point out the human catastrophe which occurs when a Southern village or rural community becomes the cheap labor of a miserable factory system. It will be a little bit harder to impress the people with the fact that the new so-called industrial "slavery" fastens not only upon the poor, but upon the middle and better classes of society, too. To make this point it may be necessary to revive such an antiquity as the old Southern gentleman and his lady, and their scorn for the dollar-chasers.[52]

The end would be to halt the chase for the dollar, to stop living by the clock, to end the dichotomy between work and play, to free the mind and relax the temper,[53] to put the private home in the place of the public gallery as the house for the arts, to value humanistic education and personal enlightenment above professional training and applied science.[54] What they opposed was, there could be little dispute, attitudes and practices prevailing in their time.

What they proposed, on the other hand, was less indisputable. They wrote eloquently about humanism and the salvation of the individual, but could allude without embarrassment to "better classes." They portrayed the old South as populated with devotees of subsistence farming indifferent to machinery and profit, but could ignore the Southern farmer's long attempt to escape from that status, the region's deeply rooted monetary ambitions, and the plantation owners' eagerness for laborsaving and profit-making devices.[55] They celebrated the free mind, but one of their most eloquent proponents of intellectual liberation, Donald Davidson, could, after the Scopes trial, defend Fundamentalism because Fundamentalism was "at least morally serious in a day when morals are treated with levity" and because it offered "a sincere, though a narrow, solution to a major problem . . . namely, how far science . . . shall be permitted . . . to determine our philosophy of life."[56] They— or at least Ransom—could after looking from a train window speak of the Pueblo Indians as happy prototypes,[57] but neither Ransom nor the other agrarians appeared to reflect upon what Southern whites, as well as Northern whites, had done to the Indians' prototypical existence, or to recognize that if tradition and cultural unity were values, then the slave system constituted a reproach.[58] As late as 1928 Allen Tate could seriously endorse with the most minor of qualifications even ante-bellum slavery itself:

The institution of slavery was a positive good only in the sense that Calhoun had argued that it was: it had become a necessary element in a stable society. He had argued justly that only in a society of fixed classes can men be free. Only men who are socially as well as economically secure can preserve the historical sense of obligation. This historical sense of obligation implied a certain freedom to do right. In the South, between White and Black, it took the form of benevolent protection: the White man was in every sense responsible for the Black. The Black man, "free," would have been exploited.

In the North, the historical sense was atrophied, and the feeling of obligation did not exist. The White man, "free," was *beginning* to be exploited. Men whose great-grandfathers had sold the Indians to the West Indian traders and had got negroes in return, whom they sold to the Virginians, did not feel themselves to be involved in the transaction. The Northern men did not feel responsible for this procedure; lacking the historical sense, they could repudiate it in the name of morality. They had come to believe in abstract right. Where abstract right supplants obligation, interest begins to supplant loyalty. Revolution may follow. When such a revolution triumphs, society becomes a chaos of self-interest. Its freedom is the freedom to do wrong. This does not mean that all men will do the wrong thing; only that no external order exists which precludes the public exercise of wrong impulses; too much, in short, is left to the individual.[59]

Yet, despite the limitation of their vision, or perhaps indeed because of it, the Southern agrarians bore witness to the absence of dignity and meaning from the activities in which their contemporaries were engaged in order to earn a livelihood.

Paradoxically, however, what they failed to perceive at the same time was that the life they advocated would ultimately have to rest upon the life they rejected. The leisurely labor they described would require either slaves or machines; in the second quarter of the twentieth century, the choice could be only machines. Moreover, they admitted that they would not scrap industrial technology: "on the contrary, further mechanization of industrial production should be encouraged, since this would mean that progressively fewer persons would be required for its processes."[60] That, however, also meant that they were willing to maintain dignity at the expense of those still enslaved in the industrial processes. Doubtless such enslaved persons were not members of the "better classes" and even if "free" would simply be exploited. Valid as was their understanding of the implications of involvement, then, no more than Schwab or Rockefeller could they conceive of any way in which industrial or business activity might incorporate ends less impersonal than the profit-making that would enable the beneficiaries to seek their fundamental personal fulfilments elsewhere than in their work.

Perhaps the individual whose sense of vocation most fully provided the possibility of the integration that the agrarians valued was ironically one who in his ignorance of history, insensitivity to the arts, and confusion in philosophy represented almost everything that the agrarians also disliked: Henry Ford. For Ford more than for any other man in his time the product rather than profit embodied the individual will. Ford possessed a desire to transform the world about him; he envisioned his car as one that would free the farmer from isolation and contribute to the well-being of the citizenry generally. The early Model A was

> Built for business or pleasure—just as you say.
> Built also for the good of your health—to carry you "jarlessly" over any kind of half decent roads, to refresh your brain with the luxury of much "out-doorness" and your lungs with the "tonic of tonics"—the right kind of atmosphere.
> It is your say, too, when it comes to speed. You can—if you choose—loiter lingeringly through shady avenues or you can press down on the foot lever until all the scenery looks alike to you. . . .[61]

The famous Model T was "a motor car for the great multitude":

> It will be large enough for the family but small enough for the individual to run and care for. It will be constructed of the best materials, by the best men to be hired, after the simplest designs that modern engineering can devise. But it will be so low in price that no man making a good salary will be unable to own one—and enjoy with his family the blessing of hours of pleasure in God's great open spaces.[62]

Ford's car would enhance living. Ford, in addition, believed in the primacy of work: "The economic fundamental is labour. . . . The moral fundamental is man's right in his labour."[63] "The day's work . . . is the basis of our self-respect."[64] On the whole, so intimately did he associate work with creation that he could not consider defining either apart from the other. From the beginning he was committed

to the production of inexpensive automobiles rather than
to the wealth they might bring him.

Money chasing is not business. . . . It is the function of business to produce for consumption and not for money or speculation. . . . If the money feature is twisted out of its proper
perspective, then the production will be twisted to serve the
producer.[65]

He meant, of course, that the money-chasing producer would
be served in terms of gain rather than in terms of the kind
of personal expression that accompanied the launching of a
product in the public realm. His own conception of business
was different: "Business is merely work. Speculation in
things already produced—that is not business. It is just
more or less respectable graft."[66] Very early in his career
he objected when he found that a company he had helped
form "was not a vehicle for realizing my ideas but merely
a money-making concern."[67] Thereafter, "I determined absolutely that never would I join a company in which finance
came before the work or in which bankers or financiers had
a part."[68] Ford's stock, once it was all his to control, was not
available to the public; his company was kept in the family.
Bankers and stockholders were for him parasites, who contributed no services or talents and who in their appetite for
profits were devoted to truly secondary concerns.[69]

The distinction between Ford's priorities and theirs was
made clear in the course of a suit instituted against him
by the Dodge brothers late in 1916, when the Dodges still
had a financial stake in Ford's operations. Ford had decided
to cut dividends to shareholders because he wished to expand
without cutting wages. The Dodge brothers argued that such
a purpose should not be at the expense of their financial
interests. On February 7, 1919, Judge Russell C. Ostrander
delivered his opinion:

A business corporation is organized and carried on primarily
for the profit of the stockholders. The powers of the directors
are employed for that end . . . and do not extend to a change in the
end itself, to the reduction of profits or to the non-distribution

of profits among stockholders in order to devote them to other purposes.[70]

Nothing could have been more alien to Ford's way of thinking. In fact, he believed in minimum profits as a matter of necessity, if not principle:

> I hold this because it enables a large number of people to buy and enjoy the use of a car and because it gives a larger number of men employment at good wages. Those are the two aims I have in life. But I would not be counted a success ... if I could not accomplish this and at the same time make a fair amount of profit for myself and the men associated with me in the business.
> ... I do not believe that we should make such an awful profit on our cars. A reasonable profit is right, but not too much. So it has been my policy to force the price of the car down as fast as production would permit, and give the benefits to users and laborers, with resulting surprisingly enormous benefits to ourselves.[71]

In 1909–10 his cars sold for $950; by 1924 he had managed to reduce the price to $290. Producing 18,664 cars at the outset, he was producing one and a quarter million in 1920–21. Meanwhile, in 1914, he had raised the average minimum wage from $2.40 per nine-hour day to $5.00 per eight-hour day.[72] Although it was always possible to argue that Ford was trying merely to keep his employees happy enough to hold them on the job and sufficiently in pocket to enable them to buy his cars, he did not at that time, as a matter of fact, regard them as tools or as nothing more than consumers; he believed profoundly that a man's job was part of the whole man, that all aspects of one's life were interrelated:

A manual labourer must have a limit on his hours, otherwise he will wear himself out. If he intends to remain always a manual labourer, then he should forget about his work when the whistle blows, but if he intends to go forward and do anything, the whistle is only a signal to start thinking over the day's work in order to discover how it might be done better.[73]

With the increase in their minimum wage, Ford's workers felt the sense of commitment and involvement that Ford

valued. There is ample testimony that from 1914 into the
early twenties the employees felt themselves part of the
business in a way that commanded institutional loyalty.
But wages alone were not responsible for their feeling. The
handicapped found Ford an employer who would hire them;
the immigrants found him one who would teach them English; the unskilled found it possible to learn skills. Ford
himself, detesting piece work, moved his workers from one
department to another both to vary their experience and to
decrease monotony. He sponsored a housing development
for them, tried to make farming an adjunct to his factory in
order to compensate for seasonal fluctuations in his output,[74]
and generally sought to enable all to acquire some sense
of responsibility for the whole: "We make the individual
responsibility complete. The workman is absolutely responsible for his work." Duties were not always defined by the
immediate supervisor. The workers "have taken particular
sections of the work to themselves. . . . They have all made
jobs for themselves—but there are no limits to their jobs."[75]
At the time he instituted his five-dollar minimum wage, he
also launched a "prosperity-sharing plan,"[76] providing for
profit-sharing that related to work as personal investment.
Ford would scarcely have told a United States Senate Committee: "I was not engaged in making cars. I was making
money." He was his car, and in some measure that car belonged for a while also to the employees.

Had Ford been able to extend through the twenties the
spirit that during 1914–19 made of his company something
of a productive community, he might have provided the
model that the decade needed. Unhappily, the very intensity
of his commitment to personal fulfilment through the association of work and creativity impaired any ability he
might have developed to understand that the ultimate validity of that commitment required its extension beyond the
limits with which he was familiar; he had to will the personal fulfilment of all associated with him as an essential
part of the fulfilment that was his own. Yet, as his produc-

tion increased, the plant became larger, the processes moved faster, and the workers became a mass of less and less individualized laborers. Whereas before 1920 he had invited and paid for suggestions from workers about technological or operational improvements, after 1920 he abandoned the policy.[77] Not only were workers "not ready for participation in the management," leaving industry to be at best "more or less of a friendly aristocracy,"[78] but, as he said after 1928: "A great business is really too big to be human."[79]

More and more removed from the problems of administration, Ford gradually left details of implementation to others. Rules against whistling, singing, talking, sitting were enforced with stony severity.[80] Friendly aristocracy gave way to Charles Sorenson and harshness and at River Rouge to Harry Bennett and his notorious brutalities. Ford's initial purposefulness became stubbornness, and stubbornness crankiness. Executive activity was directed toward keeping labor in its place. As a self-made man, Ford had always disliked the conception of rigidity implicit in class conflict; but where once he might have been able to eliminate the rigid boundaries separating the responsibilities of the employer from those of the employee, he concluded by making those boundaries more impregnable. He and his associates fought the unions viciously but did not undertake to offer workers a managerial role as the alternative to the collective security the unions promised. As absorbed with efficiency as bankers and stockholders were with profits, Ford sacrificed the vision that had motivated his productive effort to a passion for perfecting the productive process itself, which "too big to be human" could scarcely constitute a concrete vehicle for the individual fulfilment of those engaged in it. It could even be argued that by 1930 Ford's preoccupation had become so abstract, his personal will so insulated from the risks of encounter, that in relation to his employees he was finally something of an abstraction himself.[81]

There was one noteworthy attempt to move in the direction Ford's initial logic had suggested, the direction that Wilson was at the very time describing, and that was the attempt made by the Goodyear Tire and Rubber Company in 1919 to establish what a New England engineer, Paul W. Litchfield, called an industrial republic.[82] Litchfield's model was a political one: the American republic. The republican form of government presupposed "a community of interest amongst the people" and "the absence of sharply drawn class distinctions."[83] The only safe government was based on majority rule, whose effort would be toward making that majority "as efficient as possible."[84] Developing his analogy, Litchfield noted: "Capital . . . is always the result of and has its origin in the savings of labor":[85]

. . . its logical function is to be put at the disposal of mankind to be combined with labor to make that labor more productive. In other words, capital should be put at the disposal of those who labor, for the benefit of the community, and the owners of that capital should be entitled to a fair reward for its use. It is evident that this is something entirely different from the view that humanity should loan its labor to the man who owns capital for the benefit of capital. . . .[86]

Litchfield rejected the conception of there being separate communities of interest. That conception underlay industrial disputes: where there was no single community of interest, where there was a division between capital and labor, where men sold their labor, there could be only a struggle for privileges at the cost of justice.[87] In place of a separation of interests, he proposed "industrial citizenship" for all. Labor's demand to be represented in management and to share in profits was legitimate, he felt; at the same time, the satisfaction of such demands would be possible "only when the workers are prepared to take the responsibilities and duties of safeguarding the rights of capital invested in the industry, the same as they do as citizens in protecting the Government by paying taxes."[88]

Litchfield meant, by his proposal, a good deal more than

providing workers with the fringe benefits accruing to their securing a voice in the determination of working conditions; he was contemplating a new approach to fundamental control:

> We may . . . assume that the majority of industrial citizens should select a House of Representatives with certain qualifications for membership, and a Senate with still higher qualifications for membership, and that until such time as the rights of capital can be properly safeguarded, the Executives should be the representatives of capital, with veto power over such legislation as might be unfair to the rights of capital, while provision should be made for overruling the veto of Executives in such matters as might be distinctly human rights, which take precedence. It should be in the power of the majority of all industrial citizens to insist that all who wish to remain citizens and participate in representation and the rewards of industry, should make such contribution from their wages or salaries to the industry as might seem necessary or advisable properly to safeguard the rights of capital. . . .
>
> . . . In government citizens and taxpayers are one and the same. In industry, under this form, the industrial citizens would be making the laws and the common stockholders would pay the taxes, so that both would have to be represented. The only way to make both bodies the same would be to pay off all of those who furnish capital, who are not members of the organization, and insist that all common stock once owned by members of the organization could be sold only to other members of the organization. In this way the same condition would exist as in our Federal Government. It is true that each individual would not hold the same amount of stock, any more than each citizen pays the same amount in taxes.[89]

Ultimately there would be no distinctions between owners, managers, and workers:

> If all capital used by the company is properly safeguarded as to principal and interest by the savings of the working force, and through ability to tax the working force, as in the case of our National and State Governments, the passing by a two-thirds vote over the veto would be final without reference to any other body. This would be the condition of an ideal industrial republic. This condition can justly be reached only when the working force as a whole has the ability and intent to risk its own capital as a

proper safeguard for outside capital which it uses in its business.
... In such an organization all capital, except that furnished
by the laboring force, would be put at the disposal of the laboring force for the purpose of production and the general benefit
of the community, and yet due consideration of the rights of
capital would be given.[90]

Outside capital, of course, still remained a force: if funds
were misused, no further funds would be available for the
republic. Yet the decision and responsibility were in the
hands of the various "citizens"—or their elected representatives—and whatever they did with their capital,
whether it was to alter their product's design, increase the
efficiency of distribution, or pay high dividends at Christmas, was a collective decision, freely arrived at, reflecting
the purpose and values of the individuals as responsible,
involved members of the company in which they earned
their livelihood. In fact, to enable individuals to transcend
what might, in an age of specialization, become a narrow
or wholly private conception of personal interest, the Goodyear plant even developed a means of providing workers
with an educational tour of duty abroad. From 1919 to 1934
there was no strike or serious dispute in Akron.[91]

There were other approaches to reconstructing American
industry, and other proposals for extending participation in
management to workers. John A. Ryan, the most articulate
of Catholicism's social thinkers and spokesman for their
Distributist movement, was critical of a system in which
workers were kept "mere wage-earners" seeking a "maximum of return for a minimum of service" and capitalists
regarded "profit-making" as "the basic justification of business enterprise."[92] He found injustice in the existing distribution of wealth; the process was morally defective. The
criteria he proposed for determining just distribution were
"needs, efforts and sacrifices, productivity, scarcity, and
human welfare."[93] Fundamentally, he was an advocate of
fairer rewards for activity that was essentially unrewarding.
In this respect he was supported by such critics of mass

production as Ralph Borsodi, who regarded "efficiency" as "the real disease which the factory has inflicted upon mankind":[94] for the sake of efficiency men were engaged in repetitive tasks, lived out of cans instead of on home-grown foods that would take time to produce, housed themselves in slums because they could afford no alternatives, ceased producing for the family's needs in order to earn enough on the assembly line to pay for what others produced. "The world is rapidly becoming one vast factory," he said,[95] and was transforming "mankind from a race of participators in life to a race of spectators of it."[96] The remedy that he envisaged was the socialization of production and distribution. Yet, acute as were his and Ryan's perceptions, neither considered how living and working might be integrated instead of merely balanced.

Admittedly, in the twenties society was not what one businessman could call "an ideal society made up of ideal men," in which "every man must express his personal initiative, his creative urge, solely through the job out of which he makes his bread and butter."[97] For there were millions of men and women for whom freedom and self-expression could "lie [only] at the end of [the] day or a working lifetime."[98] These individuals, therefore, needed the better treatment that Ryan, Borsodi, and other advocates of similar change sought. But whether these advocates proposed that such treatment be achieved by a redistribution of wealth, by a decentralization of manufactures, or by what Edward A. Filene called "Fordizing America," enabling "the creative spirit of the engineer . . . [to] dominate our stores, our shops, our offices, our factories, and our banks,"[99] they could not, like Litchfield, go beyond palliation to imagine work as an expression of the will; instead, like those whose activities they deplored, they could see work only as the will's frustration.

Perhaps, though, they were the more clear-eyed for that. Certainly, few persons other than artists and individuals in the professions could view themselves as sufficiently identified with what they did to find expression in their livelihood. The prompt exodus from shops and offices at the conclusion of the work day proved repeatedly the degree to which satisfaction was unrelated to the particular job. Executives, some studies have indicated, often found their "greatest satisfaction from life on the job, not off the job."[100] They either stayed late in the office or brought sheafs of manila folders home in their brief cases, and on week ends, when they played golf, they often played only with those whose business interests would enhance their own. Yet, whether the desire was the clerk's to leave the job on time or the executive's to take part of the job home, the individual's involvement with it was not as radically different as surface behavior might indicate. Very often the worker or clerk who left one job early was hurrying to a second job that night;[101] the vice-president with his homework was compensating for a day spent in meetings that were occupied with transcending personal differences. The objective in moonlighting, in retiring to the den after dinner, or in completing a foursome on Sunday was not the cultivation of a more complete or more integrated life but the improvement of financial status without special regard for the content of the job that made improvement possible. For employer and employee alike, both the job and the time off from the job lacked intrinsic value.

What Hannah Arendt has said generally of modern society in the 1950's could have been said with particular appropriateness in the 1920's: "Even . . . among the intellectuals, only solitary individuals are left who consider what they are doing in terms of work and not in terms of making a living."[102] Relaxation was job-oriented, at least for the executive, and the job was reward-oriented—and the reward was finally the money that would make consumption possible. Man had become, in Sebastian de Grazia's words, "man the spender . . . a man who spends to proclaim who he is to others."[103] The attributes of "property" that enabled property to be what A. A. Berle, Jr., has defined as "a medium for . . . reception, enjoyment, and consumption" had become separated from those attributes that once had made property conjointly "a medium for creation and production and development,"[104] and once the creative attributes became less meaningful, work ceased to be self-justifying and the individual could use what he owned only in his role as a consumer. It was another way in which the modern man had lost his sense of vocation. As David Riesman has pointed out, that loss meant not only that "people [became] almost as preoccupied with getting the 'best buys' as they once were with finding their proper 'calling' in the production economy,"[105] but also that getting along with others became more important than making a distinctive mark oneself.[106] One's personal will was to be left outside the factory or office door, not in the interest of the majority decisions that Litchfield believed in, but in the interest of reducing friction in the way that John B. Watson wished to condition children to "value."[107] Only palliation or better treatment was a realistic possibility.

Andrew W. Mellon wrote in 1924: "Any man of energy and initiative in this country can get what he wants out of life."[108] But when he wrote that, energy and initiative could be devoted primarily to devising means for assuring high returns. The salesman pushed out the creator, and, if there was personal responsibility anywhere, it was for achieving the impersonal ends of business and hence a responsibility divorced from personal fulfilment. As the Southern agrarians understood, insofar as profit-making was the dominant concern within the economy the individual simply was not "there."

The decade could have had no president more appropriate than the one who declared: "The business of America is business."[109]

Chapter Four

The Individual and His Nation

The New York Stock Exchange is an affair of the State of New York, not of the Federal Government. I don't think I have any authority to interfere with its operations.

CALVIN COOLIDGE[1]

FRANKLIN D. ROOSEVELT, on June 27, 1936, accepting the Democratic Party's nomination for a second term in the White House, proclaimed his belief in "warm-hearted" government. "Better the occasional faults of a Government that lives in a spirit of charity," he said, "than the consistent omissions of a Government frozen in the ice of its own indifference."[2] Although he was clearly beginning a political campaign by reminding his audience of what he believed distinguished his first administration from the administrations of his Republican predecessors, he was at the same time emphasizing both a difference in feeling about the role of the federal government and a difference in conception of government generally, a difference in philosophy. Political tactics dictated the accusation of indifference. Historical objectivity would have substituted the idea of disinterestedness. For what the Republican presidents believed and the electorate accepted throughout the twenties was that the president and the rest of the federal government should remain dispassionate, aloof, and neutral, even if that neutrality had in fact weighted consequences.[3] It was a fundamental principle. "The government is just a business, and can and should be run on business principles," Andrew W. Mellon wrote in 1924.[4] Like the corporation, it must be impersonal.

Between the death of William McKinley and inauguration day in 1921 the presidency had been occupied by men who wanted to use the office to strengthen the federal government and to provide national leadership. Whether it was Theodore Roosevelt or Woodrow Wilson—or even William Howard Taft—the individual president had been a man committed to asserting and extending his authority, both legal and moral, and to leaving his personal mark on public policy.[5] Warren G. Harding, however, had no such passionate commitment. "I believe in party government as distinguished from personal government, individual, dictatorial, autocratic or what not," Harding said in accepting his party's nomination.[6] He would refrain, he implied clearly, from any attempt to impose his will.[7] And he thereby not only reassured the Republican leaders in the Senate who wished to regain for the Senate the prestige they felt it had lost under Roosevelt and Wilson,[8] but also defined the kind of executive influence he and his two succesors would exert.

There is something of a paradox in Harding's having been the one to restore disinterestedness to the presidential office, for Harding the man was animated by impulses as warm-hearted as any that Franklin D. Roosevelt was to try to institutionalize a decade later. He exuded joviality and wanted to do favors for friends; he loved to play golf and poker, and could imagine no evil; he was able to free the war's political prisoners, whether they were conscientious objectors or IWW organizers, without Wilsonian qualms, and released Eugene Debs in time for him to spend Christmas 1921 as a free man.[9] He wanted to be "one of the best loved [presidents]";[10] he wanted to be the small town's good neighbor who had gone to the White House;[11] he spoke in behalf of Happiness, and many Americans found him per-

sonally appealing. Even Woodrow Wilson could say: "I
really like him." [12] But he could not translate his warm feelings into a principle of government. In fact, they constituted
a kind of compensation for the impersonality that government had necessarily to embody. For Harding the personal
was restricted to the private; he no more could conceive of
using his office to direct the government than he could conceive of the government's using its power to direct private
lives. Although he was considered one of the hardest-
working of presidents, [13] the immense possibilities of the
presidency did not fully engage his mind or will, and he did
not involve his office aggressively in the resolution of particular social issues. As he shaped it, it was in effect an
office for a privileged spectator, or at best a benevolent
mediator. The interests that clamored or competed for satisfaction were for him analogous with the branches of government that the founders had kept separate. The discrete
could be satisfied discretely—each in its own realm. The in-
tricate relationships of neither American society nor the
world were sufficiently compelling to challenge the assumption that national well-being was a function of non-
partisanship and that if differences arose the appropriate
response was to compromise them without prejudice.
"America's present need," he told a Boston audience in
May 1920, "is not heroics, but healing; not nostrums but
normalcy; not revolution but restoration, not agitation but
adjustment, not surgery but serenity, not the dramatic but
the dispassionate, not experiment but equipoise. . . ." [14]

Harding did, to be sure, have a sense of presidential
prerogatives, particularly in the conduct of foreign policy,
but he took advantage of those prerogatives to provide only
minimal personal leadership, [15] leaving it to the members of
his cabinet to work out autonomous programs within their
individual areas of competence and offering as a conception
of national destiny primarily the establishment of tranquillity, or "equipoise." In practice, tranquillity was synonymous with making the world safe for American

risk capital. Although occasionally the president and the Republican leadership in the Congress were at odds, the disagreements were over privileges and legislative priorities rather than values and the definition of the country's welfare. "Less Government in Business and More Business in Government" was the title of an article that Harding wrote just before his election; in it he advocated "a closer understanding between American government and American business."[16] As one of his most recent biographers points out, Harding had long believed that business was simply "a state of independence":[17] he therefore could assert that "business has a right to pursue its normal, legitimate, and righteous way unimpeded."[18] With Andrew W. Mellon as his secretary of the treasury and Herbert Clark Hoover as his secretary of commerce, he presided over a cabinet dominated by those who fully concurred. The revival of prosperity was of the first importance, the expansion of business was the basis of prosperity, and freedom for business was the essential condition for expansion.[19] It was Harding's job to provide a president's sanction for those who sought to guarantee the essential condition. There would seem to be no bias—only healing and restoration for all—in that.

Harding and his associates provided the requisite sanction for such restoration consistently. Responding to pressures from industry to repeal the excess-profits tax and reduce the surtax, and from agriculture to provide relief through revision of the tariff, the administration undertook to do what its predecessor could not or would not do—satisfy both. It was Mellon's conviction that if wealth were taxed too heavily, capital would escape in tax-exempt securities and remain unproductive; if wealth could secure relief, it would be impelled by the "spirit of business adventure"[20] to take those risks that would increase the income of the wage earner. "Our civilization, after all, is based on accumulated capital," he wrote, "and that capital is no less vital to our prosperity than is the extraordinary energy

which has built up in this country the greatest material
civilization the world has ever seen."[21] Moreover, tax-
exempt securities would bring no revenue to the government, and the government, confronted with the financial
burdens that the war had inevitably bequeathed, needed
money.[22] Mellon did not regard taxation as other than a
source of such money, nor revenue as other than a means of
meeting past expenses. "The social necessity for breaking
up large fortunes in this country does not exist," he said,[23]
and he obviously did not expect government to compete with
private enterprise in solving social and economic problems.[24] The government had simply to free capital: "The
men capable of business success will get out of their dead
investments and put their brains and money to work."[25]
With tax relief provided by Congress on November 1921,
and with the advice and support of Hoover's Department
of Commerce, these men expanded the home-building industry, formed trade associations, developed aviation and
radio, and financed research that would enable industries
to operate with greater efficiency and greater profits.[26]
Harding and Mellon might differ in regard to the amount
of tax relief required; yet they did not disagree about the
fundamental principle,[27] and capital felt freed to take so-
called risks.

In a similar spirit the president and Congress approached revision of the tariff. At first the pressure for
revision was exerted primarily by agricultural interests, and
the Fordney Emergency Tariff Act of 1921, with its provision against dumping of foreign surpluses in the United
States and its high duties on wheat, corn, meat, wool, and
sugar, was designed primarily to arrest the postwar decline in farm prices and to restore farm income.[28] But the
following year, with the passage of the Fordney-McCumber
Tariff, high duties protected such a range of raw materials
and manufactured goods that one newspaper was prompted
to declare: "The tariff now represents the composite selfishness of the country."[29] Many understood, of course, that

the farm problem, as ancient as the weather and hunger, was not to be solved by tariff revision. But, given the belief in what freed capital would accomplish, there was little disposition to go beyond proposals to encourage farm cooperatives, extend farm credit, reduce freight rates, and improve the roads on which products were taken to market.[30] Government control of production or of prices would have been as repugnant to farmers as it would have been to manufacturers.

In conceiving of the presidency as an office in which he would refrain from exerting personal leadership but retain prerogatives primarily to sustain official objectivity, Harding promoted the view that the government must remain neutral among competing segments of the economy, and if such neutrality was more helpful to businessmen than to farmers, that made no difference; there was no presidential commitment to securing equality among contending forces, and business anyway was the basis of the nation's well-being. Labor, for example, suffering from a twelve-hour day in the steel mills, wage reductions on the railroads to compensate for deflation, and depression in the coal fields, was able to win from the president nothing better than sincere but futile attempts to conciliate and mediate. Harding deeply believed in maintaining an impartial stance; yet, when finally his persuasive power failed to terminate strikes both on the railroads and in the coal mines, he supported his attorney general's petition for what has been called "the most sweeping injunction in American labor history," restraining rail workers, shopmen, union officials, and their attorneys, throughout the United States, from encouraging continuance of the rail strike and from interfering with the operation of the railroads.[31]

Perhaps Harding did not fully understand the implications of the injunction—he had not intended to adopt an antilabor position—but from his point of view, if the way of business was "righteous" and if the spirit of business adventure was what the country needed most, the carriers or the operators could not be the ones forced to pay.[32] What was good for business was good for the country. The "close understanding" that Harding wished to establish between business and government was thus ultimately an understanding that would confer on business the benefits of untroubled unilateralism.

He might also have considered his foreign policy in an analogous way, for untroubled unilateralism was what he sought for the United States. His predecessors, beginning with McKinley particularly, had had a similar objective and had consistently rationalized American action in moral or idealistic terms that made unilateralism seem appropriate. But where that had led to military intervention in the Pacific, Latin America, and Europe and allowed the country to think of itself as the world's policeman enforcing the right,[33] it now led to a withdrawal from intervention's consequences and allowed the country to think of itself as the world's judge secure from the wrongdoing of others. From the very beginning Harding could appeal to voters who regarded postwar disagreements among European nations as parochial squabbles or products of ancient intrigues and, as though the international frontier were still open, saw no need for constraining commitments.[34] In his acceptance speech he said that he would approach postwar international relations in a way to "justify both conscience and aspirations and still hold us free from menacing involvement" and would propose to "the nations of Europe and of the earth . . . that understanding which makes us a willing participant in the consecration of nations to a new relationship, to commit the moral forces of the world, America included, to peace and international justice, still leaving America free, independent, and self-reliant, but offering friendship to all the world."[35] And with the support he had won from the electorate he could next promise in his inaugural address: "We do not mean to be entangled. We will accept no responsibility except as our own conscience and judgment may determine."[36]

Two years later, shortly before his death, Harding did reveal a modified attitude when, writing to a friend in April 1923, he said:

I have long since come to that conviction, which is inevitable when one serves as Chief Executive, that we can not be wholly aloof from the world and ought not to be, and I also have the very profound conviction that it is an unseemly thing for this nation to say to the world we are unwilling to have to do with anything which is not our own specific creation or a creation erected under our explicit specifications.[37]

But the conviction he professed in the letter did nothing other than possibly soften the tone with which the country affirmed the righteousness of its unilateralism. Article 10 of the League Covenant, pledging the League members "to respect and preserve against external aggression the territorial integrity and existing political independence of all members of the League," required precisely the sort of commitment Americans were not prepared to make. Whatever the majority of the League members might decide concerning a particular act of aggression, their judgment could not outweigh that of the United States. If it were to join the League, the United States would insist on conditions that reserved to it rights, privileges, and exemptions claimed by no other nation.[38] That did not mean that Harding was unprepared to involve the country at all in international affairs; it did mean, though, that involvement would be no more than involvement on the frontier: it would always be possible to disentangle oneself and leave.[39]

Peace meant then, as Robert Osgood has stated, "merely the avoidance of war rather than . . . a continuous process of political accommodation."[40] The United States could participate in disarmament talks, in naval treaties, in Four-Power, Five-Power, and Nine-Power agreements, but could do so only because it never considered any provision that would limit its own freedom in the degree to which the freedom of some of the other nations would be limited.[41] The United States, Great Britain, France, and Japan agreed to respect each other's insular possessions in the Pacific; but the naval ratios they were to maintain made clear that although Japan was to retain superiority in her own waters, the United States was to be enabled to have access to distant parts of the world. The United States and eight other powers contracted to respect the territorial integrity of China in return for assurance of equal commercial opportunities on the Asian mainland, but no one asked whether Japanese citizens, for example, were to enjoy comparable equality in the United States. Americans doubtless believed that they were establishing principles of international justice by insisting that all possessions be treated alike in the Pacific and that all commercial opportunities be equalized in the uncertain state of China. There was no necessity for imagining what American policy would look like from an Oriental point of view. In addition, there was no risk. As Senator Henry Cabot Lodge said of the Four-Power Treaty: "There is not a word in it which justifies calling it an alliance or which binds us to anything whatever."[42] Likewise, even Harding as a sincere advocate of American membership on the World Court had to be willing to accept senatorial reservations that included giving the United States veto power over amendments to the Court's protocol, so great was the congressional fear that the country would be trapped in an international commitment somehow limiting absolute freedom.[43] Limits of any sort were unthinkable. Where the United States enjoyed an advantage it should maintain it; where it suffered a disadvantage it should enjoy no less than equality. Open doors abroad, closed doors at home. America first, America only.

Immigration policy particularly laid the premise bare. Harding favored admitting only those aliens qualified for "easy assimilation,"[44] and Congress, of the same mind, severely restricted migrations from southern and southeastern Europe and excluded Asiatics. Immigrants must be prepared to learn English, to display enthusiasm for American holidays, to divest themselves generally of evidence of their unfortunate alien origins. Moreover, criticism of the legislation was but criticism of its details and concluded by reaffirming its intent. Arthur H. Vandenberg, in 1923, while still an editor five years away from the United States Senate, wrote: "To pretend that native-born Americans possess a monopoly on the virtues of patriotism is nonsense." But he had no intention of opening doors. For in the next paragraph he quickly declared: "Unrestricted immigration is the spawn of faction. . . . The United States has got to cease being a polyglot boarding house." What he was opposed to was, it turned out, only arithmetic formulas like quotas based on percentages, because it was absurd to suppose that "eligibility to partnership in the exalted blessings of America can be measured with a yardstick." The fundamental task, as he saw it, was "to limit diseased minds and bodies and twisted visions and treacherous hearts and unhealthy purposes" and to insure "invincible devotion to the purity of American citizenship, and . . . a rigid rule of conduct under which the importation of taint or menace would be impossible."[45] Could insistence on a protected status or a special role betoken anything except what Harding near the end of his life came to realize was "unseemly"?

Even the most enlightened measures adopted by Harding and his State Department—the measures that improved relations between the United States and Latin American states, anticipating the Good Neighbor policy of the New Deal years—disclose the taint of unseemliness. Both Harding and his secretary of state, Charles Evans Hughes, were in agreement that Wilson's practices must be changed. Military intervention and nonrecognition had created tension with Mexico, Cuba, Haiti, Santo Domingo, among others, and had constituted, as Harding said before his election, "repeated acts of unwarranted interference in the domestic affairs of the little republics of the western hemisphere," and had "not only made enemies of those who should be our friends but . . . rightfully discredited our country as their trusted neighbor."[46] Yet it was clear that what in

Harding's mind had been most wrong about American practices was less their violation of the principle of mutual
respect than their creation of a climate unfavorable to
American business. The property rights of Americans in
Mexico, the opportunities for safe investments in Cuba,
the desire of American oil interests for favors in Colombia
and Costa Rica were the primary concerns.[47] Latin American
governments were expected to be friendly to the United
States in a way that would give Americans advantages.
When Hughes sought to assure "our sister Republics" that
Washington's understanding of the Monroe Doctrine meant
that the United States would "be co-workers . . . and not
masters" and that "our purpose [was] to resist aggression,
not commit it," he was hoping to promote the sort of stability that would give American business the security it
believed it had every right to.[48]

In addition, as Robert K. Murray has pointed out, the
Harding administration "possessed a dangerous naiveté
about the ability of the United States to influence world
affairs merely by example or by indirect methods and contacts."[49] Having failed to influence world affairs by military
force in the war, it now supposed that virtuous rhetoric
about upright ways would do better. In the glaring light
of subsequent revelations about Teapot Dome[50] the belief
in the good example was a singular one for the Harding
administration to subscribe to; but it was certainly that belief, never seriously challenged, that sustained Calvin Coolidge and even Herbert Hoover, both in their use of the
presidency as an influential office and in their formulation
of domestic and foreign policies.

Calvin Coolidge did more than simply perpetuate Harding's conceptions and preconceptions, however. He elevated
them; he perfected them; he transformed them into ideality.
In fact, no one could more appropriately have occupied the
presidential office at the time than Coolidge. He was not
afflicted with warm-heartedness or a yearning for gregarious

evenings; he did not sound trumpet calls for effervescent Happiness; he did not celebrate the dangerous adventure. Each night he slept eleven hours, and each afternoon he napped for two to four hours more. He survived in his job, he reportedly told Will Rogers, "By avoiding the big problems!"[51] His father was a landowner, ran the general store, served as the notary public; his Vermont was a community of the self-sufficient; his America was one in which hard work, thrift, freedom, and public service were almost synonymous, and in which one contributed to civilization through business activity. When he had been president of the Massachusetts General Court, in 1914, he had stated:

Government cannot relieve from toil. . . . Self-government means self-support. . . .

Ultimately, property rights and personal rights are the same thing. The one cannot be preserved if the other be violated. . . .

History reveals no civilized people among whom there were not a highly educated class, and large aggregations of wealth, represented usually by the clergy and the nobility. Inspiration has always come from above [that is, God]. . . .

It may be that the diffusion of wealth works in an analogous way. As the little red schoolhouse is builded in the college, it may be that the fostering and protection of large aggregations of wealth are the only foundation on which to build the prosperity of the whole people. Large profits mean large pay rolls. But profits must be the result of service performed. . . .[52]

Service was, though, wholly compatible with profits, since, it would appear, the mere providing of opportunities for gainful employment constituted public service. Coolidge's New England milieu did not make him a worshiper of the golden calf, but it did compel him to regard material independence as the basis of the good life and the test of character. In speeches he delivered while he was vice-president, he made his values explicit:

Along with the solemn assurance of freedom and equality [provided by the American political system] goes the guarantee of the right of the individual to possess, enjoy, and control the dollar which he earns. . . . If the individual is not to have the dollar which he himself earns, then he must be forced to hand it over to some one who has not earned it.[53]

There is very little that is really worth while which can be bought or sold. The desire for gain has made many cowards, but it never made a hero. The country cannot be run on the promise of what it will do for the people. The only motive to which they will continue to respond is the opportunity to do something for themselves, to achieve their own greatness, to work out their own destiny.[54]

. . . character and ability . . . come only from grappling with the great problems of life, most usually gained by Americans in great business and administrative activities.[55]

. . . It is the doctrine of the Republican party to encourage business, not merely for its own sake but because that is the surest method of administering to the general welfare.[56]

Although there seemed to be contradiction in the deprecation of the desire for "gain," Coolidge could have meant only something excessive by the term; for what he said about earning the dollar, doing for oneself, developing character, and government's encouraging business all harmonized. To make money was to work out one's destiny; to grapple with the problems of business was to develop one's character; to enable money-making to flourish was to promote the general welfare. Earlier in his political career, when he had been in the Massachusetts House of Representatives, he had appeared to be something of a Progressive. He had favored a six-day week, setting maximum working hours for women and children, the prevention of injunctions in labor disputes, the legalization of picketing, a state income tax, and women's suffrage, among other measures. At the time there had been sentiment among his constituents for such reforms, and Coolidge had needed their votes. His conscience, however, had not needed to be troubled, for to one criterion he had remained faithful throughout: nothing must cost too much.[57]

With such a man as president it was fitting that the United States Chamber of Commerce should establish itself across the street from the White House in what William

Allen White called a "marble palace," and inevitable that the Chamber's desires and the administration's programs should continually coincide. Confirmed and guided in his predilections by Mellon, whose wealth bespoke authority, Coolidge advocated the reduction of income, inheritance, and corporate taxes, the repeal of excise taxes, the non-enforcement of antitrust laws against combinations fostering export trade, the private operation of the merchant marine, the manipulation of the tariff in the interests of domestic enterprises, the extension of Federal Reserve bank charters, the creation of a court of tax appeals, and the defeat of the McNary-Haugen bill.[58] Like Mellon, Coolidge regarded the government as just a business. "I have in mind that the taxpayers are the stockholders of the business corporation of the United States," he told Congress in 1923, "and that if this business is showing a surplus of receipts the taxpayer should share therein in some material way that will be of immediate benefit."[59] Since he defined material benefits in terms of private profits rather than social conditions, he was naturally predisposed to favor private over public works. "Never before, here or anywhere else," wrote the editors of *The Wall Street Journal* in 1925, "has a government been so completely fused with business." In fact, according to *Nation's Business,* the Chamber of Commerce's official publication, the businessman had by 1925 become "the most influential person in the nation."[60] It was only a Democratic-Progressive coalition in the Senate that prevented confirmation of Charles Beecher Warren, an agent of the sugar trust and apostle of the conservation of property, as attorney general to succeed Harlan Fiske Stone, whom Coolidge had named to the Supreme Court at a time when Stone was concerning himself actively with antitrust actions.[61] In Coolidge's mind the regulation of business could constitute only a limitation of freedom. Believing in what one of his biographers has aptly called "government by nondirective therapy."[62] Coolidge adhered to a negative conception of the federal government's role that could not

have been more satisfying to business interests, which
cherished the untroubled unilateralism they had begun to
enjoy under Harding.

It was doubtless because Coolidge saw all activity in
terms of business's self-sufficiency that he supposed that
the nondirective approach would, if firmly maintained, be
equally therapeutic everywhere, whether in the development and operation of hydroelectric power or in the improvement of the conditions of agriculture. When in 1921,
during Harding's presidency, the War Department had been
authorized to invite bids on Muscle Shoals, Coolidge had
certainly been in accord; and when he was finally president,
he gave every indication of being pleased with the prospect
of transferring the property to Henry Ford, who had made
an offer. Ford's private management would permit the large-
scale production of fertilizers without adding any burden
to the taxpayers' shoulders, and would at the same time
bring the government considerable revenue through annual
payments. Indeed, Coolidge might have been successful in
enabling the government to become simply a creditor at
Muscle Shoals had it not been that by 1924, when the proposal was before the Senate, the Teapot Dome scandals
had been exposed and the disposal of public property to a
private owner was suspect, prompting Ford to withdraw his
offer.[63] Senator George W. Norris's part in thwarting Coolidge was not negligible, but Norris did not speak for a
constituency matching Coolidge's. The country generally
shared Coolidge's desire for disengagement, as Coolidge
believed the 1924 elections showed:

I judge that the result of the election, the decisive result, indi-
cating an attachment of the people to their Constitution and the
present method of transacting their business, a desire that enterprise and business activities be left in the hands of private
individuals rather than a transfer of ownership to the control of
Government, has undoubtedly had an effect in stimulating private
enterprise.[64]

Where voters and the president did support construction of

a facility such as Boulder Dam in 1926, it was not because of a belief in extending the government's responsibilities but because of a desire to give advantages to a particular region and in return earn support for Republicans in an off-year election.[65] Large dams represented for Coolidge, in William Allen White's words,

scientific regimentation, which . . . put capital into traces. The dam controlled the land below the dam and its fertility. The dam gave power to villagers, to counties, to great valleys, to whole regions. This chained water channeled men in the new way they had to go.[66]

Large government must have seemed to Coolidge very much like a large dam.

But it was not only large governmental enterprises to which Coolidge remained opposed; it was also any degree of active involvement in the domestic economy, however small or indirect that involvement might be. Thus, on the one hand, because he had been brought up in a community surrounded by farms, he was sympathetic with farmers, who, he assumed, almost always suffered some hardship and who, he knew, deserved greater rewards than they were receiving.[67] Yet, on the other hand, when farmers wanted the federal government to extricate them from the unrewarding predicament in which the excess production of the early twenties left them, he was unable to respond other than by recommending "safe and sound economics."[68] Perhaps, from the perspective of the Vermonter, the large-scale farming of the Midwesterner was something too alien to understand. More important, however, governmental intervention was bound to be something too destructive to permit. Agriculture, he told the American Farm Bureau Corporation's annual convention in December 1925, could flourish only "on an independent business basis."[69] Although he knew, of course, that "farmers as a whole [were] determined to maintain the independence of their business," and in that respect concurred with his notion that governmental action meant "meddling,"[70] it was not that senti-

ment in itself that concerned Coolidge; it was the threat
that meddling posed for character:

> In all our economic discussions we must remember that we
> cannot stop with the mere acquisition of wealth. The ultimate
> result to be desired is not the making of money, but the making
> of people. Industry, thrift, and self-control are not sought be-
> cause they create wealth, but because they create character.
> These are the prime product of the farm. We who have seen it,
> and lived it, know.[71]

Coolidge was aware that farmers were in trouble, and
he was told by spokesmen for the farmers that some governmental action (short of meddling) was desperately required. Easy money had encouraged land speculation and
led farmers into debt; increased costs of industrial labor
had made it expensive for farmers to buy the fuel, imple-
ments, food, and clothing they needed; the substitution of
mechanical vehicles for those drawn by horses and mules
meant that feed that had once been sold in the cities no
longer found as many buyers; taxes and interest could be
paid only with borrowed money; opportunities for exporting
farm products decreased with the decline in foreign trade—
all at the very time, in the early twenties, when production
of grain and livestock both at home and in Europe so exceeded demand that the farmers could sell only at prices
so low that they had to produce even more to make what
they raised pay, and, further lowering prices, thereby decreased their financial returns still more.[72] But Coolidge
was wary lest the independence on which the farmer's character was based be eroded. "Government control cannot
be divorced from political control," he warned;[73] farmers
should solve their problems by voluntarily engaging in
cooperative marketing, by cooperating with business, by
learning, from information the government might dissemi-
nate, about crop and market conditions. It seems not to have
occurred to him that marketing was not the only problem,
or that the regulation of production in the fields differed
radically from the regulation of production in the factories.

What served business could not serve the farmer. As Donald R. McCoy has noted: ". . . for farmers, workers, and sectional interests to gain amounts of privilege equivalent to what business had gained from government inactivity alone would have required positive legislation."[74] Coolidge could not reconcile positive legislation with his conception of government as impersonal recipient of revenues, or examine his premise that no one's business was anything but business. After all, he said to Senator Burton K. Wheeler, who had visited the White House to discuss the farmer's plight, "When a man can't make any money in a business, what does he do?"[75]

What the logic of Coolidge's position meant is clarified in his treatment of the attempt by agricultural interests finally to secure for farm products economic equality with industrial products by legislative means. Once it became clear to farm leaders that more than marketing was at the root of farming's difficulties and that more than better credit facilities and lower transportation rates were what were required, they turned to a plan for positive action developed by George N. Peek and Hugh S. Johnson, of the Moline Plow Company.[76] Johnson and Peek recognized that it was because the American farmer had to buy industrial products at protected prices while he had to sell at world prices that agriculture was out of balance with industry. They therefore proposed protection for agriculture comparable to what industry enjoyed. Domestic market prices would be supported by a tariff sufficiently high to give the prices of farm commodities the same purchasing power as they had had in relation to other commodities in the prewar period (1909–14) when farmers had fared relatively well; surplus production—the amount that would, if left on the domestic market, depress domestic prices—would be purchased at the protected domestic prices by an agricultural export corporation (created by the government) to be dumped abroad on the world market at world prices; and the loss to the corporation would then be met by a small tax on the farmer, who would still receive substantially more than he was receiving.

> The question is [wrote Henry C. Taylor, chief of the Bureau of Agricultural Economics, in September 1923], shall we adhere to the policy of providing information on a basis of individual and collective action and await the very gradual recovery of agriculture through growth and readjustments of population; or, shall we undertake to bring about a more immediate solution of the problem by direct governmental action which will re-establish pre-war price relations at an early date.[77]

Senator Charles L. McNary and Representative Gilbert N. Haugen, with the endorsement of the secretary of agriculture, Henry C. Wallace, in January 1924 introduced a bill empowering the government to take such direct action.[78] Coolidge, however, despite a promise to investigate the bill's merits, could not bring himself to accept it. Listening to Hoover, his secretary of commerce, criticize it, he predictably favored Hoover's position over Wallace's. The establishment of an export corporation would put the government into business; the government should serve as only an advisor; agriculture (unlike industry) should limit itself to domestic demand.[79]

At first, Coolidge's position required no action on his part. There was a momentary rise in farm income in 1924, and when agricultural leaders disagreed as to the need for the McNary-Haugen bill, Congress rejected it.[80] Two years later, however, with the imbalance between what farmers and factory workers received once more in evidence, the bill again was on the agenda, and this time its defeat required a letter from Secretary Mellon to Haugen asserting that passage would increase the cost of living, decrease consumption, and favor "producers of the five major agricultural products."[81] Then in February 1927 and May 1928 the bill twice passed Congress, and the president had to act openly. He vetoed it both times. In his first veto message he stated that he regarded the bill as unconstitutional and partial to special interests, and that he believed it would, by involving the government in price fixing, open the way for a large governmental bureaucracy;[82] in his second veto message he reiterated his conviction of its unconstitutionality and called it "repugnant as ever to the spirit of our institutions, both political and commercial."[83] Inactivity that was helpful to business apparently favored no special interests, but activity that would accord parity to farmers would be partial.

Perhaps, despite his sympathy with farmers, he found businessmen intrinsically superior. "The man who builds a factory builds a temple. . . . The man who works there worships there."[84] But although he did not locate farmers so close to hallowed ground, he and the congressional majority that he opposed were not at odds regarding a more fundamental idea. Whatever the farm bloc's diverse motives were for pushing through the McNary-Haugen bill, one sees that the farmers generally had no greater sense of interrelatedness than Coolidge had. The followers of Johnson and Peek appeared either undisturbed or unaware that European countries would surely retaliate with high tariffs of their own or that increased profits at home would ultimately encourage overproduction once more.[85] They seemed to assume that American agriculture could be treated in an isolation as complete as the one in which Coolidge was encouraging business to develop. Before the crash of 1929 persons with power were incapable of pointing out that no interest either should or could be wholly insulated from the demands of others. Cooperation among interests might be desirable but must not be required or directed by government; government's domestic role was to remain aloof from the claims of contention, to be rather than to do; for, as Coolidge phrased it, "our American political system . . . neither seeks nor claims any justification for its existence save righteousness."[86]

This belief in righteousness was one that extended to Coolidge's conduct of foreign affairs just as consistently as it had extended during Harding's presidency, and here Coolidge encountered little dissent. Americans were generally prepared to agree with him that there was something so peculiarly elevated about their country that it ought not be expected to descend to the level of others. "To live under the American Constitution is the greatest political privilege that was ever accorded to the human race," Coolidge wrote,[87] and readers did not smile. "Those who do not want to be partakers of the American spirit ought not to settle in America," he said in endorsing restrictions on immigration. "America must be kept American."[88] He did not, like Senator Hiram Johnson of California, favor total exclusion of the Japanese, but his concern was simply to avoid offending Japan; he had no intention of swinging wide the golden gate of opportunity, and sought nothing more than an annual quota of two hundred and fifty Japanese immigrants.[89] Good will was what he wanted. Good will was necessary for stability, for comfortable relationships, for diminishing the warlike dangers that required the expense of maintaining armaments.[90] But good will was, as under Harding, still to be secured on American terms—through recognition of American standards. The Philippines, for example, could not yet be granted autonomy unless the United States decided that they were ready for self-government.[91] The war debts could not be canceled or even reduced because the Allies had "hired the money" and apparently the United States had no stake in the outcome except maintenance of its moral well-being and of its status as a creditor nation.[92]

Coolidge did perceive a need for European countries to increase their productivity if they were to pay their debts, but he could not avoid linking economic and political necessities with moral imperatives. In speaking to Congress, in December 1923, of the conditions needed for re-establishing diplomatic relations with the Russian government, he said:

Whenever there appears any disposition to compensate our citizens who were despoiled, and to recognize that debt contracted with our government, not by the Czar but by the newly formed Republic of Russia; whenever the active spirit of enmity to our institutions is abated; whenever there appear works meet for repentance, our country ought to be the first to go to the economic and moral rescue of Russia.[93]

In commenting, early in 1926, on the difficulties of coming to an understanding with Mexico concerning the property rights of American investors, he observed: "The people [of Mexico] have a different outlook on things. They haven't had the advantages that we have up here."[94] James R. Sheffield was at the time the American ambassador to Mexico and believed that it was futile to attempt "to treat with a Latin-Indian mind, filled with hatred of the United States and thirsting for vengeance, on the same basis that our government would treat with a civilized and orderly government in Europe."[95] Yet, although Coolidge was aware of the need to replace Sheffield and soon did appoint Dwight W. Morrow to the position, he was unable to regard Mexico as an equal even then, remarking to William Howard Taft: "Of course they don't like [Sheffield] particularly in Mexico, but how could a man decently act in such a way that they would?"[96] There was an inescapable disadvantage to living south of the border. In justifying the dispatching of marines to Nicaragua in December 1926, he told reporters:

There is a revolution going on there and whenever a condition of that kind exists in Central American countries it means trouble for our citizens that are there and it is almost always necessary for this country to take action for their protection.[97]

Finally, in urging Congress to support American membership in the World Court, he readily accepted senatorial reservations that would give the United States the same veto rights over advisory opinions it had not solicited as the members of the League of Nations Council enjoyed by virtue of their Council membership, but without in turn assuming any reciprocal obligations to the League. In fact, when League members sought to discuss the reservations with the United States government, Coolidge appeared affronted, stiffly stating: "We are dealing . . . directly with the nations concerned. . . . The League has nothing to do with it and can't do anything with it if it wanted to." Even the Court members, apart from the League, were rebuffed. The United States would enter the Court on its own terms, or stay out.[98]

It would be unfair to minimize Coolidge's positive and pacific contributions to international relations. His appointment of Dwight W. Morrow as ambassador to Mexico was a constructive appointment; Morrow could even *"like"* the Mexicans.[99] The appointment of Henry L. Stimson, who had been Taft's secretary of war, to negotiate American differences in Nicaragua was equally good and equally successful.[100] The United States, participating in the Sixth Pan-American Conference in Havana, December 1927–January 1928, agreed to multilateral treaties that provided for the arbitration of juridical questions and for conciliation.[101] And, jointly with France, the United States drafted a treaty —the Pact of Paris, or Kellogg-Briand Pact—for all countries to sign, outlawing war as a means of settling international differences. Yet, good augury as was the fact of American participation in Havana, the United States had still not qualified its assumption of a right to the unilateral defense of the Western Hemisphere or acknowledged any necessity for collective decision among equals.[102] And in signing the Pact of Paris, the United States incurred no new obligations. Violation of the provisions required no active response by the United States; for, as Coolidge assured the Congress, the pact

does not supersede our inalienable sovereign right and duty of national defense or undertake to commit us before the event to any mode of action which the Congress might decide to be wise [sic] if ever the treaty should be broken. But it is a new standard in the world around which can rally the informed and enlightened opinion of nations. . . .[103]

Some Senators wanted reservations attached to even that pact, but reservations were redundant. Neither Coolidge nor any substantial portion of the electorate was prepared to consider any agreement that might imply limits, and neither limits nor sanctions appeared. The Senate approved the pact, 85–1, and then, as if to emphasize how little American action would be constrained by others, voted large naval appropriations.[104]

Although the United States was not alone in shunning collective security,[105] it was surely more moralistic about its position than others were. Parties whose doctrines differed concurred in offering purity as a measure of their policies for the United States. Thus in 1924, in the platforms approved by the national conventions, some of the leftist parties rejected leagues or agreements with existing governments because these would be tainted by imperialistic purposes; the Republicans, verbalizing the thinking of the Administration, opposed "political commitments which would involve us in the conflict of European politics," and affirmed "independence without indifference"; the Democrats, although they discovered "no substitute for the league of nations as an agency working for peace," proposed mainly that the United States exert "that moral leadership in the family of nations which, in the providence of God, has been so clearly marked out for it."[106] In the same vein, in his final message to Congress, December 4, 1928, Coolidge solemnly declared: "The great wealth created by our enterprise and industry, and saved by our economy, has had the widest distribution among our own people, and has gone out in a steady stream to serve the charity and the business of the world. . . . The country can regard the present with satisfaction and anticipate the future with optimism."[107] The United States, in the enjoyment of its unique destiny, its separate peace, and its satisfying prosperity, conferred blessings on all. If later, when the blessings ceased and the depression came, Coolidge could both fix the blame on Europe and assert that Americans as private citizens could individually overcome the misfortune, he simply demonstrated how deep and generally shared was the conviction that evil was alien to the United States and righteousness was endemic, requiring nothing but liberating conditions to enable it to flourish.

Walter Lippmann criticized Coolidge's "genius for inactivity,"[108] and his "dampening down of popular interest
in popular government," but he recognized that inactivity
was considered liberating; "the country . . . [was] in the
mood for a negative administration," he noted.[109] Elizabeth
Stevenson has recalled that Senator Burton K. Wheeler,
campaigning for the vice-presidency on the Progressive
Party ticket in 1924, delighted on several occasions in under-
scoring the nature of Coolidge's presidency by placing an
empty chair on the platform and addressing questions to
it.[110] The empty chair, though intended as it was to constitute an argument, stood ultimately as a witness of the irrelevance of such argument in the twenties. "If the Federal
Government should go out of existence," Coolidge once
said, "the common run of people would not detect the difference in the affairs of their daily life for a considerable
length of time."[111]

It was no doubt evidence of Coolidge's achievement—
and, for many, proof of the soundness of his presidential
conception—that a book intended to be a campaign biography of his successor could begin in 1928 with a chapter
entitled "Why Have a President?" and ask:

> What difference does it make who is President of the United
> States? The sun will come up and the sun will go down, spring
> will follow winter and summer will follow spring—quite regard-
> less of who happens to be the tenant of the White House. And will
> not likewise the nation roll on its majestic way?[112]

Yet Herbert Hoover, with a background and perspective
strikingly different from Coolidge's, might have been expected to modify that conception in some significant manner. Born into circumstances less favorable than those in
which Coolidge had found himself, Hoover had traveled
a good deal further—physically, financially, and intellectually.[113] His father, an Iowa blacksmith, had died when
Hoover was six; his mother, having saved but some fifteen
hundred dollars, had died when Hoover was ten, one of

three children. He had then been brought up by an uncle in Oregon who was profiting from a land boom there, had become an office boy, and had qualified for study in Stanford University's Department of Geology and Mining. He had supported himself in college with odd jobs, earned the respect of classmates, and two years after graduation, after more odd jobs, both manual and clerical in mines and mining offices, succeeded in being hired by a British firm to direct new gold mines in Australia. Thereafter, with new managerial responsibilities, he had traveled in China, Mongolia, and Tibet; lived in Tientsin during the Boxer Rebellion; lived in Japan; and by 1901 become a partner in a British engineering firm with worldwide interests that took him through Asia, the Middle East, and Europe, and helped him to become, it has been said, "the richest engineer of his time,"[114] "a millionaire before he was forty."[115] During the war he had effectively directed Belgian relief; he had been an advisor at the Peace Conference; he had been given responsibility for relieving hunger throughout postwar Europe; he had, finally, become secretary of commerce under Harding as, in his own terms, "an independent progressive" rather than as an established Republican.[116] And as secretary under both Harding and Coolidge he had been immersed in international economic problems and in tasks devoted to helping business through recommendations for improving efficiency. Nevertheless, in the end, Hoover was simply a more modern embodiment of the values that Coolidge had preserved, a president who believed that society's welfare could be assured by the scientific elimination of waste and the spirit of public service but who never questioned whether welfare should be measured in any terms or promoted by any means other than those already taken for granted.

Hoover had, after all, been overwhelmingly elected president over Alfred E. Smith in large part because he could perpetuate an image of the American that Americans had cherished. Smith had certainly proved himself to be just as self-reliant. He had not lived in the backwoods, but he had lived in the back streets;[117] and although he had not pushed a miner's cart, he had at least worked in the Fulton Street fish market. He had also established himself as an able administrator. He had not distributed food abroad, but he had governed New York State well and promoted housing projects, the development of green parks, and the construction of modern hospitals.[118] He was loyal to his family; he respected business—and chose wealthy men to organize his campaign; and even though he was opposed to what he considered the hypocrisy of sending "unofficial observers" to international conferences,[119] and argued for participation with responsibility, he said: "Freedom from entangling alliances is a fixed American policy."[120] And like Hoover, he had shown how one could rise in the United States.

Unfortunately, he had risen among the wrong people. He had risen in a city whose population was heterogeneous, whose accents were glaringly polyglot and, like his own, "uncultured," whose traditions challenged in their multiplicity what William Allen White regarded as "The whole Puritan civilization which has built a sturdy, orderly nation."[121] He was associated with Tammany Hall, a symbol of urban corruption. He was concerned with the welfare of urban workers, whose origins were disturbingly different from those of storekeepers and farmers in Vermont and Iowa. He favored the repeal of Prohibition, a position connoting the saloon and the dissolute life.[122] In 1926, during the Eucharistic Congress at Chicago, he had as a Catholic kissed the ring of the papal legate and thus convinced Protestant America of his allegiance to a foreign power. And he was married to a woman who seemed so plump and plain that many newly enfranchised women, expecting the First Lady to portray their sartorial and bodily aspirations, exclaimed aghast: "Can you imagine Mrs. Smith in the White House!"[123]

It did not matter that many of his views were fundamentally conservative—that perhaps only his emphasis on the individual's need for economic security as a condition of freedom and his support of government operation of Muscle Shoals distinguished him from Hoover—or that his American Catholicism was historically less at odds with the integrity of the secular state than Hoover's Quaker faith, for which exceptions had had to be provided by law.[124] It did not matter that Tammany's scandalous reputation could be matched by what some of Harding's friends had done with the nation's oil reserves. The extent of Hoover's support among voters in all regions indicated that ideas and issues mattered far less than symbols. All that was objectionable about Smith was what bespoke Babel, the ultimate city, and its supposed indifference to the rest of the country's measured pace and comfortable immunity to alien ways. When Smith in his campaign spoke in behalf of the people against privilege, many ordinary people west of the Hudson and south of Ellis Island doubtless felt it was they who were threatened. Walter Lippmann best stated the meaning of the hostility to Smith when he wrote:

Quite apart even from the sincere opposition of the prohibitionists, the objection to Tammany, the sectional objection to New York, there is an opposition to Smith which is as authentic and, it seems to me, as poignant as his support. It is inspired by the feeling that the clamorous life of the city should not be acknowledged as the American ideal. . . .

. . . The Ku Kluxers may talk about the Pope to the lunatic fringe, but the main mass of the opposition is governed by an instinct that to accept Al Smith is to certify and sanctify a way of life that does not belong to the America they love. . . . Here are the new people, clamoring to be admitted to America, and there are the older people defending their household gods.[125]

Hoover could stand as chief defender of those gods with as much confidence as Coolidge and with more of an appearance of understanding their value. In accepting the Republican nomination he voiced an optimism that Coolidge's final message to Congress could not surpass; he declared:

We in America today are nearer to the final triumph over poverty than ever before in the history of any land. . . . We shall soon with the help of God be in sight of the day when poverty will be banished from this nation.[126]

And he was able to speak so confidently because he had some years before thoughtfully formulated a rationale concerning the nature of the American government and its relationship to the individual citizen that enabled him to believe that, with simply sound organization, the promotion of efficient practices, and an impulse to serve, the government would enable the country to run itself and prosper. In *American Individualism* (1922), written after his experience in providing relief in Europe and in observing the economic and political obstacles to European recovery, he had undertaken to define the social philosophy of Americans and to distinguish it from the principal competing alternatives in the world "not only to preserve . . . [our country's political, economic, and spiritual principles] from being fouled by false notions, but more importantly that we may guide ourselves in the road of progress." American individualism was, he emphasized, a "tried individualism."[127] This was not "individualism run riot," because it was "tempered" by a principle that required the curbing of any attempt at domination, whether by government or by industry, in order

that while we build our society upon the attainment of the individual, we shall safeguard to every individual an equality of opportunity to take that position in the community to which his intelligence, character, ability, and ambition entitle him; that we keep the social solution free from frozen strata of classes; that we shall stimulate effort of each individual to achievement; that through an enlarging sense of responsibility and understanding we shall assist him to this attainment; while he in turn must stand up to the emery wheel of competition.[128]

Rejecting "the claptrap of the French Revolution" and the "economic and spiritual fallacy and . . . moral degeneracy" of socialism, Hoover recommended "further advance in the standard of living . . . by greater invention, greater elimination of waste, greater production and better distribution of commodities and services. . . ."[129] Although he knew that no system could be founded on altruism, that huge concentrations of wealth posed dangers, that faulty distribution deprived both producers of returns and needy citizens of essentials,[130] he could not imagine any immediate need for active governmental intervention to assure the final triumph, which he clearly saw in exclusively material terms:

> To curb the forces in business which would destroy equality of opportunity and yet to maintain the initiative and creative faculties of our people are the twin objects we must attain. To preserve the former we must regulate that type of activity that would dominate. To preserve the latter, the Government must keep out of production and distribution of commodities and services. This is the deadline between our system and socialism. Regulation to prevent domination and unfair practices, yet preserving rightful initiative, are in keeping with our social foundations.[131]

The government was "the umpire in our social system."[132] Everyone was, he assumed, playing the same game.

It is significant that in concluding his celebration of American individualism he associated it with the spirit of the explorers and settlers:

> The American pioneer is the epic expression of that individualism, and the pioneer spirit is the response to the challenge of opportunity, to the challenge of nature, to the challenge of life, to the call of the frontier. That spirit need never die for lack of something for it to achieve. There will always be a frontier to conquer or to hold as long as men think, plan, and dare. Our American individualism has received much of its character from our contacts with the forces of nature on a new continent. . . . The days of the pioneer are not over. There are continents of human welfare of which we have penetrated only the coastal plain.[133]

Hoover's individual thus still lived, actually or metaphorically, in a state of nature. His problems and conflicts could still be resolved in nature rather than have to be resolved through accommodation with the contrary-minded. If human welfare was a problem, Hoover could only propose that "we . . . glorify service as a part of our national character,"[134] with a logic implying that other individuals constituted occasions for charity—occasions that ought not to be ignored but could be—rather than the obdurate conditions for the self-respect and self-discovery that ensued from one's required decisions or forced revisions of purpose. The American was, in short, deliberately to become the pioneer as Good Samaritan.

Throughout his campaign for the presidency and throughout his tenure Hoover reaffirmed his credo both in his words and in his official actions. During his campaign in 1928 he compared individualism with socialism, anarchism, and despotism:

> It is as if we set a race. We, through free and universal education, provide the training of the runners; we give to them an equal start; we provide in the government the umpire of fairness in the race. The winner is he who shows the most conscientious training, the greatest ability, and the greatest character. Socialism bids all to end the race equally. It holds back the speedy to the pace of the slowest. Anarchy would provide neither training nor umpire. Despotism picks those who should run and those who should win.[135]

There was only one kind of race to run, only one test of ability and character; hence only one test of fairness, too. For the government to interject itself in any way other than to improve the efficiency of the testing was dangerous; there was no question about the validity of the criteria: "The spread of government destroys initiative and thus destroys character. Character is made . . . by assuming responsibilities, not by escape from them."[136] Where individuals found themselves at a disadvantage, the government could suggest only cooperation on a voluntary basis.[137] Tax relief and protective tariffs were measures that released businessmen from constraints, hence did not constitute forms of governmental interference.[138] Businessmen were made responsible for what they themselves did or did not do. "Commercial business requires a concentration of responsibility [among men of ability and character]. Self-government requires decentralization," he stated.[139] Since he regarded the nation's problems in 1928 as "more than economic" and "in a much greater degree . . . moral and spiritual,"[140] he feared that any governmental attempt to limit what individuals did simply in order to improve economic conditions would subordinate moral welfare to economic welfare in the very way that socialism threatened to do. "Self-government" lay wholly "outside of political government," he insisted.[141] The extension of government was therefore a threat to the line of demarcation.

According to these principles a strong executive was as dangerous as a strong federal government. Just as responsibilities should be progressively decentralized, so should independence from dictation be preserved at the highest level. Liberty's "militant safeguard" was "legislative independence"; any "weakening of the legislative arm [must] lead to encroachments by the executive upon legislative and judicial functions, and inevitable that encroachment [was] upon individual liberty."[142] Hoover stood aloof from the legislative hurly-burly. Commentators evaluating the first months of his presidency remarked on his "strange paralysis" and his "dignified but hurt silence."[143] Addressing himself to such material problems as those afflicting agriculture, he adhered to the approach of his acceptance speech: "Farming is and must continue to be an individualistic business of small units and independent ownership. The farm is more than a business: it is a state of living. We do not wish it converted into a mass-production machine."[144] Businessmen might join forces, and might engage in mass production; but they did so on a voluntary basis. For farmers to join forces would require more governmental intervention than business had required for its welfare. At the most, he was prepared to sign the Agricultural Marketing Act in 1929 permitting the government to sustain prices by buying surpluses, on the assumption that the need would soon pass and agriculture could return to its sound ways.[145] If production was to be curtailed, the farmers would have to do so on a voluntary basis too. Their state of living must not be corrupted. Likewise when economic conditions throughout the country worsened and the need for relief was desperate, he insisted that the federal government should not substitute itself for local and voluntary agencies:

> The moment responsibilities of any community, particularly in economic and social questions, are shifted from any part of the nation to Washington, then that community has subjected itself to a remote bureaucracy. . . . It has lost a large part of its voice in the control of its own destiny.[146]

If Hoover recalled his success in distributing relief to Europe's peoples after World War I and remained without remorse at having impaired their control of their destiny, he must have supposed that what distinguished his activity then was its character as an act of charity by an agency outside the governmental structure of the countries to be aided. Hoover favored giving federal loans to agencies like the Red Cross to provide relief, but opposed giving funds outright since federal gifts, he later explained, "would have injured the spiritual responses of the American people. . . . A voluntary deed is infinitely more precious to our national ideals and spirit than a thousandfold poured from the Treasury."[147]

Textbooks point out that Hoover went beyond Harding and Coolidge in developing economic and social programs. Engineer that he was, Hoover valued scientific study and reports, and appointed a number of commissions to study problems ranging from home-building and child care to prohibition and social trends generally.[148] In addition, although he was vigorously opposed to the government's operation of facilities such as Muscle Shoals,[149] he was prepared to approve of appropriations for public works in areas where local funds had been exhausted by the need for local relief. And he argued that, as the depression worsened, profits ought to be cut before wages. Moreover, to assist banks, corporations, agriculture, state governments, and construction projects throughout the country by providing for short-term loans, he endorsed the establishment of the Reconstruction Finance Corporation, and to help banks by discounting mortgage loans he also favored the creation of Home Owners Loan Banks.[150] But the careful reports that the commissions were to take time to prepare concerned essentially how things worked—and things were already ceasing to work; loans and public works unaccompanied by direct relief presupposed that it was sufficient to stimulate the economy at the top without also directly increasing purchasing power at the bottom. And the argument against sacrificing wages to profits could not avail without executive leadership and federal compulsion that would have contradicted all that Hoover affirmed. Despite a mind and will that raised him above the level of his two predecessors, and a reflective bent that distinguished him from them, Hoover failed because of what he and they shared.

Hoover's foreign policy provides a telling confirmation of the strength of his attitude. During his 1928 campaign he was wont to stress the American "desire to cooperate with other nations for peace"; but when he considered what cooperation entailed, he made clear that he adhered to what Dexter Perkins has called "the dogma of freedom of action":[151]

. . . our people have determined that we can give the greatest real help—both in times of tranquillity and in times of strain— if we maintain our independence from the political exigencies of the Old World. In pursuance of this, our country has refused membership in the League of Nations, but we are glad to cooperate with the League in its endeavors to further scientific, economic, and social welfare, and to secure limitation of armament.[152]

Limitation of armament would save money; security would require less sacrifice than construction of battleships would; when Britain and Japan agreed to a naval treaty in 1930, the United States could maintain its defensive position without obligations. Hoover did speak in 1930 in behalf of membership in the World Court, but not on the

ground that the country ought to be party to binding commitments: indeed, he emphasized that the United States
could withdraw at any time,[153] hence there would be no risk.

Fundamentally, Hoover, and the majority of the country,
regarded commitments as antithetical to freedom of action.
Even Henry L. Stimson, his secretary of state, who ex-
plored the possibilities for collective action when Japan
invaded Manchuria in 1931, had to conclude by confronting
the facts of power in terms of moral sentiments. At the
time of the invasion Stimson reminded Japan that her action
violated the Kellogg-Briand Pact. Failing to influence Japan
with this reproach, he sought support from the League of
Nations, which now appeared to be a useful organization,
again without effect. The most that Stimson could do in the
context of Hoover's policies was enunciate the doctrine
that the United States would refuse to recognize "any situation, treaty, or agreement" achieved by means that violated
the terms of the Pact of Paris.[154] He could not propose to
support nonrecognition in any material way. The British
and French were not interested in a cooperative effort to
bring pressure against Japan, and when she next invaded
China, the president himself opposed the use of measures
as strong as economic sanctions. The Nine-Power Treaty
and the Kellogg-Briand Pact were, Hoover told the cabinet,
"solely moral instruments based upon the hope that peace
in the world can be held by the rectitude of nations and enforced solely by the moral reprobation of the world."[155]
Stimson then extended the doctrine of nonrecognition to
include any government established by force in the Far East
and later explained that what the Kellogg-Briand Pact
really meant was that war was illegal: "Hereafter, when
two nations engage in armed conflict either one or both of
them must be wrong-doers—violators of this general treaty
law. We no longer draw a circle about them and threaten
them with the punctiliousness of the duellists' code. Instead
we denounce them as law-breakers."[156] If denunciation apart
from law-enforcement meant anything, it could mean only

that the righteous would identify the wicked for the record and then treat as unthinkable even acknowledgment of the wicked's existence as a force—unless on occasion for moral rescue appeared.

In essence, Hoover's policies, like those of Harding and Coolidge, expressed a national wariness lest radical encounter or involvement should threaten American identity. The negotiations at Versailles, the potential entanglements associated with membership in a World Court, the tacit acceptance of other values implicit in any system of collective security—all suggested compromises with impurity. Virtue was an absolute that subsisted best in a cloistered state. The world, proved unworthy of salvation by force, would have to be saved simply by precept and example. If the United States engaged in good works, that was because it was animated by good will. Whether such acts proceeded from individuals in their own capacities or from individuals in their group capacity, the acts were essentially acts of charity—gratuitous, voluntary, evidence of largeness of heart, performed at the propitious moment.

Few individuals wished to bind themselves to the demands of statutes, and both the courts and the legislatures, reflecting the consensus, thwarted attempts to go beyond the modest establishment of public health centers and child welfare divisions on the state level to the larger regulation of child labor, the fixing of a minimum wage for women and their protection against exploitation, or the institution of publicly supported health insurance.[157] Some progressives wanted the government to enlarge its role to include relief for victims of material hardship,[158] but they could not secure sufficient support from the prewar radicals or the intellectuals to be politically effective. The old radicals had become deeply divided; "every radical and every liberal, apparently," Newton D. Baker wrote in the mid-twenties, "has his own theory or his own grievance."[159] And the intellectuals had turned their backs on government entirely. After the intolerance of dissent during the war and the imposition of Prohibition, they had little use for the political system that appeared to condone dictatorship by majorities.[160] "There was," as Richard Hofstadter has recorded, "a marked retreat from politics and public values toward the private and personal sphere, and even in those with a strong impulse toward dissent, bohemianism triumphed over radicalism."[161] What Hannah Arendt has called "the joy and the gratification that arise out of being in company with our peers, out of acting together and appearing in public, and out of inserting ourselves into the world by word and deed, and thus acquiring and sustaining our personal identity and beginning something entirely new,"[162] remained dormant or unknown.

Furthermore, social workers once active in efforts to reform society abandoned attempts to achieve national change politically and, affected by the new psychology's preoccupations with discovery of the Real Self, ministered to the psychological requirements of individuals to help them overcome the difficulties of adjusting to existing conditions as fixed conditions.[163] The number of such workers, together with the development of settlement houses and the growth of organizations like YMCA's, YWCA's, Scouts, and Campfire Girls,[164] showed that social concern was anything but dead, of course; yet social action was either confined to state and municipal levels or outside of government altogether. It would not be until the inauguration of the New Deal that the national government could be expected to do much more than encourage the Red Cross.

Lord Northington, an eminent eighteenth-century English judge, once stated: "Necessitous men are not, truly speaking, free men, but, to answer to present exigency, will submit to any terms that the crafty may impose upon them."[165] Insofar as Americans left it to only local government to eliminate the need that denied freedom, they indicated ignorance of both the scope of the denial and the relation of that denial to national purpose. And insofar as they left it to private individuals or private social agencies to eliminate the need, they made freedom the creature of private whim or private conscience.[166] When Calvin Coolidge remarked in a talk with reporters on March 1, 1929: "Perhaps one of the most important accomplishments of my administration has been minding my own business,"[167] he unwittingly revealed how alien to the affirmation of his own—or any American's—business was any affirmation of the business of others. Neither separately nor together did Americans will the will of others; they willed only what must be called private advantage or exclusiveness.

Chapter Five

The Individual and His Race

*A Beggar-Race can never be respected. Stop begging
for jobs, and create your own. Look around you and
wherever you see the need for factories and business,
supply it. Stop begging for a chance, make it yourself.
Remember God helps those who help themselves.*

MARCUS GARVEY[1]

AL CAPONE, NICOLA SACCO, AND BARTOLOMEO VANZETTI were
all three Italian immigrants, and all three accused of major
crimes; yet Capone, whose guilt was generally taken for
granted, was never convicted of anything except relatively
minor offenses and was treated by a considerable portion
of the public as a celebrity, to be admired even if ambiva-
lently, whereas Sacco and Vanzetti, whose guilt was at
least debatable, were electrocuted with the consent of the
highest authorities and mourned primarily by intellectuals
and radical workers. Marcus Garvey, concerned about the
conditions of black Americans, undertook to organize a nationalist movement that would give his race security and
dignity; yet, even though Harlem was at the very moment
becoming a renowned center of black awareness, he failed
to attract many black Americans to his cause and was finally
rejected by his contemporaries. On the surface, such responses might have seemed contradictory; beneath the
surface, however, they were consistent with the American
dedication to private advantage.

The glorification of Al Capone was virtually unavoidable; for in an ironic way, combining traits of the Alger hero, the frontiersman, and the scientist, he was a Representative Man. He began his life in the United States as an alien but was very quickly melted in the great pot.[2] He retained his Italian friendships and ethnic loyalties[3] but learned his adopted country's recipes for success with almost textbook fidelity. In less than a decade, and before he was thirty, he rose from a position as anonymous newcomer to that of internationally known millionaire, the more glamorous for his association with traditions diverse enough to include Robin Hood, Jesse James, and the Lone Ranger,[4] as well as the robber barons. He was sometimes respectful of "True Catholics," and ordered his henchmen not to steal cars in which images of St. Christopher were displayed.[5] He was concerned with the welfare of his neighborhood's Italians and in the early days of the depression, when, according to one of bootlegging's chroniclers, he was the Squire of Cicero, he and his gang "set up the first soup-kitchens and block-restaurants for the distribution of free food on Thanksgiving Day."[6] He distinguished himself from bankers and big businessmen because they were "crooked" and took from the poor, whereas he, as a supplier of liquor, generously performed a service for all.[7] Compared with Capone, Samuel Insull was, one lawyer declared, "a ruthless brigand." Capone was "relatively innocent,"[8] as he himself believed:

I don't interfere with big business. None of the big business guys can say I ever took a dollar from 'em. Why, I done a favor for one of the big newspapers in the country when they was up against it. Broke a strike for 'em. And what do I get for doing 'em a favor? Here they've been ever since, clamped on my back. I only want to do business, you understand, with my own class. Why can't they let me alone? I don't interfere with them any. Get me? I don't interfere with their racket. They should let my racket be.

The fact that he violated laws did not set him apart from others, whom he served: he was supplying "a legitimate demand. Some call it bootlegging. Some call it racketeering. I call it a business. They say I violate the prohibition law. Who doesn't?"[9] In fact, it was the very violation of the law that enhanced his stature. Outside the law, left to his own resources, he won the admiration of the law-abiding and the dependent. In the so-called Golden Age of Sports, he embodied a male principle, physical accomplishment enlarged to almost mythological dimensions.[10] Chroniclers note that when he attended a prize fight in Miami, he was escorted to the seat of honor by Jack Dempsey; "when [he] walked into the Charlestown Race Track, thousands rose to cheer their favorite bootlegger"; and

> When this real-life Robin Hood appeared at a Northwestern University rally, 10,000 Boy Scouts, young eyes a-sparkle with hero-worship, spontaneously set up the yell, to the embarrassment of their troop leaders: "Good old Al."

Or maybe it was "Yea, Al!" Some might argue that the boys' welcome was probably just their thanks for the tickets that Capone had given them all, but the absence of any protest by the older leaders against acceptance of the gifts in the first place suggests a regard that was more positive and more widely shared than any gratitude that the young Scouts may have felt or than any attitude that ostensible embarrassment could conceal.

His scars became fascinating in the press; his occasional jailors gave him special privileges in prison; his accomplishments placed him, in one student poll, among the ten "outstanding personages of the world," with President Hoover, Gandhi, Einstein, and Henry Ford; his meaning became the topic of a lead article in *The North American Review*; and it was thought important that during at least one sojourn in a cell he read Shakespeare and George Bernard Shaw.[11] He was called in his own time "the greatest and most successful gangster who ever lived . . . possessed of a genius for organization and a profound business sense,"[12] a man who was "not petty . . . [but] generous, foolishly so . . . [and] intensely loyal."[13] More recently one scholar has added that Capone, in his adaptation of weapons and strategies bequeathed by the war, and in his use of "the newly available mobility of the fast car," should even receive credit for the scientific way in which he modernized his calling.[14]

It was, though, less in his modernization of bloodshed than in his personal circumvention of the law that Capone captivated the Manassa Mauler and the Boy Scouts, and it was less in the circumvention of the law alone than in the circumvention for the purpose of ingeniously performing a laudable service that he attained the stature of a romantic figure. Prohibition, whatever its original purposes, had quickly lost most of its nobility. At one time its advocates were convinced that it would assure the destruction of liquor in conformity with God's ordinances and require even purging the Scriptures of references to wine and other intoxicants;[15] at another time they argued that it was helpful to the poor, especially the immigrants, who had difficulty retaining the wages of their labor in the face of clever exploitation by the liquor interests.[16] But whether the movement was inspired by divine or by social concern, it was soon, with the passage of the Volstead Act, regarded as an assault on personal freedom and resisted. Even in regions that considered urban forms of leisure sinful, and that favored prohibition because they did not share in the pleasure[17]—or, if they were white Southerners, because they did not want blacks to drink[18]—resistance flourished. In Kansas those who feared public condemnation simply drew their blinds or closed the barn door.[19] In Tennessee, at the time of the Scopes trial, William Jennings Bryan openly hobnobbed with moonshiners.[20] Everywhere, as Andrew Sinclair indicates, juries sitting in judgment dramatized hypocrisy or indifference:

In one trial in Virginia, a member of the jury dropped a half pint of liquor in court; no action was taken, and the jury as a whole found the defendant, a bootlegging Negress, guilty. On another occasion, a jury in San Francisco was itself put on trial for drinking up the evidence in a liquor case.[21]

Once personal freedom seemed threatened, it became as difficult for urban drinkers to think of bootleggers as criminals as it was for the mountaineers to aid in destroying the stills.[22] In fact, as one sociologist put it, "The people of Chicago wanted booze, gambling and women, and the Capone organization was a public utility."[23]

Not only did bootlegging cater to appetite, it also sustained individual declarations of independence of the law. Cocktail-party hosts boasted of the quality of their ingredients and the prowess of their particular bootleggers. Some adventurous citizens were even permitted to hang around the gangs.[24] Policemen who directed traffic at country-club dances were invariably invited in to share the blessings of the bar. The all-American boy who wished to be a glamorous escort had to have a hip flask when out on a date.[25] Violators of the public law became exemplars of the public will. "On one occasion," William E. Leuchtenburg reports, "thousands of bathers at Coney Island watched an encounter between Coast Guard cutters and rumrunners: they cheered the rumrunner as it opened a lead on the pursuing government boats."[26] When in 1924 the notorious Dion O'Banion lay "in state" for three days and nights in a ten-thousand-dollar coffin of bronze and silver, one newspaper woman made particular note of the "graceful hands which could finger an automatic so effectively."[27] Even the language of drinking changed to reflect what Edmund Wilson at the time perceived to be the drinker's sense of "an exceptional occurrence, a breaking away . . . from the conditions of his normal life." One was no longer simply intoxicated or drunk; one was lit, squiffy, fried, zozzled, stiff, primed, loaded for bear, ossified, embalmed, stewed to the gills, or said to have the screaming meemies or to burn with a low blue flame.[28] In such a context, Capone would scarcely have been booed.

Mabel Walker Willebrandt, who was appointed by Harding in August 1921 as assistant attorney general with responsibilities for enforcing prohibition, believed that the majority of Americans neither bought nor sold liquor and that they wanted enforcement to be successful.[29] Statistically she might have been correct; yet statistics are weaker than "Good old Al," and it is significant that public disenchantment with bootlegging and gang warfare has been attributed primarily to the St. Valentine's Day massacre of 1929, which seemed so far removed from the classic mystique, complete with Furies, that Hemingway had just commemorated in "The Killers" that it earned the judgment of being "lousy public relations."[30] If the enforcement of the law had any appeal, it was largely because of the activities of the celebrated government agents, Izzy Einstein and Moe Smith, whose lone exploits were admired as products of ingenuity and daring rather than approved as the implementation of moral consensus. Morality was, after all, a private matter; it was no one else's business who drank— and Al Capone helped keep it that way.

Yet, in a curious fashion, the conspicuous drinker's resistance to interference was but the corollary of the crusading prohibitionist's attempt to interfere. The prohibitionist sought to standardize his conception of society without regard for individual or cultural diversity or the value of social dissonance; the drinker, in return, sought to perpetuate his individual pleasures without regard for their social implications. The prohibitionist did not want his private convictions challenged by a different way of life; the drinker did not want his individual actions even questioned. Alike, they committed themselves to having their way, atomistic as that way might be.

A similar combination of commitment and rejection underlay the treatment of Sacco and Vanzetti. As everyone has recognized, their case was not so simple that it can be explained or analyzed in terms of a single factor. Unex-

amined motives, divergent ideologies, jurisdictional limits
established by law, manipulated evidence, external circumstances, all contributed to the execution of the two men in
a way that left the fairness of the verdict in undying doubt.[31]
Nevertheless, motives, ideologies, evaluations of evidence,
and responses to circumstance often proceeded from a bias
so widely shared that what to a later time could appear as
tragic prejudice scarcely ever during the critical years dis-
turbed the many sincere observers who saw nothing that
was incompatible with fairness. Although it has been difficult for most reasonable men and women to accept Judge
Webster Thayer's assertion that his personal opinions did
not affect his conduct of the trial, or to understand how
in any acceptable system of justice a judge could be permitted, as Thayer was, to rule on his own prejudice, it
is not difficult to believe that he thought that he had conducted the trial with scrupulous fairness and that the
Lowell Committee and Governor Alvan T. Fuller, when
they had the opportunity to prevent the execution, thought
not only that Thayer had been fair but also that they themselves were no less objective.

The Sacco-Vanzetti case began amid fears throughout
the United States that Attorney General A. Mitchell Palmer
was right when he declared that the country was threatened
with violent revolution by some sixty thousand alien radicals. In the spring of 1919 bombs had been mailed to
numerous high government officials, and although no individual could be found responsible for the attempted assassi-
nations, Palmer indicated that Communists, Red labor
agitators, and members of the IWW were joined in a vast
conspiracy. Despite liberal criticism of the patent and frequent abridgment of individual rights and liberties, the
government rounded up hundreds of foreign-born residents
suspected of depraved doctrines in order to deport them
and, in the spring of 1920, with the help of publicized in-
formers, proclaimed the discovery of evidence of a sinister
international plot.[32] A year later, coincident with the open-

ing of the proceedings in the Massachusetts courts against Sacco and Vanzetti, *The Delineator* began printing a series of articles entitled "Enemies of the Republic," by Calvin Coolidge, in which the vice-president equated radicals with revolutionaries and destroyers and noted that "about half of the names [of the Rand School faculty] are foreign and do not indicate a former achievement or training sympathetic with our national ideals." Sympathy with national ideals meant, he made clear, "respect" for and loyalty to existing institutions—and "correct" opinions.[33] When combined, foreign birth and radical ideas were so dangerous to the maintenance of the American order that the survival of institutions charged with assuring fair treatment received priority over the task that they were expected to perform.

Judge Thayer, accordingly, seemed to sense nothing improper in asking to preside at the Dedham trial after he had come to believe that the men should be convicted; or in telling reporters even while the jury was still being selected that he would "*show 'em*"; or in referring to the chief defense counsel as "a long haired anarchist"; or in commenting while the case was still in progress that the courts must be protected against anarchists; or in saying to a Dartmouth law professor, a fellow alumnus, also while the case was still in progress, and right after he had denied some defense motions: "Did you see what I did with those anarchistic bastards the other day. I guess that will hold them for a while. Let them go to the Supreme Court now and see what they can get out of them."[34] Accordingly, too, the governor's advisory committee, as one of the lawyers for the defense rightly saw, "knew the answers before their deliberations began,"[35] and undertook to discredit defense claims and to justify the prosecution rather than to review the case with objectivity. President A. Lawrence Lowell's questioning of witnesses and others consistently disclosed bias, and he and his colleagues criticized Judge Thayer only for "indiscretions in conversation."[36] Even Governor Fuller, who in his capacity as governor should have been more concerned with whether the conviction had been fair than with whether it agreed with his predilections, believed simply that he was to help guarantee the security of the Republic against subversives. He had, before his governorship, been one of a majority of congressmen to vote against seating Victor M. Berger, a Milwaukee Socialist, and he had replied to Berger's condemnation of the action by saying:

Berger characterizes the action of the House as a "crucifixion" and in a manner it is. It is the crucifixion of disloyalty,—the nailing of sedition to the cross of free Government, where the whole brood of Anarchists, Bolshevists, I.W.W.'s may see and read a solemn warning.[37]

To such Americans the guilt of Sacco and Vanzetti was reasonably certain. Sacco and Vanzetti were admirers of Eugene Debs;[38] they had been armed when originally apprehended; they had lied in ways suggesting "consciousness of guilt." How could they then be anything except guilty? With their broken English, radical doctrines, record of draft evasion, proved association with labor agitators, and suspected association with bomb-throwers and would-be assassins, they embodied precisely what the United States had most to fear. Neither of them could satisfy Harding's requirement of "easy assimilation" nor give the sort of assurance sought by Vandenberg of "invincible devotion to the purity of American citizenship."[39] They criticized American capitalism; they scorned Success; they questioned the validity of war; they imputed evil motives to all who held power.[40] When one supposed, as Thayer, Lowell, and Fuller did, that American processes were essentially decent and fair, one could not conceive of anyone's fearing arbitrary treatment to a point where he exhibited what would appear to be consciousness of guilt unless he were in fact guilty. And when one also supposed, as most people apparently did, that the Lowells of their society could do no wrong, one could regard criticism of the trial as simply further evidence of a radical plan of subversion and disruption and remain complacent about executing the enemy.

Where Capone's Italian provenance constituted largely a point of origin of a journey toward Americanization, the Italy of Sacco and Vanzetti was a point of ominous reference full of implications of alien threat.[41] In their undisguised disapproval of those American institutions and values that made the assurance of exclusiveness synonymous with the promotion of personal freedom, Sacco and Vanzetti became an unforgivable reproach to what H. G. Wells called "the self-righteous unrighteousness of established people."[42] So, while Capone was cheered by the many, Sacco and Vanzetti were mourned by only the few.

The general resentment of the challenge to selfish preoccupation was, then, not simply emotional self-defense; it was nothing less than a deep fear of encounters that might compel revisions of assumptions. As the indifference to doubts concerning the guilt of Sacco and Vanzetti suggests, the ordinary individual believed himself jeopardized rather than identified when he exposed his will and values to criticism and rebuff, and he accordingly gave the highest priority to personal sanctuary, often by joining groups that could act to obliterate customs and values different from his own. At its merely absurd this view perhaps sanctioned only petty inequities, such as those that one visitor from India saw as characteristic of the country he called "Uncle Sham": K. L. Gauba reported that in Seattle a man was sentenced to two hundred days in jail for saying: "To h—— with Coolidge; it's only an accident that he is President"; that in Texas the citizenry declared it immoral to wear spats and to dress for dinner; that in Alabama the Blue Laws explicitly proscribed dominoes; that in Washington fifteen Chinese men were arrested for playing mah-jongg; that in Minnesota side curtains on automobiles were prohibited unless it was raining; that in Los Angeles a city ordinance forbade bathing two babies in a single bathtub at one time.[43] At its most perverted, however, the view supported activities that culminated in the horrors of group brutality like those of the Ku Klux Klan, whose oaths of secrecy elevated the good of the Klan above that of society, whose religious and racial bigotry fostered the persecution of Catholics and Jews and encouraged the lynching and torture of Negroes in ways whose malice and sadism surpassed what had once been attributed to the Indians, whose private enforcement of private justice substituted whim and impulse for reason and due process—whose order, in short, was the Invisible Order, one beyond the reach of the public's critical scrutiny. It was not really curious, then, that the Klan inveighed against bootleggers and upheld monogamy and domestic virtue while, at the same time, they ignored moonshiners and their leaders deserted their spouses, transported whisky, and engaged in white slavery. For it was against the alien, the foreigner, the wicked urbanite, anyone who was "different"—not the WASPish "native American"—that the Klansmen were mobilized. Along with the frivolous as well as the respectable, the benighted sought refuge in a self-sufficiency that was, at the last, hermetic.[44]

This embracing of self-sufficiency was profoundly involved in the career of the Black Nationalist movement of Marcus Garvey, which foundered as much on the reluctance of individuals to sacrifice personal opportunity as it did on the personality of Garvey himself, but which at the same time contributed to a cultural consciousness that could be recovered as an alternative to exile or utter self-containment.

The postwar problem "overshadowing all" other problems was, as Harold Stearns wrote in 1919, "the impending race conflict between the black and the white which we diligently refuse to face."[45] Ever since the days of Reconstruction black Americans had been victims of atrocities that varied only in the rapidity and degree of sensible pain that accompanied death or humiliation. They had been hanged or burned, castrated or dismembered, starved or imprisoned by segregation. By the middle of the postwar decade the ruthlessly flamboyant extinction of the blacks' self-assertion in the South was being cruelly matched by its inexorably drab suffocation in the North, where unemployment, race riots, and ghettos worked as sure a disaster as the noose, the torch, and the blade. North or South, Negroes occupied no position of political authority; they were generally unable to secure the same credit, loans, and mortgages as whites could; they were excluded from most labor unions; they could not find housing readily or live without fear in what they did find. During Woodrow Wilson's presidency they had lost high government jobs, and although Harding managed to restore Negroes to some important positions, Coolidge did little to continue restitution. In his first message to Congress, December 6, 1923, he asked for funds to advance the agricultural and medical training of Negroes, and he advocated the "prevention and punishment against the hideous crime of lynching." But he took few steps to implement his own recommendations; and although he was accessible to prominent Negro spokesmen, he apparently only listened to their suggestions. He did not attempt to desegregate the civil service; he did not concern himself about civil rights beyond referring proposals to Congress and complaints to the Department of Justice; at the most he appointed a black man to be minister to Liberia. Far more interested in securing congressional support to reduce taxes than in risking division to curb white vigilantes, he did not exercise his available executive powers even to insure that federal officials would treat Negroes with courtesy.[46]

Perhaps Coolidge took comfort in statistics; for, as *The World Almanac* showed, the number of recorded lynchings was declining. Although in 1892 the number of Negroes lynched was 155, after 1901 the total never exceeded 100 and between 1922 and 1923 dropped from 51 to 29, with a low of 10 achieved for the year 1928. But if he did take such comfort, he had to do so not only by reading numbers as though they were bloodless but also by ignoring other statistics. In 1885 there had been 184 lynchings in the United States, of which 106 of the victims had been white. Thereafter the number of blacks always exceeded the number of whites, and whereas the number of black victims never fell below two figures, only twice after 1903 did the number of whites lynched rise to two figures, while during 1924, 1925, and 1927 their number fell to zero, and in the year that the low of 10 was reached for blacks, only one white victim was reported. Moreover, during Coolidge's presidency the power and prestige of the Ku Klux Klan reached its peak. In 1924 the organization enjoyed a membership of at least four and a half million, perhaps closer to six, and a gross income of approximately seventy-five million dollars a year. In 1925, on Saturday, August 8, some forty thousand white-robed Klansmen and Klanswomen (more of them from the North than from the South) proudly marched, without masks, occasionally twenty abreast, from noon to sundown along Pennsylvania Avenue, in the city of Washington, singing "Onward, Christian Soldiers" and catching in a huge American flag coins thrown by sympathetic spectators; the next year, fewer in number, they marched again.[47]

Although numerous whites were outraged by these desecrations of the national capital and the Klan was itself on the verge of a decline, there was scant evidence to support any expectation that Negroes were closer than they had been to substantially sharing at last in the fulfilments promised by American life. During the 1928 presidential campaign Republicans told Southern voters that the Democrats of Smith's city had put Negroes in charge of Harlem, where black politicians dictated to white secretaries; and Democrats told Southerners that Hoover posed a threat to their institutions.[48] Yet, because trust in the American promise was so much part of the national outlook that even those for whom it remained empty found the reality difficult to accept, the obstacles to fulfilment for Negroes were compounded.

It was in large measure the pervasiveness of this trust, especially in Harlem, that thwarted Marcus Garvey's efforts to free his oppressed people from bondage. James Weldon Johnson once referred to Harlem as "more than a Negro community; it is a large scale laboratory experiment in the race problem."[49] For Garvey, however, Harlem was less an experiment than the principal district in which to recruit those who might be persuaded to move the laboratory to Africa. A Jamaican, he had become aware of racial oppression in its West Indian and Latin American forms and, thinking in terms of rigid color and class lines, had in 1914 established in Jamaica the Universal Negro Improvement Association with the objective of creating ultimately a distinctive nation in the African "homeland." Encountering an apathy fostered by tradition and a political weakness produced by a want of financial resources, Garvey soon turned from his own country, where blacks were in the majority, to one in which they were in the minority but in which there might be money and clearly could be ferment. If, as Harold Cruse has pointed out, Garvey and his associates "wanted American Negroes to achieve the kind of nationalist unity as a minority that the West Indians could not achieve as a majority,"[50] they were perhaps not entirely mistaken in supposing that racial consciousness could become more energetic in the United States, where there was some mobility, than in the West Indies, where there was stagnation. There were grievances enough throughout the country to provide a cause, and in Harlem there was density enough to provide the nucleus for a following. In fact, during the first third of the century Harlem's population was increasing at a dramatic rate. In 1900, according to the Bureau of the Census, there were 67,304 "colored" people in New York City, of whom 41,125 were in Manhattan, concentrated in the Fifties. Ten years later there were 97,721 in the five boroughs, with 64,964 in Manhattan (which now meant Harlem), 60,534 of whom were, according to James Weldon Johnson, Negroes.[51] In 1920 the figures were 160,585 and 115,197; and by 1930, when the census bureau distinguished Negroes from others it called "colored," there were 327,706 Negroes in New York and 224,670 in Manhattan—with most of them continuing to be contained by boundaries whose expansion could barely keep pace with the increase in inhabitants.[52] This increase occurred at the very time that the total population of Manhattan was decreasing, from 2,331,542 in 1910 to 1,867,312 in 1930, which was only 17,000 more than it had been in 1900. Within the nation's largest city blackness could become a significant force, even if not in the way Garvey envisaged.

Fundamentally, Garvey was limited by his image of black destiny. Never having himself been part of the Southern migration to Harlem that during and after the war brought thousands of Negroes to New York searching for jobs left vacant by departing servicemen or pursuing dreams made glamorous by travelers and adventurers, he had not approached New York with the expectation of becoming an American success. Rather, with a conviction that the black man's liberation was linked with complete separation from the white man's society, he had entered the United States to lay the foundations for an African nation. The United States would remain white and as the population increased would eventually have no room for blacks. The blacks must live in their own place, which was of course Africa.[53] He addressed audiences of five or six thousand; he collected money for a black merchant marine, a Black Star Line; he created a corps of Black Cross nurses; he spoke eloquently of the glory and dignity of black men and women everywhere, and, in the words of one of his followers, "[gave] my people backbones where they had wishbones."[54] Yet the very form of his appeal was ultimately at odds with its spirit. He conceived of dignity and glory in terms alien to the traditions that his American audiences shared. While reminding them of the violation of their democratic rights, he established for himself a royal hierarchy. He regarded himself as "Provisional President of Africa," which was to be "the big black republic," but as James Weldon Johnson noted:

Around him he had established a court of nobles and ladies. There were dukes and duchesses, knight commanders of the

Distinguished Order of Ethiopia, and knight commanders of the Sublime Order of the Nile. There were gorgeous uniforms, regalia, decorations, and insignia. There was a strict court etiquette, and the constitution provided that "No lady below the age of eighteen shall be presented at the 'Court Reception' and no gentleman below the age of twenty-one." There was established the African Legion, with a full line of commissioned officers and a quartermaster staff and commissariat for each brigade.[55]

Rejecting a society that had placed whites in power and surrounded that power with all the panoply of rank and vanity, he then adopted the very models that in the past had kept blacks down.

Moreover, in West Indian fashion, he explicitly distinguished between blacks and individuals of lighter complexion, and thus not only countered the bias of the Blue Vein cliques but also implicitly relegated to an inferior status vast numbers of American Negroes whose sufferings had not been materially qualified by what were often very slight differences in color. He did, to be sure, in Johnson's words, "arouse a latent pride of the Negro in his blackness," but at the same time "wrought an overbalancing damage by the effort to drive a wedge between the blacks and the mixed bloods."[56] He spoke of the importance of "self-help" and "self-reliance," and stated that "God helps those who help themselves."[57] But ironically, although he thereby intended to strengthen the pioneer will to emigrate and redeem Africa, he could but strengthen the will—or the backbone—to remain in the United States, where the pioneer spirit was still celebrated. The very realization that the black man was as good as the white could only support the resolve of many blacks to claim their rightful inheritance in the only land that they had ever known or wanted to know, the only land in which opportunity was traditional and recognizable; it certainly could not persuade them to escape to a continent where mixed blood would be labeled white and government would belong to an aggressive hierarchy.[58] Doubtless for similar reasons the vaguer, less demanding (and less promising) Pan-Africanism of

Garvey's bitterest opponent, W. E. B. DuBois, would not prove attractive. "American Negroes," DuBois said, "were not interested."[59]

Essentially, "American Negroes" were Negro Americans, who, despite the atrocities, frustrations, and absence of substantial evidence that the American promise would be kept, experienced sufficient mobility and beheld enough tangible wealth to retain their faith. Black banks during 1900–28 entered what has been called their "greatest era."[60] Workers, when they joined unions like the miners' and longshoremen's, found themselves fairly treated, and when they remained aloof from associations that might benefit primarily white labor, and instead aligned themselves with employers, found themselves financially rewarded. In residential areas where hostility and threats were overt and crude, they found the glimmerings of racial self-sufficiency; for they discovered that when property and lives were in danger, other blacks were increasingly ready to mass together for purposes of defense and retaliation.[61] And wherever the black population was concentrated, as it most notably was in Harlem, they learned that they had cultural resources that were both entertaining and profitable—that, in fact, gave them a place of seeming distinction in the American scene.

Whatever racial confidence should be attributed to Garvey's eloquent strengthening of black pride, then, was inseparable from the pervasive white bourgeois values that kept the American continent more attractive than the African and that militated against collective black commitment. Like most whites, many blacks hoped to succeed on their own, and on similar terms. They were interested in status based on money; they sought acceptance by those in power, inevitably whites; they shunned visible ties with an Africa that marked them as different. They had, as E. Franklin Frazier has pointed out, "been taught that money will bring them justice and equality in American life,"[62] and whether they positively sought membership in the Blue Vein society that Charles Waddell Chesnutt had satirized, or simply negatively avoided association with "luscious black" of the sort exhibited by Emma Lou in Wallace Thurman's *The Blacker the Berry . . . ,*[63] they appeared to accept the rules and standards of the middle-class white society that surrounded them.[64] The fact that in November 1926 only 22,000 of Harlem's 225,000 inhabitants were registered to vote, and that of those eligible only 72 percent voted,[65] demonstrated not only political apathy but the absence of a sense of black community that would make claims on individual allegiance.

Claude McKay, with the sharp eye of a sensitive outsider, saw during a later period that in Harlem

there is very little group spirit among Negroes. The American Negro group is the most advanced in the world. It possesses unique advantages for development and expansion and for assuming the world leadership of the Negro race. But it sadly lacks a group soul. And the greatest hindrance to the growth of a group soul is the wrong idea held about segregation. Negroes do not understand the difference between group segregation and group aggregation. And their leaders do not enlighten them, because they too do not choose to understand. Negro institutions and unique Negro efforts have never had a chance for full development; they are haunted by the fear of segregation. Except where they are forced against their will, Negroes in general prefer to patronize white institutions and support white causes in order to demonstrate their opposition to segregation.[66]

Written of the thirties, McKay's description was nonetheless even truer of the twenties, when he himself was "in love with the large rough unclassical rhythms of American life . . . [and] fascinated by its titanic strength . . . [and when he] rejoiced in the lavishness of the engineering exploits and the architectural splendors of New York."[67] Although he consistently valued the distinction conferred by his color, and "was deeply stirred by the idea of a real Negro renaissance" and the commitment to "a common purpose" and "creating things . . . typical of their group,"[68] he too feared the segregation that "group aggregation" might produce. "I have always been a little dubious about anthologies of Negro poets and all that kind of stuff," he confessed. "Because there is a tendency to mix up so much bad with the good, that the good is hard to pick out. Of that kind of thing, some critics will say: 'Good enough for a Negro.' " He feared particularly the patronizing tone and sought to prevent it by meeting white expectations: "Though because of lack of common facilities and broad cultural contacts a Negro's work may lack the technical perfection of a white person's, intrinsically it must be compared with the white man's achievement and judged by the same standards."[69] In fact, not until his book of poems was published in 1922 in the United States—which he called "the great, difficult, hard world"—did he feel "the greatest joy of my life experience."[70] It was not surprising, then, that less intellectual Negro performers and Harlem theater managers should be more likely to measure their own achievements in like manner, and to place commercial success above cultural self-discovery for the masses.[71] The pride to which Garvey simply contributed was paradoxically pride in eligibility to share the white man's rewards.

A consequence was a burst of both self-seeking and self-expression, bourgeois commercialism and artistic discovery, combining a threat to collective black advancement with a basis for its eventual realization. It was certainly self-confidence and a belief in opportunities for material success that gave Harlem what Johnson called "a place in the list of famous sections of great cities." Harlem was, he pointed out, "known in Europe and the Orient, and . . . talked about by natives in the interior of Africa." It was "farthest known as being exotic, colourful, and sensuous; a place of laughing, singing, and dancing; a place where life wakes up at night." The inhabitants were "pleasure-loving"; the streets were "a parade ground"; and during warm evenings everyone went out strolling and socializing.[72] Moreover, as Rudolph Fisher emphasized at the time, Harlem was "superlatively rich in diversity," picturesque:

Consider the mere item of complexion, you whose choice may run only from cool white to warm rose-and-olive. Harlem offers its cool white too, with blue eyes and flaxen hair, believe it or not; proceeds on through the conventional shades to the warmth of rose-and-olive; and here, where the rest of Manhattan ends, Harlem has just begun: on through the creams, the honeys and high-browns, the browns, the sealskins and chestnuts—a dozen gradations in every class, not one without its peculiar richness. And if white be cool and olive warm, must not chestnut be downright fever? Harlemites swear that the Queen of Sheba was without doubt a sealskin brown and further insist that Cleopatra could have been but a honey at the fairest. And for evidence they will point out a dozen Shebas and any number of Cleopatras in the flesh.[73]

People came from all over to see and to hear. In Wallace Thurman's words, "The Negro and all things negroid had become a fad, and Harlem had become a shrine to which feverish pilgrimages were in order."[74] Mainly the pilgrimages were from the white sections of Manhattan and from some of the suburbs. Many whites, in search of rapture and release, turned to the night life of Harlem as though it would give them a vitality that they could find nowhere else. Whether it was the bizarre or the exotic, the sensuous or the romantic, the attraction for them was what vicarious primitivism can have for the individual looking for connections with roots or a past. The whites went to Harlem as though to a safe jungle to hear the beat of ancestral rhythms. Wealthy midtown matrons made their way north toward 135th Street and along Seventh Avenue to "doctors" reputed to possess mysterious healing powers: "He's not a regular doctor, but when he touches your feet—something about his hands: he knows just what to do—and you're really cured. She's been going to a specialist for years, but then she went to *him*, and in just two visits. . . ."[75]

It was not long before what was black meant money

from whites. The originality and spontaneity of New Orleans's Preservation Hall became the slicker, stylized program at the Cotton Club or the Savoy; potentially serious Negro drama waited in the wings of better-paying vaudeville or farce, or of white plays with black actors and black characters;[76] and the fashionable cabarets that were internationally known not only catered to white customers but eventually excluded all Negroes except waiters and performers.[77] Ambitious black entrepreneurs, encouraged by white property owners, and assured enough to exploit new ways of making good, transformed color into what would serve them as individuals isolated from a collective destiny. "I find all other peoples preparing themselves for the struggle to survive," Marcus Garvey complained as he viewed the scene, "and you, still smiling, eating, drinking, dancing and sleeping away your lives, as if yesterday were the beginning of the age of pleasure."[78] Garvey lamented "the Negro's lack of [a] racial nationalist ideal" and as a "cure" recommended "his removal to an atmosphere entirely his own, where he would be forced under rigid civil and other discipline to respect himself and his own racial authority."[79] With opportunities to prosper seemingly at hand, though, those with tangible prospects could scarcely be expected to prefer forced respect for any authority, even racial.

There would, of course, have been no success at all had there not been something of a distinctive atmosphere about Harlem whose promise Garvey ignored, an atmosphere that white society could not create; and that distinction would not have been possible apart from the large racial awakening that came to be identified with the "New Negro." For despite the commercial subordination of blacks in mass entertainment, there arrived a group of black poets, novelists, critics, and scholars that made black readers throughout the country aware of a heritage that had been but barely glimpsed in the past. White critics and scholars had consigned the few Negro writers known to them to lesser categories of literature (folk, dialect, local color, slave narratives), and black readers had had no sense of the possibility for different criteria. Now, however, in the light of beckoning postwar possibilities, younger writers, for whom stereotypes were demeaning and dialect condescending, looked at their own experiences and traditions and presented them in forms not prescribed by others. Some of the forms were, to be sure, conventional enough. There were couplets and sonnets and quatrains, for example. But there were emphases that white poets and storytellers would not have considered, and feelings that only ages of cruel suffering could have engendered, and experiments with organic form that, in relating words to the musical patterns and cadences of jazz or the blues, contributed to a sense of total art that was new and peculiar.[80] And there was a conviction that what they said would be received on its own terms.

In 1925 *Survey Graphic*, at Alain Locke's instigation, devoted its March number to a kind of symposium about Harlem, containing poems, stories, articles, drawings, and photographs by a score of contributors, most of them black. It focused on the Negro in New York with particular emphasis on his contributions in the various creative arts and their significance for postwar America. Its scope was comprehensive, its scrutiny close, and it was so popular that it had to be reprinted more than once to satisfy the demand. Finally, later the same year, it became in slightly expanded form the book entitled *The New Negro*, also edited by Locke, offering "the first fruits of the Negro Renaissance,"[81] a summary at mid-decade, a representative selection of works illustrating the main currents in Negro American literature, and an influence on other artists and on readers. Here were not manifestoes and protests, but what one student has perceived as attempts "to celebrate the fabric of Negro life."[82] Here were poetic forms as indigenous as the sermons and the blues to reaffirm identity and roots,[83] and to suggest an American continuity with traditions and cultures older than those whose absence or loss T. S. Eliot was then lamenting—a constant theme with variations.

Claude McKay was one of the poets included by Locke, and his poems—in particular those collected in his *Harlem Shadows* (1922)— have been said to mark the beginning of the Harlem Renaissance.[84] Intense, direct, and passionate, they sometimes exhibit nostalgia for the greener Jamaica from which he came, sometimes dwell on the fascination of Harlem's sensuous shapes, dusky colors, and degradation, sometimes become bitter protests against racial oppression. A view of tropical fruits recalls "dewy dawns," "mystical blue skies," and "nun-like hills" and precipitates a "wave of longing" that produces tears.[85] A Harlem dancer whose "voice was like the sound of blended flutes/Blown by black players upon a picnic day" and who "sang and danced on gracefully and calm,/ . . . /To me she seemed a proudly-swaying palm/Grown lovelier for passing through a storm," is praised by tossed coins and the devouring gaze of "wine-flushed, bold-eyed boys, and even the girls," and shows the poet a "falsely-smiling face."[86] Young street walkers "bend and barter at desire's call," victims of the

> . . . stern harsh world, that in the wretched way
> Of poverty, dishonor and disgrace,
> Has pushed the timid little feet of clay,
> The sacred brown feet of my fallen race![87]

The shut door of the white man's house challenges him "To bear my anger proudly" and "keep my heart inviolate/Against the potent poison of your hate."[88] He dares the baptism of destructive discrimination:

> Into the furnace let me go alone;
> Stay you without in terror of the heat.
>
> I will go naked in—for thus 'tis sweet—
> Into the weird depths of the hottest zone. . . .
>
> I will come out, back to your world of tears,
> A stronger soul within a finer frame.[89]

He commemorates the 1919 race riots with an exhortation:

> If we must die, let it not be like hogs
> Hunted and penned in an inglorious spot,
> While round us bark the mad and hungry dogs,
> Making their mock at our accurséd lot.
> If we must die, O let us nobly die,
> So that our precious blood may not be shed
> In vain; then even the monsters we defy
> Shall be constrained to honor us though dead!
> O kinsmen! we must meet the common foe!
> Though far outnumbered let us show us brave,
> And for their thousand blows deal one deathblow!
> What though before us lies the open grave?
> Like men we'll face the murderous, cowardly pack,
> Pressed to the wall, dying, but fighting back![90]

Yet, no matter how bitter, throughout he stands external to the action, declaring his responses, his sympathies, his identity, his connection, but less a vehement advocate of public deeds than a vigorous strengthener of individual resolve. For at heart McKay was deeply committed to the American dream:

> Although she feeds me bread of bitterness,
> And sinks into my throat her tiger's tooth,
> Stealing my breath of life, I will confess
> I love this cultured hell that tests my youth![91]

"Always I was inflamed by the vision of New York as an eye-dazzling picture," McKay said later, and emphasized that his bitterness and hate were compounded with love.[92] The qualities he praised were universal rather than racial; blackness only made them more essential and their display more of an achievement. The problem was to be a man in the face of a society that would degrade, and the solution appeared to rest with the individual—his capacity for endurance, his determination to persist, his self-confidence that meant pride.[93] Racial prejudice was a condition to be confronted not by collective action but by an attitude like that of the speaker in William Ernest Henley's "Invictus."

And the very affirmation of that attitude in material terms implied a belief in possibility within the American context.

Countee Cullen, also represented in Locke's anthology, younger than McKay and later to arrive on the literary scene—his first book, *Color*, appeared in 1925—was another poet of hope but less as the poet of stoic will than as the poet of troubled sensibility, caught between idea and feeling and, unable to give himself to either, inclined to resolution through consciousness. Cullen did not believe in a distinctive Negro tradition or Negro aesthetic. Verse might be written by Negro poets, but he questioned the reality of Negro verse. In his foreword to a collection of poetry that he edited in 1927, *Caroling Dusk: An Anthology of Verse by Negro Poets*, he declared:

As heretical as it may sound, there is the probability that Negro poets, dependent as they are on the English language, may have more to gain from the rich background of English and American poetry than from any nebulous atavistic yearnings toward an African inheritance.[94]

In principle he saw no reason to distinguish black authors from white and argued that "the double obligation of being both Negro and American is not so unified as we are often led to believe. A survey of the work of Negro poets will show that the individual diversifying ego transcends the synthesizing hue."[95] For himself he looked to Keats as a poetic ancestor and stated that all good poetry was "lofty thought beautifully expressed."[96] He could write poems bearing such titles as "Wisdom Cometh With the Years," "To My Fairer Brethren," "To One Who Said Me Nay," "Harsh World That Lashest Me," "Youth Sings a Song of Rosebuds," and "To Endymion" with the apparent belief that as late as the mid-twenties they disclosed a distinguishable ego,[97] as though a clever turn, an apt phrase, or carefully wrought truths about love, death, and time would carry out the promise implicit in a poem he wrote for his high-school magazine in 1921, "I Have a Rendezvous with Life (with Apologies to Alan Seeger)."[98] Yet he also found his precepts at odds with his needs. Although he could say in 1939 that he had "met with very few instances of discrimination during my life," he was sensitive to the complexities of being black in the United States and less ready than McKay to consign them to an assertion of will:

In spite of myself . . . [he said in 1926] I find that I am actuated by a strong sense of race consciousness. This grows upon me, I find, as I grow older, and although I struggle against it, it colors my writing, I fear, in spite of everything I can do. There may have been many things in my life that have hurt me, and I find that the surest relief from these hurts is in writing.[99]

It was this struggle that produced and informed his most memorable poems. "Heritage," for example, explicitly acknowledges both the impossibility of forgetting Africa and the impossibility of rejecting Christianity. Africa is memory, a sensuous natural setting full of wonder and appeal, but "A book one thumbs/Listlessly, till slumber comes." For "I belong to Jesus Christ,/Preacher of humility;/Heathen gods are naught to me." At the same time, the Savior, the Trinity are not his personal reality; they are abstractions: ". . . in my heart/Do I play a double part." There is a distance between him and the God he professes.

> Ever at Thy glowing altar
> Must my heart grow sick and falter,
> Wishing He I served were black,
> Thinking then it would not lack
> Precedent of pain to guide it. . . .
> Lord, forgive me if my need
> Sometimes shapes a human creed.[100]

His well-known "Yet Do I Marvel" concludes its series of instances of the inscrutability of the Divine Will by saying:

> Yet do I marvel at this curious thing:
> To make a poet black, and bid him sing![101]

And "The Shroud of Color" describes the course of the poet's anguish as, addressing the Lord, he begins by asserting: "My color shrouds me in, I am as dirt/Beneath my brother's heel," continues by lamenting that his strength is inadequate to his condition, and concludes, after a vision in which he beholds Lucifer's defiant fall from Heaven and scenes of the deathless strivings of "all dark people," by affirming: "I laughed aloud . . . / . . . I looked and saw the rising sun."[102] Even the lynching of a black boy in "The Black Christ" culminates in the image of a second crucifixion and renewal of faith.[103] If McKay leaves the black man's fate a matter of individual determination, Cullen leaves it a matter of individual awareness. The struggle with a sense of race consciousness is an inescapable part of the black condition that each individual must confront privately; his freedom and hope lie in the acceptance of mortality and contention.

Perhaps, though, it was Langston Hughes who in his poetry most completely celebrated color in America and found promise in his identity. Sharing some of McKay's belief in the dignity of the resolute stance and some of Cullen's questioning response to the double obligation imposed by race, he also conveyed an identification with what he rendered that in tone, statement, and form was more intimate than theirs. He wanted to enable "the smug Negro middle class to turn from their white, respectable, ordinary books and papers to catch a glimmer of their own beauty."

We younger Negro artists who create now intend to express our individual dark-skinned selves without fear or shame. If white people are pleased we are glad. If they are not, it doesn't matter. We know we are beautiful. And ugly too. The tom-tom cries and the tom-tom laughs. If colored people are pleased we are glad. If they are not, their displeasure doesn't matter either. We build our temples for tomorrow, strong as we know how, and we stand on top of the mountain, free within ourselves.[104]

From the beginning he spoke with love, with tenderness, with compassion, as well as with pride, of his dark heritage. His "Proem" in his first collection, *The Weary Blues*, begins:

>   I am a Negro:
>   Black as the night is black,
>   Black like the depths of my Africa.[105]

And it introduces poems about blues singers, black dancers,
black lovers, about the Harlem that Hughes called "Jazz-
onia." It announces a black man's point of view and, implicitly, his ability to hear the jazz bands sob, to translate
musical rhythms into verbal patterns, to capture the aesthetic possibilities of colloquial statement:

>   Strut and wiggle,
>   Shameless gal.
>   Wouldn't no good fellow
>   Be your pal.
>
>   *Hear dat music. . . .*
>   *Jungle night.*
>   *Hear dat music. . . .*
>   *And the moon was white.*
>
>   Sing your Blues song,
>   Pretty baby.
>   You want lovin'
>   And you don't mean maybe.
>
>   *Jungle lover. . . .*
>   *Night black boy. . . .*
>   *Two against the moon*
>   *And the moon was joy.*
>
>   Strut and wiggle,
>   Shameless Nan.
>   Wouldn't no good fellow
>   Be your man.[106]

It explains his imagery (the gentleness of night: "Dark like
me"; the tenderness of night: "Black like me."[107]), his
affinity for Southern warmth in contrast to civilized Northern cold ("We should have a land of sun,/Of gorgeous
sun"[108]), his choice of the river as metaphor in the familiar
"The Negro Speaks of Rivers" that links the Mississippi
with the Euphrates, the Congo, and the Nile and speaks
for the extent and depth of the black American's link

with original humanity.[109] Although some of the poems in Hughes's first volume are about his life as a sailor and are unconnected with the proclamation of blackness, most of those that he published in the twenties are, as he said, "racial in theme and treatment, derived from the life I know. In many of them I try to grasp and hold some of the meanings and rhythms of jazz."[110]

He did not precisely reproduce either jazz or the blues; as James Emanuel has shown, Hughes did not subordinate poetic possibilities to the limitations that a consistently faithful transcription of musical forms would have imposed; but he did attempt to embody in his work "Negro folk-song forms" and to use them to express the "black man's soul."[111] Moreover, his very attention to these forms both as subjects and as patterns for his poetry constituted an affirmation of the intrinsic value of indigenous Negro expression. "The rhythm of life/Is a jazz rhythm,/ Honey."[112] The mingled despondency and joy of the blues, whether of a homesick hobo or a crooning piano player on Lenox Avenue, consistently are the embodiment of the Negro American's condition.[113] If Cullen's poetic ancestor was Keats, Hughes's was Whitman—and perhaps the Wordsworth of the Preface to the *Lyrical Ballads*. The common experiences and language were there to be used and then must be re-created. The spectacles Hughes witnessed, the speech he heard, the rhythms he responded to, the agonies—these were his reality. "Mother to Son," the most moving of the poems in *The Weary Blues*, is on the explicit level simply an admonition, in the category of Longfellow's "Psalm of Life." Yet because the poem is not *about* the mother but is in fact the rendering of the mother herself—and because the controlling metaphor (the stairs) and the meter are means to characterize her, are "in character," that is—the admonition is not prescription; it is action.[114] And "Mulatto," included in his second volume, likewise a story simple to paraphrase, one about the dual heritage,

fully objectifies the black experience of white lust and heartless racial perfidy, while at the same time it communicates
the sweetness of the Georgia night and of dusky humanity,
because the son's dramatic claim and the father's imagined
denial and memory are, in the irregular stanzas provided,
the very form of the experience and not a form to which
the experience must be subordinated. The form of the argument is, in short, itself argument, as it is in Whitman's
"Out of the Cradle Endlessly Rocking" or "When Lilacs
Last in the Dooryard Bloom'd." The alternating of scorn
with nature's soft presence continues until the father, his
recollections and nostalgia awakened, must accept the son's
claim, which is itself an appeal to nature.[115]

Hughes's poetry, no vehicle for something external, thus
provides its own life, and insofar as it does that, it becomes
a celebration of the poet's expression of its traditions, of
its locale. The lines that constitute the Epilogue for *The
Weary Blues* could appropriately conclude any selection of
his poetry during the twenties:

> I, too, sing America.
>
> I am the darker brother.
> They send me to eat in the kitchen
> When company comes,
> But I laugh,
> And eat well,
> And grow strong.
>
> Tomorrow,
> I'll sit at the table
> When company comes.
> Nobody'll dare
> Say to me,
> "Eat in the kitchen,"
> Then.
>
> Besides,
> They'll see how beautiful I am
> And be ashamed,—
>
> I, too, am America.[116]

Far from denying the American dream, Hughes wholly affirms it, insisting only that he as Negro American share it.
In fact, as he dwells upon the condition and expression of
colored Americans—yellow, brown, black, even red—he
declares in effect that black identity is itself part of the
American opportunity, and an essential part of the beauty
of America. Paul Laurence Dunbar had worn the mask;
the mask was now there no longer. Consciousness was made
visible.

Consciousness of black identity pervaded the work of
short-story writers and novelists as well. Some examples
were included by Locke in *The New Negro* to suggest the
range of resources to be developed by black writers. They
could, like Bruce Nugent in "Sahdji,"[117] use an East African
setting to show that an African woman's faithfulness to
her slain husband, the tribe's chieftain, has greater dignity
than the sentimental conception of love that ordinarily appeals to Western readers; or like Eric Walrond, in "The
Palm Porch,"[118] expose the pretensions of a shrewd mulatto, a woman "colorful as a pheasant,"[119] who runs a
house in Panama that caters to seagoing "grimy Britishers"
and the local Colon constabulary, and show that those pretensions are still superior to the grosser appetites of the
clients who support her; or like Zora Neale Hurston, in
"Spunk,"[120] relate the fatal rivalry of two mill workers for
the favors of a susceptible girl and treat the matter with
sufficient humor to give it something of the quality of a
folk tale. Or they could, like John Matheus in "Fog,"[121] in
which a trainload of commuters, mainly workers, abandon
bigotry, prejudice, and selfishness and find solidarity when
they think that a bridge that they are crossing is going to
collapse into the Ohio River, create a parable of hope.
    Or like Rudolph Fisher, in sketches and stories about
Harlem,[122] they could with mingled humor, satire, and compassionate irony show the humanity in foibles and limitations peculiar to the Harlem scene. King Solomon Gillis, a

huge country innocent who is overwhelmed by the wonders of Harlem, where they "even got cullud policemans," and is tricked into dope-peddling, has two ambitions: to get himself a "gal" and to become a policeman; apprehended by white plain-clothes men, he begins to resist, but yields exultantly when he is finally confronted by a black man in uniform. The Reverend Shackleton Early, who has found the pulpit a less precarious means of livelihood than the gambling he once depended on, must watch the better-paying portion of his congregation forsake him for the Reverend Ezekiel Taylor, a real rural preacher from the South, and hypocritically not reveal his frustration. Jutie, a teen-age girl, becomes a seeker of wanton pleasure while her grandmother prays for her lost soul. A father inveighs against "too much learnin' " but rejoices when his daughter wins a scholarship to Teachers College. A hardened bootlegger is so affected by a revival meeting he pauses to observe that he cannot regard it as circus; for it "makes me think of the old folks or somethin' . . . it just sorter—gets me—." Naive or worldly, ridiculous or pathetic, exotic or commonplace, they are figures in a panorama of black humanity and because they are human testify to their kinship with the mankind familiar to readers—and since the readers of *The New Negro* were Americans, white as well as black, the effect was to show that these characters, too, were America.

Most of the stories in Locke's anthology have the quality of vignettes. Even the two selections from Jean Toomer's *Cane*, taken out of context, give the impression of being little more than portraits, lyric in effect.[123] Characters have no career; they have a look, they are in a situation, and that is all. Although it is in such sketches that a writer like Rudolph Fisher excels, it is in the more extended form of the novel that the implications of the lives of the individuals sketched are made meaningful. Fisher's *The Walls of Jericho*, for example, peopled though it is with stock characters that are easy to dismiss or ridicule, goes beyond the portrayal of obvious situations to show what color and prejudice can mean in the total lives of individuals. Fred Merrit, the liberal Negro lawyer who can pass; Miss Agatha Cramp, the philanthropic white old maid who would do good for whatever is remote; Joshua Jones ("Shine"), the simple piano mover who falls in love with the beautiful black maid, Linda; Henry Patmore, the vengeful black proprietor of a pool parlor; many others, among them avant-garde writers and silly members of the black bourgeoisie, all move in a society whose conflicts are conditioned by the presence of racial bias and create for themselves walls of self-illusion behind which they are secure. It is these walls that Shine in particular—the character closest to being Fisher's protagonist—must break down, and does. He ceases to be "hard" and deserves Linda, fully humanized at last.

Thurman's *The Blacker the Berry* . . . , while grimmer in tone, also makes the fact of color and color prejudice its central theme, and Emma Lou Morgan, of a "luscious black complexion,"[124] very early considers her blackness as a curse and leaves the semiwhite world of Boise, Idaho, for Los Angeles and finally New York to search for love and a livelihood. But so affected by the value of whiteness are even the men and women in Harlem that she finds her color a recurrent barrier to intimacy and ultimately, amid the promiscuous, the faithless, and the emasculated, a cause for unhappiness. It is only when she resolves "to accept her black skin as being real and unchangeable" and to fight for acceptance by herself rather than by others—to become "eminently selfish"—that she can become hard enough to hope to survive.[125] Unlike Fisher, Thurman cannot entertain the pleasurable, even satirically, lest it be deluding. Truth requires that one perceive hardness to be the prerequisite to liberation. Loneliness is the corollary of victory. One may then live without joy, but one may live with self-respect.

Less doctrinaire, but perhaps more complex and significant in defining the new consciousness, are Toomer's *Cane* and Hughes's *Not Without Laughter*. Deceptively eclectic in appearance, in its prose and verse superficially resembling something of a combination of *Spoon River Anthology* and *Winesburg, Ohio*, lyrical in tone, and often as reticent about race as Toomer himself was, *Cane* is nevertheless an artistically integrated account of the black experience that concludes in an affirmation. The poetry and prose, far from being haphazardly assembled, provide variety and modulation for a theme that is constant and a development that is systematically structured. As the most attentive critics have demonstrated, the theme is the condition and role of blackness, and the development is of a point of view necessary to the recovery of what once gave life to the "souls of slavery."[126] Through episode after episode Toomer shows the potential for individual fulfilment perverted, thwarted, or destroyed until he can force the question of how fulfilment is possible and provide an answer. The episodes are not all alike, however, and the three-part division of the book, along with the use of poetic interludes, emphasizes that Toomer has a dialectical development in mind.

The first part consists of a group of sketches rendering the loveliness, agony, possibility, and frustration of life in the South and emphasizing the warmth of the heritage to which the seldom-seen narrator, who is a kind of Camera Eye, sympathetically responds. Karintha "carries beauty, perfect as dusk when the sun goes down," but because all men want her, her soul is damaged; it "was a growing thing ripened too soon." She has an unwanted child and buries it in a smoldering sawdust pile. Becky is a white woman who has two Negro sons; treated as an outcast, she is finally entombed in a house that the righteous have set fire to. Carma, strong as a man and faithless to her husband, provokes her husband until he loses his head, murders another, and is sentenced to the chain gang. Fern, half-Jewish, desires more than men can give with their bodies, and

becomes unapproachable. Esther at the age of nine is profoundly affected by her sight of a "clean-muscled, mag-
nificent, black-skinned Negro" who comes to town as a
preacher, and dreams of fulfilment with him until, when
she is twenty-seven, she finds him drunk and hideous in a
disreputable place on a side street. Louisa, loving and loved
by both a black man and a white, finally occasions a fight
between them that ends in a lynching. Throughout the
first part, then, there is life, fertility, that comes to nothing
because, somehow, the press of feeling for expression,
consistently embodied in the Negro women, encounters the
deforming limits set by white society, which has no place
for spirit. The spirit, undefined in explicit language, is nonetheless present as a choral refrain in the poems that separate the prose sketches from each other. These poems
celebrate reapers, cotton, the sun, the Georgia dusk, pine
needles, evening—and suffering. They suggest the heritage
of natural vitality that the white man has disrupted.

The second part, set in Washington's ghetto, appropriately contains fewer poetic interludes. There is excitement on 7th Street, and money, and booze, and movement.
But there is not only impossibility of fulfilment; there is
also a loss of potential. Rhobert is crushed by a house he
must maintain. Avey goes to the city and becomes a whore.
Dorris desperately tries to awaken John, but even when
she dances he remains in shadow, withdrawn. Dan Moore
and Muriel almost come together but fail, because they
cannot yield to their feelings in an alien milieu. Paul, who
is darker than the white students he goes around with,
cannot win Bona because he cannot bring himself to accept and affirm his racial distinction. When he does implicitly do so at the last, it is too late, although in so doing he
testifies to the way false ideals have constrained and devitalized, and reveals the line along which self-liberation
lies. If in the South men and women possess a potential
that cannot be realized, in the North they lose the po-

tential in a sterile existence. In neither the North nor the South can sexual energy generate society; for society either thwarts or destroys what gives life and communion.

Toomer, however, does not conclude *Cane* there. His final section, "Kabnis," is a short play dedicated to Waldo Frank, with whom he had traveled through the South before writing *Cane* and with whom he had found, in Georgia,

the starting point of almost everything of worth that I have done. I heard folk-songs come from the lips of Negro peasants. I saw the rich dusk beauty that I had heard many false accents about, and of which till then, I was somewhat skeptical. And a deep part of my nature, a part that I had repressed, sprang suddenly to life and responded to them. Now, I cannot conceive of myself as aloof and separated.[127]

Toomer's long unwillingness to place himself in a racial category, as an individual and as a writer, is common knowledge now. His mixed heritage, his pale skin, his belief that art required no racial adjective all presented him with a dilemma.[128] It was, for him, fundamentally a question of the relation of art to the artist's roots, of the relation of personal liberation to personal heritage. The dedication to Frank indicates that the trip to Georgia had provided the answer, and "Kabnis" objectifies Toomer's struggle even as it offers hope within the framework of the fiction. For as the characters argue about what the Negro race can be— shall it settle for an assigned "place"? shall it become indistinguishable from the white?—they must come to terms not only with each other's ideas but also with Father John, the deaf and blind old man who lives in the cellar of Fred Halsey's workshop and is either "A mute John the Baptist of a new religion—or a tongue-tied shadow of an old."[129] In fact, he symbolically connects them. He lives in the cellar like a neglected racial memory—"symbol, flesh, and spirit of the past," as Lewis, the most perceptive of the characters, a Northerner who would establish black solidarity, calls him[130]—and represents the Negro experience through history:

> Slave boy whom some Christian mistress taught to read the Bible. Black man who saw Jesus in the rice fields, and began preaching to his people. Moses—and Christ—words used for songs. Dead blind father of a muted folk who feel their way upward to a life that crushes or absorbs them.

Lewis bids him "Speak, Father!" and wonders: "Suppose your eyes could see, old man. . . . Suppose your lips . . ."[131] Eventually, unable to stand the pain with which others struggle, Lewis flees the cellar; but Carrie K., Halsey's sister, who feeds the old man and who remains behind with Kabnis, the Northern "professor," hears him finally speak. He says: "Sin." He says: "Th sin whats fixed . . . upon th white folks—f tellin Jesus—lies. O th sin th white folks 'mitted when they made th Bible lie."[132] Kabnis does not understand, but Carrie does. She kneels before the old man, murmuring: "Jesus, come." The light "streaks through the iron-barred cellar window. Within its soft circle, the figures of Carrie and Father John." Outside: "The sun arises."[133] Blind and deaf, old Father John has begotten awareness in young Carrie, who sees and hears. The old is the life-giving source of the new; the black links are there to be acknowledged, not broken. Although Toomer provides no prescription for action, he affirms the book's epigraph: "Oracular./Redolent of fermenting syrup,/Purple of the dusk/Deep-rooted cane." Cane, the embracing metaphor, defines the prophecy, sweetness, racial beauty, history, and generation that consciousness can take possession of to become the agent of liberation.

Not Without Laughter, although it does not dwell on the problem of acknowledging the heritage of the black race, does focus upon the question of how to continue that heritage. Hughes was from Lawrence, Kansas, and "wanted to write about a typical Negro family in the Middle West, about people like those I had known in Kansas."[134] He did not regard his own family as typical enough to provide details, but he did know how it felt to be "a typical Negro boy."[135] So he created a story about characters more typical than his family could produce, yet informed by values that clearly his family shared with him. It is a story of growing up, and it is a lesson. Sandy Rodgers's grandmother, Aunt Hager Williams, is the determined, strong embodiment of the tradition of endurance and stability that more recent generations could dismiss as subservient but that Hughes shows to be strong enough to confront and survive adversity. She is the first character to appear in the story, and her first act is to hold Sandy close to her as a cyclone descends upon the village, shakes and tugs at the house, and then passes on to leave the dwelling standing. Sandy's mother works, and sometimes has to go away to find a job. His father Jimboy comes home on occasion, but more often is elsewhere. His aunt, Harrietta, is restless and rebellious, does not like white people, and runs off to become a popular blues singer. Sandy himself studies, works, does chores, and when Aunt Hager dies, finally goes to live with his mother. With her he visits Aunt Harrie and Billy Sanderlee, her accompanist, and reveals to Harrie that although his mother wants him to get a full-time job to help support the family, he really wants to continue his education. Harrie, having found that "all of us niggers are too far back in this white man's country to let any brains go to waste," sides with him: "He's gotta be what his grandma Hager wanted him to be—able to help the black race . . . the whole race!"[136] She commits herself to providing whatever any job he could find would provide—and gives him a ten-dollar bill for his books. On the way home he and his mother pass a church where the singing of worshipers reminds them of the "old folks." "It's beautiful!" Sandy cries.[137] The link is forged; what Grandma Hager wanted is to be fulfilled by Sandy—he is to study, to rise, to help the race. It is an echo of Hughes's "Mother to Son"; the strength of the old generation is reasserted in the new.

Color, instead of being a condition to struggle against, is a condition to accept as part of oneself. "I am the darker brother. . . . I, too, am America." The individual comes to terms with himself through acceptance and, because he too is then America, preserves his individuality.[138]

The black American's individuality was then as self-centered as the white American's but distinguished by its conscious relationship to group expression and common effort. On the one hand, there was the "tide of Negro migration, northward and city-ward," that Dr. Locke indicated was a tide toward a beachhead for individual success:

With each successive wave of it, the movement of the Negro becomes more and more a mass movement toward the larger and the more democratic chance—in the Negro's case a deliberate flight not only from countryside to city, but from medieval America to modern.[139]

On the other hand, there was the awakening of a racial consciousness in the city, most notably in Harlem, that was comparable to the national awakening that had not much earlier occurred in Dublin[140]—although in this instance the consequence would be integration, not separatism:

The racialism of the Negro is no limitation or reservation with respect to American life; it is only a constructive effort to build the obstructions in the stream of his progress into an efficient dam of social energy and power.[141]

This racial concern fostered, as the historically minded Arthur A. Schomburg could see, the Negro's "thinking more collectively, more retrospectively than the rest,"[142] and led to an emphasis on what Arthur Huff Fauset called the value of the "nearness to nature" and "universal appeal" of Negro folklore.[143] It stimulated Negro painters and critics of the plastic arts to scrutinize the nature of viable traditions and to argue about indigenous form and content very much as the participants in the Irish Renaissance had argued and very much as those earlier Americans had similarly argued when they decided to listen to muses other than Europe's courtly ones. Aided by the growing respect for African art among painters and sculptors everywhere, it encouraged respect for the black man's personal idiom and for the transcription of experience peculiar to a variety of black Americans.[144] In addition, it attracted some white writers and intellectuals who seemed to find in a shared sense of a past linked to nature a picturesque spiritual and aesthetic resource, a connection between art, life, and personal identity missing from their own milieu, and they in turn sympathetically encouraged its development. Carl Van Vechten particularly, because of his widespread acquaintance among editors and publishers, enabled numerous Negro authors to see print.[145] Had there been no crash and depression, the literary development that was later continued by Richard Wright might not have been interrupted. For black writers by the end of the twenties were clearly beginning to acquire a group sensibility that could survive the political preoccupations of the thirties more successfully than could anything bequeathed by most of their widely celebrated, lighter brothers and that could enable them to become more profoundly aware of the isolation and privacy latent in the prevailing notions of self-advancement that they had shared.

Chapter Six

The Individual and His Protagonists

"I had made a separate peace. I felt damned lonely. . . ."

FREDERIC HENRY IN *A Farewell to Arms*[1]

IT IS AN IRONY but characteristic of epochs that the major poets and novelists, even when they are critical of their society, usually share the principal assumptions responsible for what they reject. The Negro writers, as has been shown, were despite their new awareness unable to perceive the need to challenge the narrow self-concern pervading the decade's economic, social, and political thinking. The white writers, lacking the kind of social sensibility that was evolving in Harlem, could perceive that need even less and remained so committed to individualism as self-enclosure—a kind of Emersonian self-reliance without either the Oversoul or a recognition of contingency—that they simply treated their own peculiar outlook as a universal given. T. S. Eliot, for example, imagined he was speaking for modern man when in *The Waste Land* he lamented the absence of a viable tradition, used fragmentary scenes and discontinuity to assert the meaninglessness of history and the irrelevance of time, and displayed the pickle-laden Thames as an image of the disappearance of spiritual glory. He doubtless supposed himself an exemplar when he portrayed the futile fisher concluding that there was nothing left but to set his own lands in order. "The river sweats/Oil and tar." Elizabeth and Leicester in their gilded shell appear no more.

Langston Hughes knew more rivers than that, and perceived a connection, and the flow of history into his time; but he was Negro, which could mean little to Eliot, who was circumscribed without awareness of circumscription.

It was in large measure, perhaps, a question of how to define nobility, or the hero. In the twenties the hero was not an individual who had unified a nation, integrated a society, or promoted a sense of mutual concern. He was not an individual who risked a display of feeling in behalf of his own purposes—which is an acknowledgment of the presence of others. He was the lone individual, the individual whose accomplishments appeared to have been unaided, the individual whose attitude was cool to a degree that surpassed even the rational self-containment celebrated by Jane Austen long before. "The Coolidges never slop over," declared the president of the mid-twenties,[2] revealing the utter self-sufficiency that made of him what William Allen White labeled "a sort of midget Yankee Paul Bunyan," "an ideal . . . a hero in fact."[3] Self-sufficiency, insulation from the claims of others, was what the country could admire.

Fittingly, the most notable of the decade's heroes was called the Lone Eagle. Much has been written about the extent to which Charles A. Lindbergh's flight embodied the triumph of mechanical skill, of organized technology. He himself praised his "wonderful motor."[4] But no one who remembers the occasion can equate anything with the fact that Lindbergh was seen as having done it all himself. It had, after all, been a race. Two Frenchmen were to attempt the westward flight; Commander Richard E. Byrd and three other rivals, all with copilots, and Byrd himself with a third member for his crew, were to attempt the eastward one. Lindbergh, unknown, later than the others to reach the East Coast, was seen as one who came from behind and who, when his competitors suffered mishaps, or delays, or catastrophes, proceeded without hesitation to do what needed to be done and succeeded. And, unlike the others, alone. He referred to himself and his plane as "we," but his fans regarded that as simply an excess of modesty. "Lucky Lindy/Up there in the blue. . . ." There were songs; there were lucky coins. Charles A. Lindbergh was everyone's personal talisman, his good-luck charm—a token of the potential of the unaided man. Newspapers stressed his freedom from "comrades, moneyed chums . . . boards . . . councils. . . . He plans ALONE. . . ."[5] Magazine writers described him as another pioneer, whose boyhood had been characterized by his doing things "by himself" and who exhibited the "natural simplicity" of Cooper's Leatherstocking.[6] His ego was without offense, determined, boyish, quiet, modest to such a degree that he seemed to embody the fullest possibilities of self-possession. Describing his "whole-hearted welcome" in France that "touched me beyond any point that any words can express," he writes in *We*, his account of his life and trans-Atlantic flight:

I left France with a debt of gratitude which, though I cannot repay it, I shall always remember. If the French people had been acclaiming their own gallant airmen, Nungesser and Coli, who were lost only after fearlessly departing in the face of conditions insurmountably greater than those that confronted me, their enthusiastic welcome and graciousness could not have been greater.[7]

The self-deprecation in the moment of triumph, the acknowledgment of the power of nature after that power had been overcome—this was heroism.

At the same time, since the admiration for Lindbergh was for his qualities rather than for the unique person, it was an admiration that could be extended with only lesser intensity to others who similarly distinguished themselves as individuals. The decade has often been alluded to as "The Golden Age of Sports," meaning the age of sports "heroes": Big Bill Tilden, Bobby Jones, Jack Dempsey, Gertrude Ederle, Babe Ruth, Red Grange, even the racehorses Man o' War and Zev—individuals whose disciplined performance would set the standards for all successors.[8] The

Golden Age also meant a decade in which college team-sports became immensely profitable, because, in part, they provided week-end displays of individual exploits. Even Notre Dame's famous eleven with its Four Horsemen became the exploit of a single man, the coach Knute Rockne. In fact, the very success of these individuals was ultimately in their unprecedented and unequaled attraction for spectators, for whom spectator sports were in themselves invitations to the fantasies of vicarious individualism. The spectator participated without risk; he personally was exposed to no consequences. Like the employee who could express himself only as a consumer rather than as a producer, the devotee of sports committed what feelings he had to the activities of others rather than to engagements of his own. It was a result of what Arthur Mizener has called "the childish absurdity of our American preoccupation with athletics,"[9] or a way of perpetuating the freedom from responsibility enjoyed by those who had not made the passage beyond puberty. It was the "hero-worship" that Ring W. Lardner regarded as "the national disease that does most to keep the grandstands full and the playgrounds empty."[10] It was part of the passivity to which the phonograph and radio were contributing by luring people away from the singing societies and pressing them into armchairs from which they could give form to the spontaneous act by twisting a dial and listening, vocal chords at rest.[11] H. L. Mencken defined the position with sardonic satisfaction in his "Catechism":

Q. If you find so much that is unworthy of reverence in the United States, then why do you live here?
A. Why do men go to zoos?[12]

Whether to ridicule or to worship, the individual was a safe observer and admired others who either extricated themselves from, or insulated themselves from, human entanglements. Lindbergh and his motor. The Watsonian child.

The fictional hero could, once he considered all his alternatives, participate no more fully, and his creator could imagine no other choice. This does not mean that participation was rejected as an ideal; it means that it was rejected as a possibility. In the major novels of the decade—central works by Sinclair Lewis, John Dos Passos, F. Scott Fitzgerald, Ernest Hemingway, and E. E. Cummings, writers who can scarcely be disregarded on any ground—the characters who try to participate either cannot be fully respected for their point of view or, if they can be respected, conclude by rejecting the opportunity to enter the society. Carol Kennicott is, ostensibly, Lewis's protagonist in *Main Street*; but Lewis refuses to sustain her through even the first paragraph of Chapter I:

> On a hill by the Mississippi where Chippewas camped two generations ago, a girl stood in relief against the cornflower blue of Northern sky. She saw no Indians now; she saw flour-mills and the blinking windows of skyscrapers in Minneapolis and St. Paul. Nor was she thinking of squaws and portages, and the Yankee fur-traders whose shadows were all about her. She was meditating upon walnut fudge, the plays of Brieux, the reasons why heels run over, and the fact that the chemistry instructor had stared at the new coiffure which concealed her ears.

He excites a sentimental response to the landscape; he despoils the scene with flour-mills; he belittles his observer by making her equate the frivolous with the serious, and he foreshadows all her difficulties by making the serious irrelevant to what she sees. It is of little use to go on to call her "a rebellious girl" or "the spirit of that bewildered empire called the American Middlewest"; for over and over what is merely girlish subsumes what is rebellious, and what is grandly imperial is lost in bewilderment. Gopher Prairie is dull—"dullness made God"—not because in any absolute sense dullness can be defined and condemned, but because Carol finds it so. Yet for hers to be a significant judgment, her point of view needs to be given some stature, and consistently Lewis prevents it. In activity after activity, in group after group, whatever their age and whatever their sex, Carol shows herself full of a spirit of uplift that is essentially as puritanical and smug as what she opposes. She wants to make others over in some image of her own. Vida Sherwin tells her: ". . . you have to work from the inside, with what we have, rather than from the outside, with foreign ideas. The shell ought not to be forced on the spirit."[13] The more sympathetic Miles Bjornstam shortly afterward restates this in other terms: ". . . you got the wrong slant. You aren't one of the people—yet. You want to do something for the town. I don't! I want the town to do something for itself."[14] And after talking with Mrs. Bogart she herself is able to wonder:

"If that woman is on the side of the angels, then I have no choice; I must be on the side of the devil. But—isn't she like me? She too wants to 'reform the town'! She too criticizes everybody! She too thinks the men are vulgar and limited! *Am I like her?* This is ghastly!"[15]

Nonetheless, she cannot find worth in Gopher Prairie unless there is a Little Theater group that can go beyond *The Girl from Kankakee* to perpetuate the Irish Renaissance or at least recover the classics,[16] and she can only ruefully accept Will's limitations when she finds that he prefers the rhythms of Rudyard Kipling to "the world of lonely things" in Yeats.[17] Individuals have little worth for her when they cannot conform to her conception of individuality.

Lewis's treatment is patently deliberate, and the reader is never deluded into supposing that Lewis regards Carol's idea of freedom as anything other than an adolescent idea or her approach to reform as anything other than cultural righteousness. Moreover, as if to define Carol's limitations beyond those revealed by self-exposure, Lewis offers the figure of Will Kennicott as the one—the only one—who is endowed with a touch of heroism. Gopher Prairie is full of what Lewis can expect his readers to agree are ugliness, petty materialism, smugness, and bigotry; and Will, when he is part of the society, loquaciously socializing, is simply like the rest, weak, deplorable. But when he is the country doctor, the man on the job alone with his task—when he is amputating Adolph Morgenroth's arm in the Morgenroth kitchen, and there is no occasion for small talk—he is laconic, resolute, strong, full of dignity.[18] It is this man whose "personality" later strides out of the letters to recall Carol to him.[19] Yet Lewis, no happier with Will's defects than he is with Carol's, must finally undercut him, too. For the source of his strength is his essential practicality, his immunity to dreams. Carol at the end says: "I may not have fought the good fight, but I have kept the faith!" Will replies with a perfunctory "Sure" and ponders whether or not to put up the storm windows.[20] The immediate and tangible provides a shelter from reality rather than an acknowledgment of it.

Part of Lewis's problem in presenting his characters may be simply that he cannot envisage a fulfilling role for women.[21] More fundamental, however, is that he appears unable to envisage any satisfactory relationship between any individuals within society. It is significant that when Will goes hunting and takes Carol along "to see the country round here" early in the book, Lewis never renders their responses absurd. After Will bags some prairie chickens, the two of them eat sandwiches by a prairie slew, and while Will smokes his pipe, Carol "[leans] back in the buggy and let[s] her tired spirit be absorbed in the Nirvana of the incomparable sky." At the close of the day, Will has "a dramatic shot at a flight of ducks whirling down from the upper air, skimming the lake, instantly vanishing." Then:

> They drove home under the sunset. Mounds of straw, and wheat-stacks like bee-hives, stood out in startling rose and gold, and the green-tufted stubble glistened. As the vast girdle of crimson darkened, the fulfilled land became autumnal in deep reds and browns. The black road before the buggy turned to a faint lavender, then was blotted to uncertain grayness. Cattle came in a long line up to the barred gates of the farmyards, and over the resting land was a dark glow.

Carol had found the dignity and greatness which had failed her in Main Street.[22]

Man finds nobility in the context of nature, not society. Society can only destroy. Where the Chippewas camped beneath the cornflower-blue sky are the flour-mills. Where the pioneers confronted perils alone are the devitalized members of the Thanatopsis Club. Ezra Stowbody has superseded Erasmus, and provincialism has become universalized. Freedom cannot survive in Gopher Prairie, because individuality is not respected. It cannot be fulfilled in Washington, to which Carol flees, because there individuals are not even recognized. There is only loneliness, either way.[23]

But in *Main Street* Lewis does not then suggest that fulfilment in any positive sense is to be found apart from society. He cannot even propose a fulfilling deed. Perhaps the reason is the one that Walter Lippmann once suggested, that Lewis always cared less about human beings than about his own attitude toward them.[24] Or one might add, less about his own attitude than about what others might believe that attitude to be. For Lewis resists implying any commitment that would be vulnerable to exposure. Finding only a denial of self in human relationships, he arrives at the wisdom that Carol tells herself is an answer:

Not individuals but institutions are the enemies, and they most afflict the disciples who the most generously serve them. They insinuate their tyranny under a hundred guises and pompous names, such as Polite Society, the Family, the Church, Sound Business, the Party, the Country, the Superior White Race; and the only defense against them . . . is unembittered laughter.[25]

Gopher Prairie is thus one of the zoos to which men go.

In *Babbitt* Lewis restates rather than develops this idea, although he does so with more of a tone of positive affirmation. George F. Babbitt, a pygmy beneath the aspiring towers of Zenith, "prosperous, extremely married and unromantic,"[26] dreams of personal freedom, of love with a fairy child who regards him as "gallant youth," of a total escape from society, but is consistently unable to achieve lasting independence of any sort from his wife, his business associates, or the Middlewest Republican consensus. He dreams of romantic love, and is awakened by an alarm clock to hear his wife scratchily brushing her hair; he goes with Paul Riesling on a trout-fishing expedition to find serenity, and returns to the Saturday golf game required of the Successful Man and to the joys and obligations of the Solid Citizen and Booster; he tells his son that "we've got to have Vision" and cease to be "material," and criticizes courses in French and poetry because they "never brought in anybody a cent."[27] On the one hand, he wishes he had read Dante; on the other, he warms to the praise of Vergil Gunch.[28] A creature of routine and standardized thought, he cannot fully be the figure of his dreams. He is sympathetic with Paul's desire to be free of social and domestic ties; he plots to free Paul long enough to go camping with him; he responds to Paul's poetic perceptions and in Paul's company discovers "something sort of eternal" in the Maine woods.[29] And after he visits Paul in prison he becomes rebellious and tries to find himself—by taking a trip alone to Maine, by having an affair with the manicurist Tanis Judique, by supporting Seneca Doane and rejecting the Good Citizens' League. But Lewis denies him fulfilment. Babbitt "can't seem to get away from thinking about folks!"[30] He makes a fool of himself with Tanis and the Bunch. He confronts the possible death of his wife and realizes that he really "needs" her. Where Paul's rebellion leads to a crime, Babbitt's leads to the peril of ultimate loneliness. Although in *Main Street* nature beckons as a kind of spiritual salvation, in *Babbitt* nature is closer to offering an escape that is without solace and that finally does not beckon at all.

Partly, this desolation of nature comes from Lewis's inability quite to renounce the humanity implicit in Babbitt's loyalty to Myra. Partly, it comes from his inability to create a Babbitt strong enough to renounce consolation.[31] In his conclusion, Lewis evades a radical choice by blurring the radical issue. Babbitt's son violates conventional expectations by contracting an early marriage, and Babbitt stands by him, becoming a vicarious rebel, a spectator who can say: ". . . I've never done a single thing I've wanted to in my whole life! . . . But I do get a kind of sneaking pleasure out of the fact that you knew what you wanted to do and did it."[32] The pleasure is both sneaking and not sneaking; the rebellion is formally a rebellion but, even allowing for dates, not substantially a very serious rebellion. And Lewis is clearly sympathetic both with the Babbitt who returns to his wife and the behavior expected by his old associates and with the Babbitt who would for once do what he wants. Yet in that very ambivalence Lewis indicates that the social limit is the crippling limit and that the self is free and definable only in the degree to which it can withstand and perhaps even disregard the demands of other persons.

In *Arrowsmith* Lewis carries this view to its logical conclusion. As in *Main Street* and *Babbitt* the central character moves in a society peopled with promoters, self-servers, social climbers, and materialistic institutionalists, the most representative of whom is Dr. Almus Pickerbaugh, the creator of Swat the Fly Week, Tougher Teeth Week, Banish the Booze Week, Better Babies Week, the Health Bee, and the Health Fair, and eventually a Representative in Congress.[33] But there is a difference; for although Lewis cannot refrain from making caricatures of such characters, the tone of the novel is less satirical than is that of its predecessors, and the treatment of Martin Arrowsmith himself is more unwaveringly compassionate than is that of either the Kennicotts or Babbitt. Lewis may try to obscure his own partisanship by referring to his story as "this biography of a young man who was in no degree a hero, who regarded himself as a seeker after truth yet who stumbled and slid back all his life and bogged himself in every obvious morass,"[34] but he enables Arrowsmith to share his understanding: "Gradually Martin's contemplation moved beyond Almus Pickerbaugh to all leaders, of armies or empires, of universities or churches, and he saw that most of them were Pickerbaughs."[35]

Certainly the admiration that Martin feels for Max Gottlieb is Lewis's, too. And certainly, although Lewis supports Martin's concern for social welfare and his attempt to provide free medical services for the poor, he much prefers having Martin engage in basic research to having him behave like "a good citizen."[36] Martin's progress is, in fact, away from all organization, even clinics for the poor and institutes for biological research, toward complete disaffiliation. Martin sees the way the scientist is used by institutes; he sees the way expediency wins priority and thus excludes concern with finalities; wherever human beings act in groups, or as groups, he finds that personal integrity is compromised by commercial considerations. So he says No to others. He learns, in short, to become the kind of religious figure that Gottlieb tells him the true scientist is:

"He must be heartless. He lives in a cold, clear light. Yet dis is a funny t'ing: really, in private, he is not cold nor heartless— so much less cold than the Professional Optimists. The world has always been ruled by the Philanthropists: by the doctors that want to use therapeutic methods they do not understand, by the soldiers that want something to defend their country against, by the preachers that yearn to make everybody listen to them, by the kind of manufacturers that love their workers, by the eloquent statesmen and soft-hearted authors—and see once what a fine mess of hell they haf made of the world! Maybe now it is time for the scientist, who works and searches and never goes around howling how he loves everybody!

"But once again always remember that not all the men who work at science are scientists. So few! The rest—secretaries, press-agents, camp followers! To be a scientist is like being a Goethe: it is born in you. Sometimes I t'ink you have a liddle of it born in you. If you haf, there is only one t'ing—no, there is two t'ings you must do: work twice as hard as you can, and keep people from using you. . . ."[37]

He learns to love "humanity as he loved the decent, clean rows of test-tubes" and to pray "the prayer of the scientist":

"God give me unclouded eyes and freedom from haste. God give me a quiet and relentless anger against all pretense and all pretentious work and all work left slack and unfinished. God give me a restlessness whereby I may neither sleep nor accept praise till my observed results equal my calculated results or in pious glee I discover and assault my error. God give me strength not to trust to God!"[38]

There is, for a while, one potential obstacle to his achieving the purity he comes to value; it is not that he is greedy or that he is ambitious, but that he is married to Leora, who is as much without pretense and egotism as any character that Lewis can imagine. But Lewis removes Leora before her presence can create a need for a choice. In fact, Lewis has himself no choice other than to remove her, since for Martin to have abandoned her as he abandons his second wife, Joyce Lanyon, and their child would have made him heartless in a way quite other than Gottlieb meant. Leora dies of the plague; the claims of genuine love cease; and toward Joyce, who lacks understanding, well able to maintain herself and their son in comfort, he needs to feel no claims of conscience either. With Terry Wickett, "in a clumsy boat, an extraordinarily uncomfortable boat," on a secluded lake, he dedicates himself to "work": "This new quinine stuff may prove pretty good. We'll plug along on it for two or three years, and maybe we'll get something permanent— and probably we'll fail!"[39] If Terry should marry, that "could break me," Martin admits; but the effect of the conclusion is to minimize the threat and to affirm the decision not to give hostages to fortune.[40] "Keep people from using you," Gottlieb said. Martin Arrowsmith finally removes himself from "people." Self-containment becomes the alternative to involvement.

Dos Passos placed his characters in more densely populated settings—during the twenties it is the army, or Manhattan—but he imposed on them no less a need to extricate themselves. The pattern of their stories is appropriately first depicted in Dos Passos's first book, appropriately entitled

One Man's Initiation: 1917; for each story is essentially one
of initiation and each initiate substantially achieves the wisdom that Martin Howe, the "one man," does. Howe sets
out "to see the damn show through," as the American Ex-
peditionary Force's lyrics had it, but he soon becomes aware
of the devastation, "the brown hurt eyes of the soldier, and
the triangular black patch where the nose should have
been,"[41] and sees that America has "turned traitor" to the
ideal of securing "freedom from the past" and become "a
military nation, an organised pirate like France and England
and Germany."[42] "We are slaves of bought intellect," he
concludes, and agrees with those who say that they "have
all been dupes."[43] For Martin and his friends the future
contains only death. Dos Passos himself at the time he was
writing the book was appalled by the war's "horror" and
the "goddamned mess" that "the bankers and brokers and
meatpackers and business men" had "made of organized
society." "Down with the middleaged. . . ."[44] Yet he regarded the American mind as a "stagnant puddle" in which
it was almost hopeless to make more than a small "splash,"
and confided to his friend Arthur McComb: "Our life is
a wake over the corpse of an elaborately garbed liberty that
I suspect was purely mythical anyway."[45] When Richard
Norton in a farewell speech to the drivers in his Norton
Harjes Volunteer Ambulance Service called them "gentlemen volunteers," Dos Passos half-humorously reported the
incident to McComb and said:

> But all this is merely to announce that I have sworn solemn
> vows to remain for the rest of my days a gentleman volunteer—
> Let us all be gentlemen volunteers in life and rollick through
> it mindless of the insane gibberish talked about us, of the musket
> barrels they threaten us with—.
> Doesn't the phrase make you think of the bands of gentlemen-
> volunteers, gentlemen-adventurers who swaggered over to the
> continent in the time of Elizabeth to fight for liberty and con-
> science in the Netherlands—They drank and roistered and
> whored their way through the wars to the consternation of their
> allies and to the great edification of posterity— We of the Nor-

ton Harjes ambulance are much like that—we refuse the yoke.
. . .[46]

But the humor is at the expense of "gentlemen," not "volunteer"; a volunteer can always "refuse the yoke" of any restriction.

The cost of the yoke is, in general terms, the theme of *Three Soldiers* and is clearest in the desertion of John Andrews, the most important of the characters. Andrews, as he begins his training, wants to "fix [his experience] in himself," and "make it into music."[47] Although he knows he should "forget himself,"[48] he cannot do so and is increasingly aware of being engaged in an enterprise that denies his humanity and freedom. Once during a rest on a march, when he goes for a swim with Chrisfield, he says, almost as though he were Huck Finn on the raft: "It's great to feel the sun and the wind on your body, isn't it, Chris?" He tells his friend, as they undress: "Chris, come away from those stinking uniforms and you'll feel like a human being with the sun on your flesh instead of like a lousy soldier." He remarks, when they have finished their swim: "God, I can't make up my mind to put the damn thing on again; I feel so clean and free. It's like voluntarily taking up filth and slavery again." And when a "Y" man asks: "D'you call serving your country slavery, my friend?" he replies: "You're goddam right I do."[49] Later, wounded and hospitalized, he lies on his cot reflecting that this is freedom:

He was free. The thought came to him gleefully, that as long as he stayed in that cot in the hospital no one would shout orders at him. No one would tell him to clean his rifle. There would be no one to salute. . . . He would lie there all day long, thinking his own thoughts.[50]

Until now he has never questioned his easy submission to the army, but now his condition enables him to see that he has been "a coward," lacking "the strength to live" or "the courage to move a muscle for his freedom"; he has risked "his life as soldier, in a cause he believed useless."[51] He finally decides that "civilization" is "nothing but a vast edi-

fice of sham, and the war . . . its fullest and most ultimate
expression"; and resolves that once out of the hospital "he
would desert." "It seemed the first time in his life he had
ever determined to act."[52] But his determination produces
no action; it only foreshadows it; for Andrews will respond
to symbolic rather than social provocation.

What Andrews wants is not simple relief from unpleas-
antness or mounting outrage, but relief from the need to
salute and all that that need implies. Comfort and gaiety
do not particularly interest him. Self-expression does. ". . .
what's the use of just seeing and feeling things if you can't
express them?" he asks. And he is "greedy for solitude."[53]
In solitude he can be himself, be John Andrews, thinking
his own thoughts and giving them form—musical form.[54]
Although, with the help of an acquaintance who is able to
"arrange" matters, Andrews can, after the armistice, be
sent by the army to study music at the Sorbonne, Dos Passos
will not let him fulfill himself at the army's expense. There
must be no claims, no indebtedness, no benefit from the system that is sustained by duties, ranks, and restrictions. Significantly, it is no hatred of fighting or fury at inhuman conduct that provokes Andrews's desertion, but what he sees
as unjust and intolerable punishment for being found without his papers and for failing to salute—for, that is, a plain
disregard of symbols of a procedure designed to institutionalize human relations. By making Andrews a deserter from
the system rather than a dissident within it, Dos Passos
compels Andrews to define his individuality as completely
separate from his social identity. Henslowe reproaches Andrews for subordinating his work, his music, to an "abstract
idea of asserting your right of individual liberty," and Wal-
ters reminds him that there are such things as family and
patriotism and duty. But Andrews can only reply: "I can't
explain it. . . . But I shall never put a uniform on again."[55]
There can be no good in society. Geneviève Rod, the girl
who comes closest to providing love, must fail him and con-
vince him that he is "alone."[56] Geneviève's family and

friends must form a barrier between her and Andrews, and her own understanding must be inadequate: "people were always alone, really; however much they loved each other, there could be no real union."[57] The music he begins to compose must almost inevitably celebrate the destruction of institutions, and it commemorates the spirit of John Brown.[58] The story of human society has always been, according to Andrews, "organizations growing and stifling individuals, and individuals revolting hopelessly against them, and at last forming new societies to crush the old societies and becoming slaves again in their turn. . . ."[59]

Dos Passos might have posed a choice between the military life and the wartime civilian life, but instead he shows them as complementary parts of a single machine: the individual is "molded" and eventually crushed "under the wheels," as the book's division titles indicate.[60] There is a "world outside"—outside the life of the barracks and the trenches—but there is no "world" outside the system. If one renounces the system, abdication is the choice that remains. Although Andrews would celebrate John Brown, he cannot emulate John Brown's action or sympathize with his social orientation. If he refuses the yoke, it is in order to be, not in order to do. Thinking of Brown does not impel him to make common cause with others; it leaves him in only lonely contemplation. Such contemplation is the sole sanctuary, and even that is invaded and destroyed at the last by society's emissaries.

Civilian life in peacetime, as Dos Passos demonstrates in his account of prewar and postwar New York in *Manhattan Transfer*, may contain less of a threat to physical liberty, but, even when there is no war for it to support, civilian life is just as destructive as the military and leaves only secession from all involvements as the way to self-preservation. Dos Passos's city has a vitality that the army cannot have; he, like many of his contemporaries, found the New York of rising architecture and jazzy noises full of the excitement that rhythmic energy can stimulate. And influenced by the cinematic techniques of D. W. Griffiths and Sergei Eisenstein, he regarded urban life as a picturesque montage, rich with the color and dissonance that the nation's drab Gopher Prairies lacked.[61] Here certainly dullness was not made God. Yet he also could see what Carol Kennicott discovered in Washington—that energy is impersonal and that human relationships are consumed inside a generator. In Dos Passos's Manhattan individuals cannot fulfill themselves in relation to each other as persons or even maintain an identity. They reach the city "*through the manuresmelling wooden tunnel of the ferryhouse,*" as the first epigraph states, and "*like apples [are] fed down a chute into a press.*" Or, like Ellen Thatcher, they are born on the island and treated by the nurse in the maternity ward as though they were objects in a bedpan, resembling to a detached observer a feebly squirming "knot of earthworms."[62] Against a backdrop of fires, murders, unemployment, abortions, and promiscuity, they earn their livings as lawyers, actors and actresses, or reporters who have no deep commitment to their work, contract loveless marriages and momentary liaisons, and if they do not take their own lives or perish in burning buildings, end simply by drifting from one emptiness to another.

Ellen Thatcher and Jimmy Herf are, of course, the two central characters. What other characters are and what they do matters only insofar as they establish a milieu for Ellen and Jimmy. Bud Korpenning, the Cooperstown farm boy who has killed his brutal father and, failing to find work in the city, drops from the Brooklyn Bridge; Stan Emery, the student and dilettante who attracts Ellen and dies in a fire; George Baldwin, the ubiquitous lawyer and bedroom companion who has casual relations with numerous female clients; Joe Harland, the poor relative who, once known as the Wizard of Wall Street, loses his touch and becomes the family reprobate; James Merivale, the respectable relative who says after the armistice that "it was a great war while it lasted"[63]—these, along with many others, serve primarily to define New York, which as it becomes what the newspapers proclaim as the "WORLD'S SECOND METROPOLIS" is to be seen as a *"steel, glass, tile, [and] concrete"* version of Babylon and Nineveh, *"built of brick,"* of Athens, with its *"gold marble columns,"* of Rome, *"held up on broad arches of rubble,"* and of Constantinople, with minarets that flamed *"like great candles round the Golden Horn."* [64] Within this new Nineveh, Ellen and Jimmy can enjoy no saving satisfaction. Either they try to find a place in the social organization and deny their individuality, or they try to preserve their individuality and find no place that can be peculiarly theirs. Ellen, resisting the demeaning categorical subordination of women and craving an independent social status, with money and freedom from obligation, is unable to establish any personal relationship to which she can devote herself. "I guess I dont love anybody for long unless they're dead," she says. [65] She can be permanently wedded to only the impermanences of New York and, appropriately, maintains herself by being an actress, playing different roles, becoming someone else—achieving only the identity of her changing functions. Jimmy, pampered by his widowed mother and orphaned at sixteen, rejects the opportunity to acquire wealth and be hustled through the revolving doors of office buildings to rise in the world, and takes up journalism in order to be himself. But since the position of detached observer is possible only because of an attitude that rejects the values of what he observes, Jimmy can be no more successful than Ellen in reconciling self-sufficiency with social involvement. Ellen herself, of course, cannot permanently attach herself to him, and when he loses his job, he awakens to his alienation—he has "lost his twenties," as he mentally phrases his delayed coming of age—and, ties severed, begins hitchhiking westward with no destination other than "pretty far." [66]

What he renounces is a lot more than what an earlier innocent, Huck Finn, renounced when he lit out for the territory. This is more than the "civilization" of manners and games. Jimmy is heading for no place in particular; he is simply leaving as far behind as he can all the attachments of organized society for a vast and lifeless landscape. To remain is to be depersonalized and part of a mechanism, like Ellen; to leave is to be adrift with no expectations of warmly human contact but with at least a sense of integrity. As yet Jimmy's integrity is somewhat abstract. He is no Mencken, who can consider it all a zoo, or even a Carol Kennicott, who can prescribe unembittered laughter. He can, however, begin to laugh. What he needs to develop—and may now develop—is a capacity wholly to externalize society, a capacity that Dos Passos reserves fully developed for Congo Jake, who may have inspired Jimmy to secede.[67] Jake has a sense of humor and lives the good life. Jake is without roots or binding ties. He has become a bootlegger. He is outside the law. "Moi je suis anarchiste vous comprenez monsieur."[68]

It is a philosophy of disengagement without the *air dégagé*. Fitzgerald, Hemingway, and Cummings contemporaneously illustrate how much the view comprehends. No one could be more ashamed of the human race than Nick Carraway, for example, who perceives that it is people as social beings who destroy, "careless people, Tom and Daisy—they smashed up things and creatures and then retreated back into their money or their vast carelessness, or whatever it was that kept them together, and let other people clean up the mess they had made. . . ."[69] These careless people are the constituents of the society; they are the "rotten crowd"[70] who give the society its character. In their world no relationships are possible beyond the tacit agreements made for strategic purposes. No one will accept a personal limit in the interest of something transcendent. Although it has often seemed that Fitzgerald created Jay Gatsby as a protagonist advocating infinite personal commitment, opposing the callous expediencies of the world of the Buchanans, the fact is that Gatsby is so completely unaware of any point of view other than his own that he cannot, any more than they, treat others as anything but egotistical extensions of his desire, objects whose humanity he denies. He utterly dismisses the objective reality of other persons and even of time. The segment of the past that he rejects must be simply erased or discarded,[71] and a new one supplied or bought. He would have Daisy assert not only that she does not love Tom but that she never loved Tom. If there was any feeling between them, "it was just personal,"[72] as his own feeling significantly is not. He has been part of "that bunch that hangs around with Meyer Wolfsheim," as Buchanan labels it, engaging in affairs outside the law to further a dream that can acknowledge no laws; but he is corrupt in only a conventional sense: his dream is, Carraway reports, "incorruptible."[73]

Yet, if Gatsby with "his capacity for wonder"[74] is "worth the whole damn bunch [the 'rotten crowd'] put together," there is a question of how "great" he really is—how acceptable his dream. Solipsism must have consequences, and Gatsby finally pays the price for it. Unprepared to accept circumstance, unwilling to grant to others the desires or ambitions he himself possesses, he cannot grow beyond an adolescence for which the world is fantasy, and must be annihilated by the requirements of maturity. Carraway reflects that it has been a story of the "West" showing that all of them, "Westerners, . . . possessed some deficiency in common which made us subtly unadaptable to Eastern life."[75] Insofar as their view was innocently romantic, he is right. But the challenge of how to come to terms with what Eastern life represents is one that his awareness still does not permit him to meet. He can only leave New York for the region that was the source of the impossible dreams, "where the dark fields of the republic rolled on under the night,"[76] green with virginal possibility. In *The Great Gatsby* Fitzgerald cannot show any fulfilment save in a withdrawal to dream immaturely about it, a longing one century too late.[77]

Hemingway similarly shows the need for withdrawal but offers no consolation in wonder. The principal characters of his two central novels, *The Sun Also Rises* and *A Farewell to Arms*, although seeking fulfilment in relationships with others, ultimately realize that they cannot succeed and, instead of escaping in dreams or contemplation, must finally settle for stoical endurance. *A Farewell to Arms*, the later of the two novels, dramatizes the experiences out of which the earlier one emerged. Frederic Henry has learned to distrust society, to see the hollowness of its pretensions. "I was always embarrassed," he says, "by the words sacred, glorious, and sacrifice and the expression in vain."[78] He drives an ambulance for an army whose nationality he does not share. He commits himself to no cause beyond his job. He maintains his integrity by remaining aloof from emotional involvements—until he meets Catherine Barkley and falls in love with her. Although Hemingway suggests from the very beginning that Henry is secure against the claims of feeling—Henry finds stability in the landscape, purity in the mountains, and all perceptions equal in value, as Hemingway's joining those perceptions with coordinating "and's" repeatedly makes obvious—Henry cannot withstand the appeal of one who shares his dislike of sham. Not hardened enough to dispense with all society, he is vulnerable to compromising for a closed one. He and Catherine against the world. Within this closed society, Hemingway makes clear, the ordinary conventions are unimportant. It is a society that is pure, a society without sin, a society with conventions of its own. The man, not the woman, is the one who wants to get married. And it is the woman who prevents it. Catherine Barkley is strong. She wants no lies, no sweet words; sometimes no words at all, since experience itself is what possesses vitality and true love is to be translated in deeds for another, not in the verbal sentimentalizing of sensations. There must be no ceremonies for relationships, no medals for brave acts—they are akin to the embarrassing words. It is, indeed, only in the self-disciplined relationship between Henry and Catherine that there is any society at all. With the disintegration of the Italian army, the institutions of society become absurd. The social order is no longer one within which peace is negotiated; it is one with which to make peace. And Henry does make "a separate peace," free to join Catherine and then "feel alone . . . against the others" but "never lonely and never afraid when we were together."[79]

Catherine's death, of course, constitutes the final enlightenment. There is no necessary connection between the feelings the two of them have for each other and the catastrophe that befalls them. There is only the inevitability of death:

Now Catherine would die. That was what you did. You died. You did not know what it was about. You never had time to learn. They threw you in and told you the rules and the first time they caught you off base they killed you. Or they killed you gratuitously like Aymo. Or gave you the syphilis like Rinaldi. But they killed you in the end. You could count on that. Stay around and they would kill you.[80]

But whatever Henry could have learned with more time, he does learn that there is no way in which knowledge can alter anything. In Catherine's words, "It's just a dirty trick."[81] The absence of necessary sequence and of justice and of consolation is the great fact; to deny it or to complain is folly and weakness. One can only passively accept encounters and prove oneself by acceptance, by self-control. One can only walk "back to the hotel in the rain,"[82] and tell about it as dispassionately as possible. The narration of *A Farewell to Arms* is patently the "action" that establishes Henry's recognition of destiny, and its style just as patently transforms that recognition into an affirmation of what Ralph Ellison has called "a morality of technique."[83]

This is a morality that emphasizes manner rather than substance, and in its definition of manner implicitly repudiates the conventional sanctions of society. Thus Jake Barnes in *The Sun Also Rises*, destined to suffer from a trick as dirty as the one played on Henry and Catherine, must celebrate the technique of acceptance by continually exhibiting the strength and dignity of self-containment. Victim of a war-time injury that has left him with the capacity to feel sexual desire but deprived him of the means to fulfill it, Jake must learn to adopt the right attitude toward his predicament in order "to be," as Joseph Conrad might have put it. He must be able to contemplate his injury with humorous irony rather than self-pity; he must be able to struggle with anguish and not succumb to it; he must be able to subject himself to a variety of personal relations and temptations—which his sexual predicament finally symbolizes in acute form—without evincing the self-indulgence of either distress or enthusiasm. The group within which he moves is, to some degree, a closed society within the larger society, but even within the enclave there are differences among which Jake must distinguish himself. Mike Campbell, a bankrupt playboy and unresisting drinker, readily yields to the temptation to bait Robert Cohn and shows himself weakly self-indulgent. Cohn, full of the expectations of finding the world as romantic as his Princeton education and W. H. Hudson's *The Purple Land* have persuaded him it is, cannot refrain from complaining about disappointments and betrayals or from striking out in public gestures of literary manliness that simply prove his inability to understand the finalities of circumstance. Lady Brett, whose lack of scruple and fascinating immorality earn her the label of Circe, cannot help seducing Pedro Romero. In his relations with these and the others Jake must maintain an equipoise that demands as strict a self-discipline as any that Jane Austen ever demanded of Elizabeth Bennett. But where Jane Austen was establishing a basis for society, Hemingway is suggesting how to live without one.

Pedro Romero is, it is generally agreed, the noblest of the characters. He has become Belmonte's successor in the bull ring. He can do "always, smoothly, calmly, and beautifully, what he, Belmonte, could only bring himself to do now sometimes."[84] And even when he is under Brett's spell, he can maintain a self-possession that testifies to his integrity:

> Pedro Romero had the greatness. He loved bull-fighting, and I think he loved the bulls, and I think he loved Brett. Everything of which he could control the locality he did in front of her all that afternoon. Never once did he look up. He made it stronger that way, and did it for himself, too, as well as for her. Because he did not look up to ask if it pleased he did it all for himself inside, and it strengthened him, and yet he did it for her, too. But he did not do it for her at any loss to himself. He gained by it all through the afternoon.

Every movement of his "was all so slow and so controlled."[85] His grace in confronting possible annihilation is the embodiment of the technique of aceptance that Jake must practice. Whether he is knocked down by Cohn or seduced by Brett or threatened in the ring, Romero confronts his situation with an attitude that bespeaks the freedom of the private man. Display must remain minimal. One does not look up to ask if it pleases; one does it for oneself and keeps it within oneself. Yet, although Romero clearly has "the greatness," the importance of it lies in its effects upon Jake and Brett, and upon their relationship to each other. Brett makes Jake her pimp in seducing Romero, but finally realizes Romero's nearly sacred quality and resolves, at least for once, "not to be a bitch. . . . It's sort of what we have instead of God."[86] And Jake, having yielded to Brett, is able to recover what Romero represents and remind her of the limits no one can disregard. When the two of them are being driven onto the Gran Via in Madrid at the end, Brett says: "Oh, Jake, we could have had such a damned good time together." But Hemingway places a policeman in their path to raise a baton that stops not only the traffic but also wishful thinking about personal relations.[87] Both of them feel good in reflecting upon Romero, but they must not succumb to the temptation to believe that mutual fulfilment might have been possible. To wish for what might have been is to behave like Robert Cohn. Jake understands the warning of the raised hand and with cauterizing irony provides the last words: "Yes. Isn't it pretty to think so."[88] The social conditions are at the conclusion the same as they were at the beginning, but the need to maintain individual integrity—even immunity from personal relationships—has been intensified, and through Romero the voices of Jake and Brett have been joined to bear witness.

Hemingway leaves his characters no alternatives. When Jake and his friend, Bill Gorton, who functions as an authenticating minor commentator, go into the mountains, they can abandon their defensive irony and open themselves to what will survive them. "One generation passeth away, and another generation cometh; but the earth abideth forever." But Hemingway sends them there on only a holiday excursion, not in search of another way of life. He shows them, however, something to revere akin to what the Kennicotts see in the sunset, to what Martin Arrowsmith and Terry Wickett find in the woods, and to what Frederic Henry and Catherine Barkley feel in the Alps—something that transcends society and can, when one understands it as Jake does, strengthen the capacity to define oneself independent of the claims of mortals who do not recognize the limits of their mortality.[89]

Perhaps the most unqualified expression of reverence for the natural as against the social is E. E. Cummings's *The Enormous Room*, in which every vestige of the institutional world is reduced to absurdity and progress is measured by the narrator's appreciation of inarticulate spontaneity. It is, as Cummings frequently makes explicit, a modern and personal version of John Bunyan's allegory.[90] His equation of the *Section Sanitaire Vingt-et-Un* with the Slough of Despond, his putting down his burden at the foot of a cross, his baptism in a cold bath, his purification through filth, his encounters with the hypocritical Count Bragard, the Three Wise Men, and Apollyon, and identification of the characters who most fully embody love and humanity as The Delectable Mountains—all suggest parallels, some exact, some inverted, that contribute to Cummings's presentation of his experience as a spiritual journey.[91] The tone is generally ironic and satirical, and religious institutions are often subjected to ridicule, but the narrator does not attack the values that Bunyan believed in so much as he exposes the corrupting character of the forms that were historically intended to preserve the values. At the same time, though, Cummings is exposing more than the institutional expression of religious conceptions; he is concerned with all formalized social conceptions and the dehumanizing effect produced by the acceptance of form. At a time when semanticists were criticizing the use of language that was detached from actual experience, Cummings was likewise criticizing forms that negated substance. His pilgrim's progress is thus toward awareness that the natural man or the natural self—as distinct from the social self—is the true self and that art as against intellect is the means for self-realization.

The Enormous Room, then, is in a large sense an account of the discrepancy between language and experience in which, as Marilyn Gaull has convincingly demonstrated, the narrator becomes disenchanted with the language of society and learns to value something that is beyond conventional discourse.[92] Yet, because the story is told retrospectively, the narrator recounts his experience in terms of his final awareness and from the beginning makes evident in his tone what the outcome must be. In a vein that pervades his poetry, which in its very shape and use of lower-case letters is an attack on public speech, Cummings mocks the official rhetoric of "the characteristic cadence" of "Our Great President," of the belief in *"La Gloire* and *Le Patriotisme"* professed by "the inimitable and excellent French Government," of the popular appeal in behalf of "This Great War For Humanity."[93] He exhibits over and over the absurd syllogisms of petty French functionaries who cannot understand how one can love the French without hating the Germans,[94] and displays the thoughtless brutalities of the guards at La Ferté Macé who are unconcerned with understanding anything at all. He lays bare the anachronistic character of chapel services and religious rituals in the prison and the irony of engraving "*Liberté. Egalité. Fraternité.*" upon the public buildings of a nation that imprisons individuals without reason, denies suspected persons equal rights, and violates all the rules of common humanity.[95] Repeatedly he portrays the humiliation of individuals by agents of the social will and the futility of trusting to supposedly rational procedures for redress. For within the social organization communication has become impossible. Just as slogans have violated truth for Frederic Henry, so have all words become mere counterfeits for the coin of genuine human relationships. Outside The Enormous Room, where the niceties of orderly procedures are maintained, it is impossible to convey meaning to the officials who preside over the processes.

Only inside the Room, where nearly a dozen languages are spoken in loud confusion, does communication become possible. When Cummings enters the chamber from the outside he feels a sense of liberation: "I was myself and my own master."[96] "By God, this is the finest place I've ever been in my life."[97] For here with no common language there is no common deceit. It is, in fact, significant that the hypocritical Count Bragard is a man whose French is "glib and faultless,"[98] that the most treacherous inmate, "Judas," is one who "talks in French; converses in Belgian; can speak eight languages,"[99] and that the humane ones are usually illiterate, primitive, and inarticulate. The Wanderer cannot read.[100] Surplice is "utterly ignorant. He thinks America is out of a particular window on your left as you enter. . . . He cannot understand the submarine. He does not know that there is a war."[101] The Bear can speak only awkwardly.[102] Jan has immense difficulty in imparting or receiving an idea.[103] The Orange Cap is silent.[104] Zulu employs signs.[105]

Jean le Nègre has the mind and vocabulary of a child.[106] Where, as one of Cummings's poems says, "feeling is first/ who pays any attention/to the syntax of things/will never wholly kiss you. . . ."

The book's meaning, however, does not lie any more completely in the consistency of its tone and characterization than it does in the mechanical application of allegorical parallels. It lies in the way impressions, tone, characters, and allegorical reverberations produce a cumulative effect on the reader's own progress through the book.[107] First he sees the parochial insensitivity within the *Section Sanitaire*; he hears the empty and discordant rhetoric; he observes the hollowness of those encased in uniforms; he senses the imprisonment of spirit and natural feeling among the forces of "the great and good" governments.[108] Then he proceeds to share the narrator's feeling of liberation from the ordinary world as he enters The Enormous Room, while he increases his understanding of the nature of society by perceiving how society's power is applied: order is maintained without reason, the law is applied like a logical proposition in frequent defiance of common sense, life is subordinated to discipline, persons are official objects, forms are shells— there is no soul. Then he meets The Delectable Mountains as positive examples of the possibilities of fellowship. The Wanderer is a gypsy, with loyalties to only his wife and children, not to the organized state; Zulu is gentle, selfless; Surplice is dirty, simple-minded; and Jean le Nègre is childlike, imbued with an elemental life force—and has been arrested for, irony of ironies, allegedly impersonating an officer. Enabled to feel his humanity at last through association with these individuals, the narrator takes the reader through the darkness of the Room to the light outside at the conclusion, as through a nightmare to an awakening, even while showing that it is in the Room that the true light exists and that in the lowest social depths the spirit can most readily rise. At one point Cummings says that the "secret of [Zulu's] means of complete and unutterable com-

munication lay in that very essence which I have only defined as an IS. . . ."[109] IS means giving oneself to natural
responses; it means utter indifference to the social order
with its bureaucratic categories; it means yielding to the
spontaneous, uncalculating, innocent self that resides deep
in the spirit. Knowing this, the narrator can emerge into
daylight a separate person and go forth confidently into a
world vibrant with the promise of life; he can take the
reader from the enormous room of reflection into a life
where he will be a healthy observer.

The elevation of observation is essentially the elevation
of the artist, the one who can conceive of his own value,
the only one who can assert the value of the destruction of
the rational categories. Jean le Nègre cannot speak for himself. It takes Cummings to appreciate him, in the same way
as it takes Jake Barnes to appreciate Romero, and it is
through Cummings that nature must speak. So speaking,
nature might thus declare the primacy of its interpreter,
but if it does, the interpreter must always remain withdrawn. Malcolm Cowley has noted that at the outbreak of
the war Americans became ambulance drivers and reporters,
symbolically appropriate positions for those with a spec-
tatorial bent. "The War created in young men a thirst for
abstract danger, not suffered for a cause but courted for
itself. . . ."[110] And it is noteworthy that as a consequence
of their experience the writers did not plunge into reform
but rushed to claim their observation posts. There they could
maintain their integrity. "Thanks to I dare say my art I am
able to become myself," Cummings states in his introduction.[111] The Greenwich Village Bohemianism of the prewar
years became what Cowley has described as a doctrine: the
spirit of childhood was to be perpetuated, untrammeled self-
expression was the goal, the body was a temple, the moment
was the time to live for, liberty was superior to and independent of all laws, conventions, or rules of art.[112] Yet the
articles of belief clearly militated against common commit-

ments that would mean the subordination of differences. Although the Village, the salons, the "evenings" were full of radicals of various hues, the radicals were not solemn reformers united by programs for restructuring society but joyous polemicists sharing a desire simply to subvert the social order for the sake of individual and separate purposes,[113] or refugees from established communities who wished to conduct personal experiments in new ways of living.[114]

There was indeed a question of whether society as such was worth saving. What was worthy in men and women was precisely only what could be sequestered—the unattached ego. The indifference of authors of the twenties to the social texture that preoccupied their nineteenth-century precursors, together with the resolutions that the characters in their books achieved in removing themselves from the demands of their milieu, make clear that there was in their minds no fulfilment for the individual who was not detached. Edmund Wilson, looking back at the decade, found the view pervading the journalism of the time as well, where Mencken and George Jean Nathan and Alexander Woollcott adopted and developed "the self-assertive approach" of George Bernard Shaw, Gilbert Keith Chesterton, and Max Beerbohm—and where, he might have noted, *The New Yorker* and *Time* came into being as magazines whose styles would call more attention to the editorial presence than to the material presented. Like the novelists, these journalists were a long way from respect for "the best that has been thought and said":

All these writers were everlastingly saying "I": the exploitation of personality had become an integral part of criticism. It all stemmed, I suppose, from Oscar Wilde, who had a genius for self-dramatization and was imitated in this respect by Bernard Shaw. In the twenties a young man who was still nobody made a point of saying "I"—"I don't like so-and-so," "I can't read so-and-so," "I have always thought so-and-so,"—in the hope of being taken for somebody.[115]

In their glorification of the first person singular the literati were akin to the spectators in the grandstands who glorified the sports heroes, and vicariously themselves, and to the Village Bohemians who wished to explore ways of life devoid of impositions. What Floyd Dell called the Vagabond overwhelmed the social reformer, and those who hated capitalism and wished to create a more equitable society proved to be far less important than those who, as Joseph Freeman would recall, hated "the responsibilities which any highly developed social system imposes upon its members."[116]

A devotion to self-assertion can be a devotion to discovering distinctive ways of expressing community values, social purpose, mutual regard, or, as some Negro writers and artists were about to find, of affirming a collective experience. It can dwell upon the value of the play of individual upon individual within the social context and celebrate the self-discovery consequent upon limiting relationships. But in the twenties what was shared by whites was only the attempt to express the value of individual distinctiveness for its own sake, and the implications of the "I" asserted by the prose writers were enforced and reaffirmed by work done by other artists—most notably painters and sculptors —with forms that would serve private need rather than public communication. In a sense what was communicated was that the private person was a meaning unto himself alone. The world that Jean-Baptiste Chardin had once found interesting or, closer to the twenties and the United States, the world that the Ashcan school had considered worthy of attention was no longer an acceptable subject for the many new artists who, after the Armory Show of 1913, wanted to do more than modify the old style. Artistic reality was not to be defined by consensus, or related to "life"; the generally recognizable was, apparently, but a reminder of conventions long found inadequate and now judged fraudulent. The presence of the traditional signified the presence of the social—the world to break away from. If an artist looked at an individual he did not see that individual in his social guise but in a unique configuration of shapes and colors. The artist did not serve his subject; the subject was the occasion for the artifact. Art was, in other words, not a vehicle for representing persons and objects; it was itself an object, a design—and not a design *of*, but a design suggested *by*. The private eye's composition—the private character of its interest—gave greater importance to the original beholder than it did to what was composed. Line, color, and space were not attributes of what he painted but were themselves his subject.[117] If there were discernible common objects or familiar human forms, they were without associative value. What was generally called "modern art" purged itself of externals.

The modern artist, in other words, did not refer to a fixed or agreed-upon reality. Cubism, for example, as E. H. Gombrich has explained, sought "to prevent a coherent image of reality from destroying the pattern in the plane. . . . a still life by Braque will marshal all the forces of perspective, texture, and shading, not to work in harmony, but to clash in virtual deadlock." There was no "correct" perspective on nature; there was only the "one reading of the picture—that of a man-made construction, a colored canvas."[118] The canvas was the total reality.[119] Or, as one student has phrased it, "The visual presence of the object was replaced by the sensory presence of the painting."[120] Form and light were seen in place of their occasion, which meant, in turn, that art was, in the sense proposed by José Ortega y Gasset, dehumanized. It was "not for men in general."[121] It avoided "living forms" and social importance.[122] If a painter chose to paint a man, he must destroy "the human aspect" and "paint a man who resembles a man as little as possible."[123] The new emphasis required a shift from "the outer world" to "the subjective images in his own mind."[124] The human figure—most often the nude—was not delineated as a stimulus for desire but as a symbol of desire. It was not there to arouse but to be. If the Greek idealized the anthropomorphic, the modern idealized the relation of the human to that order that transcends the merely social. Sir Kenneth Clark has summed up the difference:

The Greeks perfected the nude in order that man might feel like a god, and in a sense this is still its function, for although we no longer suppose that God is like a beautiful man, we still feel close to divinity in those flashes of self-identification when, through our own bodies, we seem to be aware of a universal order.[125]

It is with that order and within that order that each one is separately at peace. If, then, an individual happened to be portrayed by a modern artist, he could have found satisfaction not in the way the artist related him to or elevated him above other men and women, magnifying his human qualities, but in the way the artist perceived in him an element of absolute design.

The logic of modernity should perhaps have culminated in the rejection of even design, and among many in Europe in the twenties it did in fact so culminate. Expatriate Americans, who like Robert McAlmon liked to live in a foreign country where deracination guaranteed a wholly free private life,[126] or like Harold Loeb found excitement in contemplating American energy from a distant Paris, where they did not have to experience the limits of national philistinism,[127] helped sustain the European artists who carried the assault on all rational structures to a point where they promoted surrealism and even Dada. What modernity meant was, as Daniel Bell has stated,

the destruction (in the ideal-type sense) of rational conceptions— of time as an orderly sequence of events; of space as an ordered composition of figure and background—which had been the dominant mode since the Renaissance, and what had achieved its classic definition of appropriate genre in Lessing's *Laokoön*.

And that finally meant breaking "existing genres and traditional distinctions between the arts" and establishing "all experience, or happenings, without any shaping, as art."[128]

Thus freedom became the concern of André Breton's "Manifeste du surréalisme" of 1924:

Le seul mot de liberté est tout ce qui m'exalte encore. Je le crois propre à entretenir, indéfiniment, le vieux fanatisme humain. Il répond sans doute à ma seule aspiration légitime. Parmi tant de disgrâces dont nous héritons, il faut bien reconnaître que la *plus grande liberté* d'esprit nous est laissée.[129]

And thus, too, Antonin Artaud could speak for the surrealists collectively when the following year he said that they protested "against any interference with the free development of a delirium as legitimate, as logical as any other sequence of ideas or human acts. . . . All individual acts are anti-social."[130] Surrealism was dedicated to "total liberation of the mind."[131] Dada, of course, with its uproar, cacophonies, and public exhibition of private spontaneity marked what Malcolm Cowley, one of the American exiles, came to regard as "the extreme of individualism." The Dada Manifesto declared:

The new painter creates a world. . . . The new artist protests: he no longer paints (*i.e.* reproduces symbolically and illusionistically), but creates directly, in stone, in wood, in iron and tin, rocks and locomotive organisms that can be turned in every direction by the limpid winds of his momentary sensation. Every pictorial or plastic work is useless. . . . Order-disorder; ego-non-ego; affirmation-negation: all are supreme radiations of an absolute art. . . . Art is a private matter; the artist does it for himself; any work of art that can be understood is the product of a journalist.[132]

American artists generally, to be sure, did not become Dadaists or surrealists. In fact, even their cubism was less than abstract. As art historians have pointed out, the native American tradition was too deeply rooted in realism to permit abandonment of all vestiges of the particularized.[133] Yet, even when they focused on the particular, they did so in ways that subordinated it to the patterns of their own shaping eye. The New York scenes of John Marin and Joseph Stella, the still lifes of Charles Demuth and Morton

L. Schamberg, the industrial subjects of Charles Sheeler,
the flower-pieces of Georgia O'Keeffe, and the *collages* of
Arthur G. Dove are, for example, essentially expressions of
a highly individual "visual excitement, an exceptional sensi-
tivity to nature's colors, forms, and shifting patterns of
motion."[134] Repeatedly, whether they were cubists or real-
ists, synchromists or futurists, the artists tended to translate
the human into the natural, and the natural into the abstract. There are no harried citizens in Marin's Manhattan;
there is no dirt, or even a human face, on Sheeler's boat
decks or downtown El. The social vitality of the work of
George Bellows, John Sloan, and William Glackens, significant before the war, yields to moving light, dancing cubes,
contrasting stillnesses, or simply the purest energy. The
modern American artist in his response to the insufficiency
of his society and its forms rejected whatever because of its
commonplace realism preserved belief in the insufficiency,
and undertook to affirm the primacy of his means over the
actuality they once served. The painter came to depend on
paints, colors, canvases, not on the American social scene.
"Using paint *as* paint is different from using paint to paint
a picture," Marin once wrote.[135] The modern painter was,
then, interested in the world of objects and persons only
insofar as they gave him an occasion to explore his medium.
And what he did with his medium was transcend the botani-
cal and physiological to objectify his present response to
his vision—whence the fact that it was both in the present
and a vision peculiarly his—rather than record historical
characteristics of what he saw.[136]

Ultimately it was a rejection of the historical that the
American artists shared with the European and that the
painters and the sculptors shared with the writers. For
many writers, as has been shown, the rejection was implicit in their attitudes toward nature and their preoccupation with the ego. For others—like Gertrude Stein and T.
S. Eliot—it had to be more explicit. Gertrude Stein, begin-

ning even before the war to purge language of traditional associations that might produce conventional responses, labored with consistent determination through the twenties to dissociate her characters from temporal and spatial contexts so that they could cease to have histories or be subjected to the kind of classification she regarded as inimical to individuation. Words must be like a painter's colors and contribute to detached designs suspended in what she called a "continuous present," in which moments are not discrete or divisible except as the individual's psychological state makes them so. For she believed, very much as Henri Bergson did, that the individual's mind is the unifier of all time at any moment of perception and is thus independent of the contingencies of the external world. Her writing, accordingly, tirelessly attempted to render everything all at once directly rather than to represent an order already given.[137] And T. S. Eliot, incapable of discovering any evolution in time as meaningful as temporal contrasts within a permanently present moment, created *The Waste Land* to assert, in part, that history constituted no categorical limit, and so he placed his narrator, complaining of the present, outside of time to criticize it, as though he, Eliot, were himself annoyed with the limiting claims of the finite. It was surely ironic that Eliot never understood how parochial and time-bound that annoyance was,[138] and yet characteristic that he should suppose that the obliterating encompassment of history was a satisfactory alternative to the acknowledgment of its inexorable power.

The collective artistic attempt was in behalf of self-liberation, but it left the individual aloof from his society, negotiating his separate peace, untouched by other persons, and of no importance to them. He could function by his own laws autonomously: he was his own fixed quantity. He could sit in Arrowsmith's boat, follow Mencken to the zoo, or self-sufficiently look at the city as a dynamic arrangement in space.

Chapter Seven

The Individual and Himself

I am of the sort that takes nothing very seriously. . . .

GEORGE JEAN NATHAN[1]

THEORETICAL SUPPORT for the morality of avoiding entangling alliances came from those who emerged as the decade's principal moral philosophers. John Dewey, Joseph Wood Krutch, and Walter Lippmann, though they might differ about details, all rejected overriding purposes, schemes of inexorable retribution, and even relatively fixed entities that individuals might acknowledge as more important than themselves. They were convinced that each individual could look only to his own experience as the source for sanctions.

For John Dewey the problem was to define a standard that would give meaning to the present moment and dignity to the present act. In his central statement of the early twenties, *Human Nature and Conduct*, he deplores the tyranny of the arbitrarily prescriptive, the failure of moralists to take account of actuality or changing circumstance. He has found that codes of conduct and the arena of action have in his time become lamentably separated. Nineteenth-century standards, often invoked, are irrelevant to twentieth-century situations, and when applied they require individuals to live divided lives, with the consequence that society suffers.

But morals based upon concern with facts and deriving guidance from knowledge of them would at least locate the points of effective endeavor and would focus available resources upon them. It would put an end to the impossible attempt to live in two unrelated worlds. It would destroy fixed distinction between the human and the physical, as well as that between the moral and the industrial and political. A morals based on study of human nature instead of upon disregard for it would find the facts of man continuous with those of the rest of nature and would thereby ally ethics with physics and biology. It would find the nature and activities of one person coterminous with those of other human beings, and therefore link ethics with the study of history, sociology, law and economics.

Such a morals would not automatically solve moral problems, nor resolve perplexities. But it would enable us to state problems in such forms that action could be courageously and intelligently directed to their solution.[2]

The "facts" are what scientific observation shows human nature to be and what experience reveals the environment to be. Morals must take account of both and adjust to them rather than contend with them, for the moral concern is always "the future. It is prospective." The individual must address himself to "modifying the factors which now influence future results,"[3] employing the intelligence he has been equipped with to apply what he knows of people and conditions to the fulfilment of his purposes. Since modification means change, and since change is natural, not to be arbitrarily dictated, the presupposition is that change itself is beyond judgment and that only its utilization can be at issue. In fact, in the optimistic milieu from which Dewey came, change was inseparable from hope for society generally. In the words of one of Dewey's most astute critics, Arthur E. Murphy, "Social change was naturalized as evolutionary growth, and to make it 'progress' all that was required was the free use of coöperative intelligence by progressively educated men in the solution of their common problems."[4] A consensus could be assumed, and the exercise of intelligence by individuals, proceeding from common premises, would necessarily bring about the social integration that was in jeopardy. If one could reason from causes to consequences, and if there was no disagreement about the desired consequences, reason would produce the good society.

Insofar as change meant growth, the individual confronted with particular or alternative changes would choose among them in terms of the availability of the means for achieving them, and among the means in terms of the probability of achieving the desired change. In fact, Dewey insisted that the means really were the ends:

> Means are means; they are intermediates, middle terms. To grasp this fact is to have done with the ordinary dualism of means and ends. The "end" is merely a series of acts viewed at a remote stage; and a means is merely the series viewed at an earlier one. The distinction of means and ends arises in surveying the *course* of a proposed *line* of action, a connected series in time. The "end" is the last act thought of; the means are the acts to be performed prior to it in time. To *reach* an end we must take our mind off from it and attend to the act which is next to be performed. We must make that the end.[5]

In performing the next act the individual would take account of the nature of the world and attempt what was most likely to succeed. He would determine the character of the immediate facts of life and the direction of existing trends, and seek to conform with the actualities. He would, as Harold Stearns put it, hope "to control events by abandoning [himself] to them."[6] Values were, in this context, indistinguishable from the means for their realization. For just as academic standards were subordinated to the self-expression of individual children in the Progressive Schools, so were ethical standards subordinated to evolution's expression of the stubborn process of social change.

In insisting on the worth of possibility Dewey might, as Murphy suggests, have adopted the slogan, "Hitch your conscience to a trend."[7] But which trend to hitch to and what moral judgment to make of it Dewey could scarcely have defined without appealing to an accepted community of interest, and when that community of interest was itself no longer real—when the very idea of community was being undermined by the definition of the individual as one with-out binding affiliations—then his argument in behalf of serving all became one in behalf of any interest, private or special or simply powerful and manipulatory, that under-took to assert itself.

The question of how to define or give status to value judgments, which Dewey begged, was one to which both Krutch and Lippmann undertook to propose answers. More sensitive to the tone of the twenties than he, they could see more clearly the inadequacies of his approach. The con-templative individual who came of age in the second decade of the twentieth century found it not only impossible to share Dewey's assumption about the reality of common objectives, but also difficult to identify any objectives as so generally compelling that they ought to be shared. As Krutch argued in his summary of the decade's attitude, *The Modern Temper*, the expectations of changes for the better that science was to effect had been disappointed. Men had long ceased supposing that their ancestry was divine, and now they discovered that even their feelings were not sacred, that they were not set apart in significance from the rest of nature, that no mysteries remained to be revered. Standards of conduct were cultural data, love was a biologi-cal function or psychological reaction, choice was the product of determining conditions. What beliefs human beings had held deeply enough to base values upon were but quaint illusions, now happily susceptible to explanation, and as Krutch noted, fatally so, since "to understand any of the il-lusions upon which the values of life depend inevitably destroys them."[8] In this predicament the individual could neither act with conviction in the objective importance of his purpose nor simply observe with hope that his contem-plation had meaning. For he saw neither purpose nor mean-ing in his existence. Only "those . . . too absorbed in living to feel the need for thought" could offer affirmations of life, and they could resemble "barbarians . . . , absorbed in the

processes of life for their own sake, eating without asking if
it is worth while to eat, begetting children without asking
why they should beget them, and conquering without asking for what purpose they conquer."[9] Akin to Cummings's
celebration of Jean le Nègre, Krutch's statement was a cultivated endorsement of the uncultivated; and akin to Cummings's concluding resolve to *be* as an artist rather than to
do as a primitive, Krutch's closing assertion that he would
choose "always rather to know than to be" declared an even
more disengaged outlook as the ultimate sanctuary. "Ours
is a lost cause," he said, "and there is no place for us in the
natural universe, but we are not, for all that, sorry to be human. We should rather die as men than live as animals."[10]
Worth lay, then, in the recognition of the worthlessness of
encounters, and recognition was what Gatsby's vocabulary
called "personal."

Lippmann, concurring in much of Krutch's analysis of
modern distress, declined to treat the human cause as really
lost. He agreed that questions of worth had become moot,
that a special place for human beings in the universal scheme
was now inconceivable, that art had ceased to be a vehicle
for prophecy and had been transformed into formal expression deliberately purified of socially significant content, that
all sanctions had lost authority and unhappiness was an
inevitable consequence. But he also agreed with Dewey that
experience could provide a solution, that in experience
sanctions generated themselves. Modern "humanism," he
wrote in *A Preface to Morals*, "takes as its dominant pattern
the progress of the individual from helpless infancy to self-
governing maturity."[11] Like Dewey, Lippmann advocated
the study of human nature for the purpose of developing
"exact knowledge" about it, and also like Dewey, he equated
maturity with the acknowledgment of actuality—the way
human nature works. "The process of maturing consists,"
he explained, ". . . of a revision of . . . desires in the light
of an understanding of reality."[12]

The revision Lippmann advocated was in the interest of

softening, even eliminating, encounters with limit. The individual who is mature will do only what is "appropriate."[13] What is appropriate is what can be done in the light of an exact knowledge of reality that will help the individual achieve harmony between desire and possibility. To make certain that desire will not become frustration in its encounter with what may be impossibility, the individual must learn that no desire should matter too much. Just as the moralist is to revise his code to suit occasions, so is the individual then to outgrow "naive desire" and cultivate "disinterestedness," which will "render passion innocent and an authoritative morality unnecessary."[14] He will "become detached from [his] passions and . . . understand them consciously."[15] When he finds out what it is "appropriate for [him] to believe," he will accordingly have succeeded in "opening his mind to a true vision of the good life."[16] In fine, he will repudiate passionate commitment and instead of risking the pain of limitation will be ready to liquidate any commitments to a point at which he experiences no limitations at all. He will live in and of himself.

And so the mature man would take the world as it comes, and within himself remain quite unperturbed. When he acted, he would know that he was only testing an hypothesis, and if he failed, he would know that he had made a mistake. He would be quite prepared for the discovery that he might make mistakes, for his intelligence would be disentangled from his hopes. The failure of his experiment could not, therefore, involve the failure of his life. For the aspect of life which implicated his soul would be his understanding of life, and, to the understanding, defeat is no less interesting than victory. It would be no effort, therefore, for him to be tolerant, and no annoyance to be skeptical. He would face pain with fortitude, for he would have put it away from the inner chambers of his soul. Fear would not haunt him, for he would be without compulsion to seize anything and without anxiety as to its fate. He would be strong, not with the strength of hard resolves, but because he was free of that tension which vain expectations beget. Would his life be uninteresting because he was disinterested? He would have the whole universe, rather than the prison of his own hopes and fears, for his habitation, and in imagination all possible forms of being. How could that be dull unless he brought the dullness with him? He might dwell with all beauty and all knowledge, and they are inexhaustible. Would he, then, dream idle dreams? Only if he chose to. For he might go quite simply about the business of the world, a good deal more effectively perhaps than the worldling, in that he did not place an absolute value upon it, and deceive himself. Would he be hopeful? Not if to be hopeful was to expect the world to submit rather soon to his vanity. Would he be hopeless? Hope is an expectation of favors to come, and he would take his delights here and now. Since nothing gnawed at his vitals, neither doubt nor ambition, nor frustration, nor fear, he would move easily through life. And so whether he saw the thing as comedy, or high tragedy, or plain farce, he would affirm that it is what it is, and that the wise man can enjoy it.[17]

Here is Watson's child come of age, the pupil in the Progressive School immunized against contradiction, the worker unconcerned with his production, Coolidge minding his own business, the nation celebrating its self-sufficiency, the citizen asking that the law and justice not involve him, the member of the black minority disinclined to subordinate his personal self-advancement to a larger cause, the literary hero achieving aloofness, the artist looking on beauty bare. Here is a belief in freedom defined as the absence of friction, a conception of the personal that congeals the self in privacy. Here is the denial of nemesis. One does not meet the consequences of what one is; instead, one is always there to avert those consequences, or deprecate them, or repair them, or modify the goals in the interests of minimizing what is consequential. Had Lippmann wanted a concrete illustration of maturity, he could have logically—if not comfortably—chosen George Jean Nathan, who in 1923 wrote of his role as a drama critic:

I am, constitutionally, given to enthusiasm about nothing. . . . The theatre is, to me, a great toy; and upon the toys of the world what Mr. Mencken alludes to as my lingering residuum of boyish delight concentrates itself. What interests me in life . . . is the surface of life: life's music and colour, its charm and ease, its humour and its loveliness. The great problems of the world— social, political, economic and theological—do not concern me in the slightest.[18]

I do not take [the theatre] very seriously, for I am of the sort that takes nothing very seriously; nor on the other hand do I take it too lightly. I take it simply as, night in and night out, it comes before my eyes: a painted toy with something of true gold inside it. And so it is that I write of it. I criticize it as a man criticizes his own cocktails and his own God.[19]

Hyperbole, perhaps; but logic nonetheless.

It was poetically just that this self-detachment became self-destruction. The last frontier was closed; there were no islands any more. The country could not remain isolated, the decade could not detach itself from the claims of history, deeds did—as in ancient and Elizabethan tragedy—come home to doers as the Crash brought retribution.

> My candle burns at both ends;
> It will not last the night;
> But ah, my foes, and oh, my friends—
> It gives a lovely light![20]

The catastrophe, however, was not utter. Throughout the society there had been a commitment to discrete individuality that was doomed—a commitment that gave the decade its distinctive mark. Yet latent in that very commitment was the affirmation of a value that could not be destroyed. The Progressive Era, full of hope for a society dedicated to the general welfare, had culminated in American participation in a world war that many Americans felt subsumed the individual in abstractions and divorced the social good from personal interest. The twenties exposed the slogans; those years reinstated the personal. Moreover, in the reinvigoration of the personal they reinvigorated the creative spirit in the arts, which without an emphasis on the personal could not exist. If the personal then became private, that was, perhaps, the historical price to be paid. And if the privacy in turn carried its fatality, it nonetheless announced that any restoration of social awareness—domestic and international—would be unable to ignore the basis of all society, the source of all freedom: the interested, selfish individual with his secular concerns.

Notes

THESE NOTES are confined to citations of source material and therefore contain no textual commentary. Where I have quoted from texts containing typographical errors, I have made corrections silently.

1. The Individual and His Family

1. *Psychological Care of Infant and Child* (New York: Norton, 1928), p. 3.
2. *Ibid.*, pp. 78–79.
3. *Ibid.*, p. 70.
4. *Ibid.*, p. 44.
5. John B. Watson and William Mac-Dougall, *The Battle of Behaviorism* (New York: Norton, 1929), pp. 16–17; Watson, *Psychological Care*, pp. 38–41.
6. Watson and MacDougall, pp. 19–20.
7. *Ibid.*, pp. 66–73, 33, 38. See also John B. Watson, "The Unconscious of the Behaviorist," in *The Unconscious, a Symposium* (New York: Knopf, 1927), pp. 91–113; A. A. Roback, *Behaviorism and Psychology* (Cambridge, Mass.: University Bookstore, 1923).
8. John B. Watson and Will Durant, "Is Man a Machine?: A Socratic Dialogue," *Forum*, LXXXII (November 1929), 264–70.
9. Watson, "The Unconscious," p. 113.
10. Watson, *Psychological Care*, pp. 81–82.
11. *Ibid.*, pp. 5–6.
12. *Ibid.*, pp. 186–87.
13. *Ibid.*, p. 41.
14. John B. Watson, *Behaviorism* (New York: Norton, 1925), p. 82. See also John B. Watson and Will Durant, "Can We Make Our Children Behave?: A Socratic Dia-

logue," *Forum*, LXXXII (December 1929), 349.
15. Watson, *Psychological Care*, pp. 47, 58–62.
16. *Ibid.*, pp. 81–82.
17. *Ibid.*, p. 113.
18. *Ibid.*, p. 8.
19. *Ibid.*, p. 89.
20. *Ibid.*, pp. 9–10.
21. *Ibid.*, p. 186.
22. George Santayana, "Living Without Thinking," *Forum*, LXVIII (September 1922), 735.
23. Cf. Mary R. Melendy and M. Henry Frank, *Modern Eugenics for Men and Women: A Complete Medical Guide to a Thorough Understanding of the Principles of Health and Sex Relations* (New York: Preferred Publications, 1928), pp. 119–22.
24. Lucille C. Birnbaum, "Behaviorism in the 1920's," *American Quarterly*, VII (Spring 1955), 18, 29–30.
25. Orville G. Brim, *Education for Child Rearing* (New York: Russell Sage Foundation, 1959), pp. 328–29.
26. Geoffrey H. Steere, "Freudianism and Child-Rearing in the Twenties," *American Quarterly*, XX (Winter 1968), 759–67; Watson, "The Unconscious," pp. 91–113.
27. Cf. F. H. Matthews, "The Americanization of Sigmund Freud: Adaptations of Psychoanalysis before 1917," *Journal of American*

Studies, I (April 1967), 39–62.

28. *The Psycho-Analytic Study of the Family* (London: International Psycho-Analytical Press, 1921), pp. 40–47, 61–65.

29. *Ibid.*, pp. 237, 119–20.

30. Cf. Stanley Coopersmith, "Studies in Self-Esteem," *Scientific American*, CCXVIII (February 1968), 106.

31. Ernest W. Burgess and Harvey J. Locke, *The Family: from Institution to Companionship* (New York: American Book, 1945), pp. 21–22.

32. Havelock Ellis, "The Family," in *Whither Mankind: A Panorama of Modern Civilization*, ed. Charles A. Beard (New York: Longmans, 1928), pp. 210–12.

33. Miriam Van Waters, *Parents on Probation* (New York: *New Republic*, 1927), p. 9.

34. *Ibid.*, pp. 15–16.

35. M. F. Nimkoff, *The Family* (Boston: Houghton, 1934), p. 205.

36. *Ibid.*, pp. 180–220; William M. Kephart, *The Family, Society, and the Individual*, 2nd ed. (Boston: Houghton, 1966), p. 60; Robert S. Lynd and Helen Merrell Lynd, *Middletown: A Study in American Culture* (New York: Harcourt, 1929), pp. 99n., 111–12, 134–35, 144–52; Ernest R. Mowrer, *Family Disorganization: An Introduction to a Sociological Analysis* (Chicago: U. of Chicago Press, 1927), pp. 4–7; Van Waters, pp. 29–39, 116; William E. Leuchtenburg, *The Perils of Prosperity, 1914–32* (Chicago: U. of Chicago Press, 1958), p. 162.

37. Ruth Benedict, "The Family: Genus Americanum," in *The Family: Its Function and Destiny*, ed. Ruth Nanda Anshen (New York: Harper, 1949), p. 168; Max Horkheimer, "Authoritarianism and the Family Today," in *The Family*, pp. 363–64; Ellis, pp. 218–19.

38. Lynd and Lynd, p. 116.

39. Beatrice M. Hinkle, "Marriage in the New World," in *The Book of Marriage: A New Interpretation by Twenty-four Leaders of Contemporary Thought*, ed. Count Hermann Keyserling (New York: Harcourt, 1926), pp. 217–36; Marta Karlweis, "Marriage and the Changing Woman," in *ibid.*, p. 213; Willystine Goodsell, *Problems of the Family* (New York: Century, 1928), pp. 405–407; Ernest R. Groves, *The Marriage Crisis* (New York: Longmans, 1928), pp. 37–43, 58–59.

40. Groves, p. 32; Mowrer, pp. 159–60; William L. O'Neill, *Divorce in the Progressive Era* (New Haven: Yale U. Press, 1967), p. 225.

41. Denis de Rougemont, "The Crisis of the Modern Couple," in *The Family*, pp. 324–25.

42. Grant Allen, quoted in O'Neill, p. 109.

43. Lynd and Lynd, p. 121; Mowrer, chs. 3–5.

44. Durant Drake, *The New Morality* (New York: Macmillan, 1928), p. 114.

45. Goodsell, p. 308.

46. George Jean Nathan, *Land of the Pilgrims' Pride* (New York: Knopf, 1927), p. 53.

47. *Ibid.*, p. 61.

48. *Ibid.*, p. 63.

49. Philippe Ariès, *Centuries of Childhood: A Social History of Family Life*, trans. Robert Baldick (New York: Knopf, 1962), pp. 10, 285, 369–73, 404–407.

50. *The Law of Civilization and Decay* (1896; rpt. New York: Knopf, 1943), pp. 338–39. See also Robert Morison, "Where Is Biology Taking Us?" *Science*, CLV (January 27, 1967), pp. 429–33.

51. Ben B. Lindsey and Wainwright Evans, *The Companionate Marriage* (New York: Boni & Liveright, 1927), p. v.

52. *Ibid.*, p. 97.

53. *Ibid.* (rpt. with Foreword, Garden City, N.Y.: Garden City Publishing, 1929), p. xx.

54. Mowrer, p. 160.

55. Goodsell, p. 413.

56. Lindsey and Evans (1927), p. vii.

57. Cyrena Van Gordor, quoted in Mowrer, pp. 11n.–12n.

58. Groves, p. 43.

59. Felix Adler, "Marriage," *Hibbert Journal*, XXII (October 1923), rpt. in *Selected Articles on Marriage and Divorce*, comp. Julia E. Johnson (New York: Wilson, 1925), pp. 69–70.

2. The Individual and His School

1. *Modern Educational Theories* (New York: Macmillan, 1927), p. 11. I am indebted to Clifford R. Josephson for calling this passage to my attention.

2. National Education Association of

the United States, *Journal of Proceedings and Addresses*, XLIX (1911), 560.

3. Lawrence A. Cremin, *The Transformation of the School: Progressivism in American Education, 1876–1957* (New York: Knopf, 1961), p. 127; Merle Curti, *The Social Ideas of American Educators* (New York: Scribner, 1935), pp. 194–95.

4. Richard Hofstadter, *Anti-intellectualism in American Life* (New York: Knopf, 1963), pp. 326–29.

5. Elisabeth Irwin and Louis A. Marks, *Fitting the School to the Child: An Experiment in Public Education* (New York: Macmillan, 1924), pp. 3–4.

6. William Heard Kilpatrick, *Education for a Changing Civilization: Three Lectures Delivered on the Luther Laflin Kellogg Foundation at Rutgers University, 1926* (1926; rpt. New York: Macmillan, 1932), pp. 39–41.

7. Curti, pp. 194–200, 221–22.

8. *Ibid.*, pp. 205–207. See also George S. Counts, *Secondary Education and Industrialism* (Cambridge, Mass.: Harvard U. Press, 1929), pp. 18–49.

9. Curti, pp. 223–25, 253 ff.; Lynd and Lynd, *Middletown*, pp. 190–91.

10. *Education: Intellectual, Moral, and Physical* (1861; rpt. New York: Appleton, 1866), pp. 31–32. The material first appeared in four review-articles, 1854–59.

11. *Ibid.*, pp. 37–49.

12. *Ibid.*, pp. 55–56.

13. *Ibid.*, pp. 67–70.

14. *Ibid.*, pp. 76–77.

15. *Ibid.*, p. 79.

16. *Ibid.*, pp. 83–84.

17. *Ibid.*, p. 88.

18. *Ibid.*, p. 61.

19. *Ibid.*, pp. 105–106.

20. *Ibid.*, p. 157.

21. *Ibid.*, pp. 108–109.

22. *Ibid.*, p. 163.

23. *Ibid.*, p. 109.

24. *Ibid.*, pp. 212–13.

25. See also Cremin, pp. 100–104.

26. Cremin, pp. 75–78.

27. Abraham Flexner, *I Remember: The Autobiography of Abraham Flexner* (New York: Simon, 1940), pp. 74–81.

28. *Ibid.*, pp. 250–52; Abraham Flexner, *A Modern School*, Occasonal Papers, No. 3 (New York: General Education Board, 1916).

29. Charles W. Eliot, *Changes Needed in American Secondary Education*, Occasional Papers, No. 2 (New York: General Education Board,

1916), p. 11.

30. *Ibid.*, p. 9.

31. *Ibid.*, pp. 5–6.

32. Flexner, *A Modern School*, p. 8.

33. *Ibid.*, p. 23.

34. James Earl Russell, *The Trend in American Education* (New York: American Book, 1922), p. 23. See also Cremin, pp. 280–81.

35. Cremin, pp. 110–13.

36. Edward L. Thorndike, *Individuality* (Boston: Houghton, 1911), pp. 19–20.

37. *Ibid.*, p. 26

38. Cremin, p. 186 ff.

39. See William C. Bagley, *Determinism in Education* (Baltimore: Warwick, 1925), pp. 24–31, 46, 157–60.

40. Edward L. Thorndike, *The Principles of Teaching. Based on Psychology* (New York: Seiler, 1906), p. 39.

41. *Ibid.*, p. 51.

42. *Ibid.*, p. 4.

43. *Ibid.*, p. 58.

44. *Ibid.*, pp. 3–4.

45. Curti, p. 484.

46. Edward L. Thorndike, "Education for Initiative and Originality," *Teachers College Record*, XVII (November 1916), 408, 414.

47. See above, p. 7.

48. John Dewey, "Mediocrity and Individuality," *New Republic*, XXXIII (December 6, 1922), 35, and "Individuality[,] Equality and Superiority," *New Republic*, XXXIII (December 13, 1922), 63.

49. Cremin, pp. 115–26; Curti, pp. 503–504.

50. John Dewey, *My Pedagogic Creed* (1897; rpt. Washington, D.C.: Progressive Education Association, [1929]), pp. 3–8.

51. *Ibid.*, p. 14.

52. Cremin, p. 136.

53. Quoted in *ibid.*, p. 140.

54. John Dewey and Evelyn Dewey, *Schools of Tomorrow* (New York: Dutton, 1915), p. [iii].

55. *Ibid.*, p. 23; Cremin, p. 149

56. Dewey and Dewey, p. 18.

57. *Ibid.*, p. 5.

58. *Ibid.*, p. 7.

59. *Ibid.*, pp. 20–22.

60. *Ibid.*, p. 147.

61. *Ibid.*, pp. 109–10.

62. *Ibid.*, p. 31.

63. *Ibid.*, p. 140.

64. *Ibid.*, pp. 68–69.

65. *Ibid.*, pp. 98–101.

66. *Ibid.*, p. 79.

67. *Ibid.*, pp. 24, 137, 153–55, 162, 191–92.

68. *Ibid.*, p. 292.

69. *Ibid.*, p. 301.

70. *Ibid.*, p. 303.

71. *Ibid.*, pp. 70–73.
72. *Ibid.*, p. 315.
73. Agnes de Lima, *Our Enemy the Child* (1925; rpt. New York: *New Republic*, 1930), p. 125.
74. Quoted in *ibid.*, p. 130.
75. *Progressive Education*, III (January–March 1926), 22.
76. de Lima, pp. 12–31.
77. *Ibid.*, p. 5.
78. Cremin, p. 279; de Lima, pp. 256–57.
79. Kilpatrick, p. 125.
80. *Progressive Education*, I (April 1924), 2.
81. Margaret Naumburg, *The Child and the World: Dialogues in Modern Education* (New York: Harcourt, 1928), p. 252.
82. Caroline Pratt and Jessie Stanton, *Before Books: Experimental Practice in the City and Country School* (New York: Adelphi, 1926), p. viii.
83. *Ibid.*; Caroline Pratt, ed., *Experimental Practice in the City and Country School* (New York: Dutton, 1924).
84. Pratt and Stanton, pp. 4, 6.
85. *Ibid.*, p. 14.
86. Pratt, *Experimental Practice*, p. 21.
87. *Ibid.*, p. 12.
88. Agnes Burke *et al.*, comps., *A Conduct Curriculum for the Kindergarten and First Grade*, directed by Patty Smith Hill, intro. Patty Smith Hill (New York: Scribner, 1923), pp. x–xii.
89. *Ibid.*, pp. xiv–xvi
90. *Ibid.*, p. 15.
91. *Ibid.*, p. 41.
92. *Ibid.*, pp. 122–23.
93. *Ibid.*, pp. vii–viii.
94. Irwin and Marks, p. v.
95. *Ibid.*, p. xxv.
96. Elisabeth Irwin, "Personal Education," *New Republic*, XL (November 12, 1924), pt. 2, pp. 8–9.
97. Irwin and Marks, pp. 116–17.
98. *Ibid.*, ch. 3; de Lima, p. 39.
99. Irwin and Marks, pp. 28–38, 110, 314–16.
100. Irwin, "Personal Education," p. 9.
101. de Lima, pp. 204–205.
102. Helen Parkhurst, "The Dalton Laboratory Plan," *Progressive Education*, I (April 1924), 14–18; de Lima, p. 86; Naumburg, pp. 253–54.
103. Mabel R. Goodlander, *Education Through Experience: A Four Year Experiment in The Ethical Culture School*, 2nd ed. (New York: Bureau of Educational Experiments, 1922), pp. 5–7.
104. Carleton W. Washburne, "The Winnetka System," *Progressive Education*, I (April 1924), 11; de

Lima, p. 92.
105. Naumburg, p. 252.
106. *Ibid.*, pp. xix–xx.
107. Columbia University: Teachers College: Lincoln School, *Curriculum Making in an Elementary School by the Staff of the Elementary Division of the Lincoln School of Teachers College, Columbia University* (Boston: Ginn, 1927), p. 28.
108. *Ibid.*, pp. 240–42.
109. Cremin, pp. 284–85.
110. Columbia U., *Curriculum Making*, pp. 257–58.
111. Cremin, pp. 283, 286.
112. Columbia U., *Curriculum Making*, p. 22.
113. *Ibid.*, p. 31.
114. Hughes Mearns, *Creative Power* (Garden City, N.Y.: Doubleday, 1929), p. 119.
115. Hughes Mearns, "The Creative Spirit and Its Significance for Education," in *Creative Expression: The Development of Children in Art, Music, Literature, and Dramatics*, ed. Gertrude Hartman and Ann Shumaker (New York: Day, 1932), p. 18.
116. Florence E. House, "Creative Expression Through the Block Print," in *ibid.*, p. 37.
117. Florence Cane, "Art in the Life of the Child," in *ibid.*, p. 43.
118. Mearns, *Creative Power*, pp. 6–7.
119. *Ibid.*, pp. 18–19.
120. *Ibid.*, pp. 30–31, 33, 35, 37, 88.
121. *Ibid.*, p. 41.
122. *Ibid.*, pp. 75, 112, 192.
123. *Ibid.*, p. 237.
124. *Ibid.*, p. 113.
125. *Ibid.*, p. 118.
126. *Ibid.*, p. 119.
127. *Ibid.*, p. 203.
128. Columbia U., *Curriculum Making*, pp. 285–86.
129. *The Child-Centered School: An Appraisal of the New Education* (Yonkers, N.Y.: World Book, 1928), p. 35. See also John Dewey, "Progressive Education and the Science of Education," *Progressive Education*, V (July–September 1928), 197–98.
130. Rugg and Shumaker, pp. 36–37.
131. *Ibid.*, p. 89.
132. Cremin, p. 183.
133. Rugg and Shumaker, p. 64.
134. Mearns, *Creative Power*, pp. 275–76.
135. Harold Rugg, *Foundations for American Education* (New York: American Book, 1922), p. 552.
136. John Dewey, *Democracy and Education* (1916; rpt. New York: Macmillan, 1942), pp. 231–35.

137. Franklin Bobbitt, *How to Make a Curriculum* (Boston: Houghton, 1924), p. 9 *et passim*, and *The Curriculum* (Boston: Houghton, 1918); Boyd H. Bode, *Fundamentals of Education,* Modern Teachers' Series, ed. William C. Bagley (New York: Macmillan, 1921), pp. 30–31.

138. Bobbitt, *How to Make a Curriculum,* pp. 1–2.

139. Eugene Randolph Smith, *Education Moves Ahead: A Survey of Progressive Methods* (Boston: *Atlantic Monthly* Press, 1924), p. 52.

140. William Heard Kilpatrick, introduction to Ellsworth Collings, *An Experiment with a Project Curriculum* (New York: Macmillan, 1923), p. xvii.

141. Ellsworth Collings, *Progressive Teaching in Secondary Schools* (Indianapolis: Bobbs-Merrill, 1931), pp. 4–21, ch. 5.

142. Rugg and Shumaker, pp. viii–ix.

143. *Ibid.*, p. 8.

144. David Snedden, *Cultural Educations and Common Sense: A Study of Some Sociological Foundations of Educations Designed to Refine, Increase, and Render More Functional the Personal Cultures of Men* (New York: Macmillan, 1931), p. 305.

145. David Snedden, "Sociology, a Basic Science to Education," *Teachers College Record,* XXIV (March 1923), 105–106. See also "Dewey's Philosophy of Education," *Nation,* CII (May 4, 1916), 481; Hofstadter, *Anti-intellectualism,* pp. 381–83.

146. Bode, *Fundamentals of Education,* p. 9.

147. Conversation with author, 1936.

148. Dewey, "Progressive Education and the Science of Education," p. 201, quoted in Cremin, pp. 234–35.

3. The Individual and His Livelihood

1. *Beauty Looks After Herself* (New York: Sheed, 1934), epigraph.

2. Quoted in Thomas C. Cochran and William Miller, *The Age of Enterprise: A Social History of Industrial America,* rev. ed. (New York: Harper, 1961), p. 70.

3. Woodrow Wilson, *The New Freedom: A Call for the Emancipation of the Generous Energies of a People* (1913; rpt. Garden City, New York: Doubleday, 1921), pp. 5–6. See also Garet Garrett, "Business," in *Civilization in the United States: An Inquiry by Thirty Americans,* ed. Harold E. Stearns (New York: Harcourt, 1922), p. 411.

4. Wilson, pp. 10–11. See also George E. Roberts, "Things to Tell Your Men: A Series on Economics in Homespun," *Nation's Business,* XII (June 1924), 17.

5. Quoted in Arthur M. Schlesinger, Jr., *The Crisis of the Old Order, 1919–1933,* Sentry ed. (Boston: Houghton, 1964), p. 40.

6. Garrett, p. 397.

7. *Ibid.*, p. 411.

8. Lynd and Lynd, *Middletown,* p. 70.

9. Roberts, p. 17.

10. William Miller, "The Business Elite in Business Bureaucracies: Careers of Top Executives in the Early Twentieth Century," in *Men in Business: Essays in the History of Entrepreneurship,* ed. William Miller (Cambridge, Mass.: Harvard U. Press, 1952), p. 287.

11. Cochran and Miller, p. 315.

12. Miller, "The Business Elite," p. 294.

13. Quoted in James Warren Prothro, *The Dollar Decade: Business Ideas in the 1920's* (Baton Rouge, La.: Louisiana State U. Press, 1954), p. 65.

14. *Ibid.*, p. 26.

15. *Ibid.*, p. 85

16. *Ibid.*, p. 61.

17. *Ibid.*, p. 44.

18. *Ibid.*, p. 34.

19. *Ibid.*, p. 63.

20. Charles W. Wood, *The Myth of the Individual* (New York: Day, 1927), p. 179.

21. Thorstein Veblen, *Absentee Ownership and Business Enterprise in Recent Times: The Case of America* (1923; rpt. New York: Viking, 1954), p. 85.

22. Drake, *New Morality,* p. 163; André Siegfried, *America Comes of Age: A French Analysis,* trans. H. H. Hemming and Doris Hemming (New York: Harcourt, 1927), pp. 178–79; Morrell Heald, "Business Thought in the Twenties: Social Responsibility," *American Quarterly,* XIII (Summer 1961), pt. 1, pp. 126–39.

23. Charles Cason, quoted in Heald, p. 127.

24. Edward A. Filene, quoted in Heald, pp. 129–30.
25. Heald, pp. 131–36; D. W. Malott, "Business Advancing as a Profession," *Iron Trade Review*, LXXIV (June 12, 1924), 1565; Edwin Mims, *Adventurous America: A Study of Contemporary Life and Thought* (New York: Scribner, 1929), pp. 55, 69, 78–79. See also Williams Haynes, "Better Ethical Standards for Business: The Purpose of the Commercial Standards Council," in "The Ethics of the Professions and of Business," ed. Clyde L. King, *Annals of the American Academy of Political and Social Science*, CI (May 1922), 221; King, in *ibid.*, p. vii.
26. Heald, pp. 128–31.
27. David Brody, "The Rise and Decline of Welfare Capitalism," in *Change and Continuity in Twentieth-Century America: The 1920's*, ed. John Braeman, Robert H. Bremner, and David Brody (Columbus, O.: Ohio State U. Press, 1968), pp. 149–51, 159–60.
28. Quoted in Colston E. Warne, ed., *The Steel Strike of 1919*, Problems in American Civilization (Lexington, Mass.: Heath, 1963), p. 32.
29. Carl L. Becker, *Freedom and Responsibility in the American Way of Life* (New York: Vintage, 1955), pp. 100–101.
30. Miller, "The Business Elite," p. 289; Mabel Newcomer, *The Big Business Executive: The Factors That Made Him, 1900–1950* (New York: Columbia U. Press, 1955), p. 19.
31. Prothro, p. 69.
32. Lynd and Lynd, p. 75.
33. Irving Bernstein, *The Lean Years: A History of the American Worker, 1920–1933* (Boston: Houghton, 1960), ch. 1; Mark Perlman, "Labor in Eclipse," in *Change and Continuity*, pp. 119–44.
34. Siegfried, p. 349.
35. *Ibid.*, pp. 152–54; Lynd and Lynd, p. 41. Cf. Peter F. Drucker, *The Future of Industrial Man: A Conservative Approach* (New York: Day, 1942), pp. 102–12.
36. Siegfried, p. 182.
37. Quoted in William Allen White, *A Puritan in Babylon: The Story of Calvin Coolidge* (New York: Macmillan, 1938), p. 335.
38. John D. Rockefeller, Jr., *The Personal Relation in Industry* (New York: Boni & Liveright, 1923), pp. 12–26; Bernstein, pp. 157–89; *The Portable Veblen*, ed. Max Ler-
ner (New York: Viking, 1948), pp. 318–23. See also Ida M. Tarbell, *Owen D. Young: A New Type of Industrial Leader* (New York: Macmillan, 1932), pp. 125–26, 144, 148–57, 180–82.
39. Quoted in Arthur Pound, *Industrial America: Its Way of Work and Thought* (Boston: Little, 1936), p. 50.
40. William Z. Ripley, *Main Street and Wall Street* (Boston: Little, 1929), pp. 83, 96–119; John H. Sears, *The New Place of the Stockholder* (New York: Harper, 1929), pp. 215–19; Julius Klein, "Business," in *Whither Mankind*, p. 100; Brody, p. 154; Pound, p. 16; Drucker, pp. 80–83; Alfred P. Sloan, Jr., "Modern Ideals of Big Business. As Described to French Strother by Alfred P. Sloan, Jr.," *World's Work*, LII (October 1926), 695–98; Chester I. Barnard, *The Functions of the Executive* (Cambridge, Mass.: Harvard U. Press, 1946), p. 6.
41. Quoted in R. L. Bruckberger, *Image of America*, trans. C. G. Paulding and Virgilia Peterson (New York: Viking, 1959), p. 159.
42. *I'll Take My Stand: The South and the Agrarian Tradition. By Twelve Southerners*, Harper Torchbooks (New York: Harper, 1962), pp. xix, xxvi.
43. *Ibid.*, p. xxiv.
44. *Ibid.*, pp. xxii–xxiii.
45. *Ibid.*, p. xxviii.
46. John Crowe Ransom, "Reconstructed But Unregenerate," in *ibid.*, p. 12.
47. *Ibid.*, p. 10.
48. *I'll Take My Stand*, p. xxix,
49. Ransom, p. 20.
50. *Ibid.*, p. 23.
51. *I'll Take My Stand*, pp. xxiv–xxv.
52. Ransom, pp. 22–23.
53. Donald Davidson, "A Mirror for Artists," in *I'll Take My Stand*, p. 34.
54. See, for example, *ibid.*, pp. 37–40; John Gould Fletcher, "Education, Past and Present," in *I'll Take My Stand*, pp. 115–20; Stark Young, "Not in Memoriam, But in Defense," in *ibid.*, p. 339.
55. Alexander Karanikas, *Tillers of a Myth: Southern Agrarians as Social and Literary Critics* (Madison, Wisc.: U. of Wisconsin Press, 1966), pp. 65–72.
56. Donald Davidson, "First Fruits of Dayton: The Intellectual Evolution in Dixie," *Forum*, LXXIX (June 1928), 898.
57. Karanikas, pp. 111–13.

58. *Ibid.*
59. Allen Tate, *Stonewall Jackson: The Good Soldier*, Ann Arbor Paperbacks (1928; rpt. Ann Arbor, Mich.: U. of Michigan Press, 1957), pp. 39–40.
60. Lyle H. Lanier, "A Critique of the Philosophy of Progress," in *I'll Take My Stand*, pp. 151–52.
61. Henry Ford, in collaboration with Samuel Crowther, *My Life and Work* (Garden City, N.Y.: Doubleday, 1923), pp. 55–56.
62. *Ibid.*, p. 73.
63. *Ibid.*, p. 9.
64. *Ibid.*, p. 120.
65. *Ibid.*, p. 12.
66. *Ibid.*, p. 7.
67. *Ibid.*, p. 36.
68. *Ibid.*, p. 40.
69. Allan Nevins and Frank Ernest Hill, *Ford: Expansion and Challenge, 1915–1933* (New York: Scribner, 1957), pp. 88–89, 95–101; Bruckberger, pp. 205–206.
70. Quoted in Nevins and Hill, *Ford: Expansion*, p. 103.
71. Quoted in *ibid.*, p. 97.
72. Frederick Lewis Allen, *The Big Change: America Transforms Itself, 1900–1950* (New York: Harper, 1952), pp. 113, 111–12.
73. Ford, pp. 45–46.
74. Allan Nevins and Frank Ernest Hill, *Ford: The Times, the Man, the Company* (New York: Scribner, 1954), pp. 519–28, 541–49, and *Ford: Expansion*, pp. 227, 340–48, 525.
75. Ford, pp. 92–93.
76. *Ibid.*, pp. 126–28.
77. Nevins and Hill, *Ford: Expansion*, p. 517.
78. Quoted in *ibid.*, p. 508.
79. *Ibid.*, p. 525.
80. *Ibid.*, p. 514.
81. Cf. the psychological interpretation in Anne Jardim, *The First Henry Ford: A Study in Personality and Business Leadership* (Cambridge, Mass.: M.I.T. Press, 1970).
82. Paul W. Litchfield, *The Industrial Republic: A Study in Industrial Economics* (Boston: Houghton, 1920).
83. *Ibid.*, p. 11.
84. *Ibid.*, p. 14.
85. *Ibid.*, p. 18.

86. *Ibid.*, pp. 20–21.
87. *Ibid.*, pp. 22–24, 28–29.
88. *Ibid.*, pp. 52–53.
89. *Ibid.*, pp. 60–62.
90. *Ibid.*, pp. 75–76.
91. Pound, pp. 60–61, 57. See also Drucker, pp. 149, 155, 157, 166–67, 298.
92. John A. Ryan, *Social Reconstruction* (New York: Macmillan, 1920), pp. 235, 237. These phrases are from "The Bishops' Program for Social Reconstruction," issued by the National Catholic War Council in 1919 and reprinted as an appendix to Ryan's book. Inasmuch as Ryan drafted the document, authorship is essentially his.
93. John A. Ryan, *Distributive Justice: The Right and Wrong of Our Present Distribution of Wealth* (New York: Macmillan, 1916), p. 429.
94. Ralph Borsodi, *This Ugly Civilization*, 2nd ed. (New York: Harper, 1933), p. 33.
95. *Ibid.*, p. 31.
96. *Ibid.*, p. 15.
97. Edward A. Filene, *The Way Out: A Forecast of Coming Changes in American Business and Industry* (Garden City, N.Y.: Doubleday, 1925), p. 216.
98. *Ibid.*, p. 219.
99. *Ibid.*, p. 272.
100. Sebastian de Grazia, *Of Time, Work, and Leisure* (Garden City, N.Y.: Anchor, 1964), p. 256.
101. *Ibid.*, p. 64.
102. Hannah Arendt, *The Human Condition* (Chicago: U. of Chicago Press, 1958), p. 5.
103. de Grazia, p. 236.
104. Adolf A. Berle, Jr., *The 20th Century Capitalist Revolution*, Harvest Books (New York: Harcourt, 1954), pp. 29–32.
105. David Riesman, "The Saving Remnant: An Examination of Character Structure," *Individualism Reconsidered and Other Essays* (Glencoe, Ill.: Free Press, 1954), p. 104.
106. *Ibid.*, pp. 109–11.
107. *Ibid.*, p. 104.
108. Andrew W. Mellon, *Taxation: The People's Business* (New York: Macmillan, 1924), p. 12.
109. Quoted in White, *A Puritan*, p. 253.

4. The Individual and His Nation

1. Quoted in White, *A Puritan*, p. 336.
2. *The Public Papers and Addresses of Franklin D. Roosevelt* (New York: Random, 1938), V, 235.
3. See James Marlow, "The World

Today:/Roosevelt Inauguration 30
Years Ago/Brought Great Changes
to U. S.," Associated Press column,
Ithaca Journal, March 4, 1963, p. 6.

4. Mellon, *Taxation*, p. 17.

5. Sidney Warren, *The President as
World Leader* (Philadelphia: Lip-
pincott, 1964), p. 139; John Chynoweth Burnham, "Psychiatry, Psychology and the Progressive Movement," *American Quarterly*, XII
(Winter 1960), 458–59.

6. Quoted in Andrew Sinclair, *The
Available Man: The Life Behind
the Mask of Warren Gamaliel Harding* (New York: Macmillan,
1965), p. 152.

7. See Warren, p. 145, for evidence of
his consistency to the last.

8. White, *A Puritan*, p. 207.

9. Robert K. Murray, *The Harding
Era: Warren G. Harding and His
Administration* (Minneapolis: U.
of Minnesota Press, 1969), pp. 166–
69; Samuel Hopkins Adams, *In-
credible Era: The Life and Times
of Warren Gamaliel Harding* (Boston: Houghton, 1939), pp. 189,
254–56.

10. Quoted in Murray, p. 123.

11. Warren, p. 142; Sinclair, *The Available Man*, pp. 4–6.

12. Quoted in Murray, p. 110.

13. *Ibid.*, p. 123.

14. Quoted in Elizabeth Stevenson,
*Babbitts and Bohemians: The
American 1920s* (New York: Macmillan, 1967), pp. 81–82; Murray,
p. 70.

15. Murray, pp. 127–28, 144; Wilfred
E. Binkley, *President and Congress*,
3rd rev. ed. (New York: Vintage,
1962), pp. 267–73.

16. Quoted in Murray, p. 171.

17. *Ibid.*, p. 170.

18. Quoted in *ibid.*, p. 172.

19. *Ibid.*, p. 192.

20. Mellon, p. 18.

21. *Ibid.*, pp. 71–72.

22. Murray, pp. 182–83.

23. Mellon, p. 123.

24. Murray, p. 183.

25. Mellon, p. 172.

26. Murray, pp. 195–98.

27. *Ibid.*, p. 381.

28. *Ibid.*, pp. 206–207.

29. *Ibid.*, pp. 278–79. See also John D.
Hicks, *Republican Ascendancy,
1921–1933* (New York: Harper,
1960), pp. 57–59.

30. Murray, pp. 212–14.

31. *Ibid.*, pp. 255–56.

32. *Ibid.*, pp. 258–64.

33. See, for example, J. William Ful-
bright, *The Arrogance of Power*
(New York: Vintage, 1967), p. 6;
Dwight Lowell Dumond, *America

in Our Time: 1896–1946* (New
York: Holt, 1947), pp. 135, 245;
Otto H. Kahn, *Our Economic and
Other Problems: A Financier's
Point of View* (New York: Doran,
1920), pp. 356–57.

34. See Selig Adler, *The Isolationist
Impulse: Its Twentieth-Century Reaction* (London and New York:
Abelard-Schuman, 1957), p. 106;
Stevenson, p. 31; Eric Goldman,
*Rendezvous with Destiny: A His-
tory of Modern American Reform*,
rev. and abr. ed. (New York: Vintage, 1956), pp. 208–209; Kahn,
pp. 356–58; Walter Lippmann,
Men of Destiny (New York: Macmillan, 1927), p. 222.

35. S. H. Adams, p. 175.

36. Quoted in Warren, p. 144.

37. Quoted in Sinclair, *The Available
Man*, p. 275.

38. Harold W. Cary, "The United
States Rejects the League of Nations," in *Main Problems in American History*, ed. Howard H. Quint,
Dean Albertson, and Milton Can-
tor (Homewood, Ill.: Dorsey,
1964), II, 175–76.

39. See Dexter Perkins, "The Department of State and American Public Opinion," in *The Diplomats,
1919–1939*, ed. Gordon A. Craig
and Felix Gilbert (Princeton, N.J.:
Princeton U. Press, 1953), pp. 284–
85, 288–89.

40. Quoted in Leuchtenburg, *The Perils of Prosperity*, p. 107.

41. Robert H. Ferrell, *American Di-
plomacy in the Great Depression:
Hoover-Stimson Foreign Policy,
1929–1933* (New Haven, Conn.:
Yale U. Press, 1957), pp. 67, 72–73;
Murray, pp. 150–63.

42. Quoted in Murray, p. 160.

43. *Ibid.*, pp. 368–73.

44. Quoted in *ibid.*, p. 267.

45. Arthur Hendrick Vandenberg, *If
Hamilton Were Here Today:
American Fundamentals Applied to
Modern Problems* (New York:
Putnam, 1923), pp. 216–23.

46. Quoted in Murray, p. 333.

47. *Ibid.*, pp. 327–44.

48. Quoted in *ibid.*, p. 343.

49. Quoted in *ibid.*, p. 374.

50. Burl Noggle, *Teapot Dome: Oil
and Politics in the 1920's* (Baton
Rouge, La.: Louisiana State U.
Press, 1962).

51. Quoted in White, *A Puritan*, p.
371; Irwin Hood (Ike) Hoover,
*Forty-Two Years in the White
House* (Boston: Houghton, 1934),
p. 268, cited in Ferrell, p. 40.

52. Quoted in Donald R. McCoy, *Calvin Coolidge: The Quiet President*

(New York: Macmillan, 1967), pp. 54–55.

53. Calvin Coolidge, *The Price of Freedom: Speeches and Addresses* (New York: Scribner, 1924), p. 234.
54. *Ibid.*, p. 281.
55. *Ibid.*, p. 22.
56. *Ibid.*, p. 112. See also William Allen White, *Calvin Coolidge: The Man Who Is President* (New York: Macmillan, 1925), p. 34, and *A Puritan*, p. 73.
57. McCoy, pp. 38, 49. Cf. White, *Calvin Coolidge*, p. 76.
58. White, *A Puritan*, pp. 395–97.
59. Quoted in McCoy, p. 202.
60. Quoted in Schlesinger, *The Crisis of the Old Order*, p. 61.
61. White, *Calvin Coolidge*, pp. 148–51, and *A Puritan*, pp. 322–23; McCoy, pp. 276–78.
62. McCoy, p. 177.
63. *Ibid.*, pp. 226–29; Hicks, pp. 62–66.
64. Quoted in Howard H. Quint and Robert H. Ferrell, eds., *The Talkative President: The Off-the-Record Press Conferences of Calvin Coolidge* (Amherst, Mass.: U. of Massachusetts Press, 1964), p. 123.
65. McCoy, p. 333.
66. White, *A Puritan*, p. 363.
67. Quint and Ferrell, p. 124.
68. Quoted in McCoy, p. 308.
69. Quoted in Claude M. Fuess, *Calvin Coolidge: The Man from Vermont* (1940; rpt. Hamden, Conn.: Archon, 1965), p. 383.
70. Quoted in McCoy, p. 308.
71. Quoted in Fuess, p. 384.
72. White, *A Puritan*, pp. 343–44; Gilbert C. Fite, "The Farmers' Dilemma, 1919–1929," in *Change and Continuity*, pp. 67–75.
73. Quoted in Fuess, p. 383.
74. McCoy, p. 315.
75. Quoted in *ibid.*, p. 234.
76. Fite, pp. 82–86.
77. Quoted in *ibid.*, p. 86.
78. *Ibid.*, pp. 84–87.
79. *Ibid.*, pp. 91–92.
80. McCoy, pp. 234–35.
81. Quoted in *ibid.*, p. 309. See also Fuess, p. 384.
82. Fuess, p. 388.
83. Quoted in Fite, p. 96.
84. Quoted in Schlesinger, p. 57.
85. Fite, pp. 100–102.
86. Coolidge, *The Price of Freedom*, p. 229.
87. Foreword to James M. Beck, *The Constitution of the United States: Yesterday, Today—and Tomorrow?* (New York: Doran, 1924), p. vi.
88. Quoted in McCoy, p. 200.
89. *Ibid.*, p. 229; Quint and Ferrell,

p. 91; White, *A Puritan*, pp. 261, 279.
90. McCoy, pp. 177–78.
91. *Ibid.*, pp. 346–47. See also Murray, pp. 344–48; Hicks, pp. 254–57.
92. Quoted in McCoy, p. 337.
93. Quoted in *ibid.*, p. 183. Cf. White, *A Puritan*, p. 324; Quint and Ferrell, p. 255.
94. Quoted in Quint and Ferrell, p. 234.
95. Quoted in *ibid.*, pp. 237–38.
96. Quoted in Fuess, p. 411n.
97. Quoted in McCoy, p. 352.
98. Quoted in *ibid.*, p. 363. See also *ibid.*, pp. 360–62; Warren, pp. 148–49.
99. Quoted in McCoy, p. 355.
100. Fuess, pp. 414–17.
101. White, *A Puritan*, p. 373.
102. Hicks, pp. 161–62.
103. Quoted in McCoy, p. 378.
104. Adler, p. 237.
105. Gordon A. Craig, "The British Foreign Office from Grey to Austen Chamberlain," in *The Diplomats*, p. 40.
106. Quoted in Kirk H. Porter and Donald Bruce Johnson, comps., *National Party Platforms, 1840–1960* (Urbana, Ill.: U. of Illinois Press, 1961), pp. 251 ff.
107. Quoted in McCoy, p. 392.
108. Lippmann, *Men of Destiny*, p. 12.
109. *Ibid.*, pp. 21–22.
110. Stevenson, p. 111.
111. Quoted in Schlesinger, p. 57. See also Lynd and Lynd, *Middletown*, pp. 416–18.
112. Samuel Crowther, *The Presidency vs. Hoover* (Garden City, N.Y.: Doubleday, 1928), p. 3.
113. Richard Hofstadter, *The American Political Tradition and the Men Who Made It* (New York: Vintage, 1954), pp. 286–88; Gene Smith, *The Shattered Dream: Herbert Hoover and the Great Depression* (New York: Morrow, 1970), pp. 18–31.
114. G. Smith, p. 31.
115. Hofstadter, *The American Political Tradition*, p. 288.
116. Quoted in *ibid.*, p. 290.
117. White, *A Puritan*, pp. 410–11.
118. Oscar Handlin, *Al Smith and His America* (Boston: Little, 1958), p. 186; Leuchtenburg, p. 234; Hicks, p. 208; Schlesinger, p. 126.
119. Alfred E. Smith, *Progressive Democracy: Addresses and State Papers of Alfred E. Smith*, ed. Henry Moskowitz (New York: Harcourt, 1928), p. 69. See also Adler, pp. 215–17.
120. Alfred E. Smith, *Campaign Addresses of Governor Alfred E. Smith, Democratic Candidate for*

President, 1928 (Washington, D.C.: Democratic National Committee, 1929), p. 11.

121. Quoted in Edmund A. Moore, *A Catholic Runs for President: The Campaign of 1928* (New York: Ronald, 1956), p. 107. See also Roy V. Peel and Thomas C. Donnelly, *The 1928 Campaign: An Analysis* (New York: New York U. Book Store, Distr., 1931), p. 99.

122. See Paul W. Glad, "Progressives and the Business Culture of the 1920s," *Journal of American History*, LIII (June 1966), 87.

123. Moore, pp. 158–59; author's recollections.

124. Professor Richard H. Shryock suggested this last point in a lecture, University of Pennsylvania, during 1939–1941.

125. Lippmann, *Men of Destiny*, pp. 8–9.

126. Quoted in Hofstadter, *The American Political Tradition*, p. 295.

127. Herbert Hoover, *American Individualism* (Garden City, N.Y.: Doubleday, 1922), pp. 4–5, 7–8.

128. *Ibid.*, pp. 9–10.

129. *Ibid.*, pp. 19, 36, 33.

130. *Ibid.*, pp. 17, 37–41.

131. *Ibid.*, pp. 54–55.

132. *Ibid.*, p. 50.

133. *Ibid.*, pp. 63–64.

134. *Ibid.*, p. 71.

135. Herbert Hoover, *The New Day: Campaign Speeches of Herbert Hoover, 1928* (Stanford, Cal.: Stanford U. Press, 1928), p. 42.

136. Quoted in Albert U. Romasco, *The Poverty of Abundance: Hoover, the Nation, the Depression* (New York: Oxford U. Press, 1965), p. 17.

137. Hoover, *The New Day*, pp. 23, 53, 202; Romasco, p. 19; William Appleman Williams, "What This Country Needs...," *New York Review of Books*, XV (November 5, 1970), pp. 7–11.

138. Hicks, pp. 64, 67.

139. Hoover, *The New Day*, p. 157.

140. *Ibid.*, pp. 30–35.

141. Quoted in Romasco, pp. 17–18.

142. Herbert Hoover, *The Challenge to Liberty* (New York: Scribner, 1934), pp. 126, 125–26.

143. Quoted in Binkley, p. 282.

144. Hoover, *The New Day*, p. 19.

145. Hofstadter, *The American Political Tradition*, pp. 305–306.

146. Quoted in *ibid.*, p. 307.

147. Quoted in *ibid.*, pp. 307–308.

148. See, for example, Dumond, pp. 432–33, 538.

149. Hicks, p. 64.

150. Dumond, pp. 438–39.

151. Perkins, p. 298; Hoover, *The New Day*, p. 39.

152. Hoover, *The New Day*, p. 39.

153. Warren, p. 157.

154. Quoted in Dumond, p. 443.

155. Quoted in Warren, p. 161.

156. Quoted in Dumond, p. 444.

157. Clarke A. Chambers, *Seedtime of Reform: American Social Service and Social Action, 1918–1933* (Minneapolis: U. of Minnesota Press, 1963), pp. 33, 50–51, 61–71, 157–58.

158. Kenneth Campbell MacKay: *The Progressive Movement of 1924* (New York: Octagon, 1966), pp. 16–17.

159. "Where Are the Pre-War Radicals?" *Survey*, LV (February 1, 1926), 556–57; George Soule, "Radicalism," in *Civilization in the United States*, p. 272.

160. Arthur S. Link, "What Happened to the Progressive Movement in the 1920's?" *American Historical Review*, LXIV (July 1959), 844.

161. Richard Hofstadter, *The Age of Reform: From Bryan to F.D.R.* (New York: Vintage, 1960), p. 286.

162. Hannah Arendt, "Truth and Politics," *New Yorker*, XLIII (February 25, 1967), 88.

163. Chambers, pp. 89, 93–105; John Chynoweth Burnham, "The New Psychology: From Narcissism to Social Control," in *Change and Continuity*, pp. 367–74, 392–93.

164. Chambers, p. 53.

165. Quoted in *ibid.*, p. 81. See also Roosevelt, *The Public Papers*, V, 233.

166. Lynd and Lynd, pp. 458–70.

167. Quoted in Quint and Ferrell, p. 19.

5. The Individual and His Race

1. Quoted in Amy Jacques Garvey, *Garvey and Garveyism*, intro. John Henrik Clarke (New York: Collier, 1970), p. 29.

2. See Philip Gleason, "The Melting Pot: Symbol of Fusion or Confusion?" *American Quarterly*, XVI (Spring 1964), esp. pp. 40–45.

3. Kenneth Allsop, *The Bootleggers and Their Era* (Garden City, N.Y.: Doubleday, 1961), p. 238.

4. Fred D. Pasley, *Al Capone: The*

Biography of a Self-made Man (London: Faber, 1966), p. 79; Allsop, pp. 259, 293.

5. Richard Wright, conversation with Theodore Dreiser and author, June 2, 1944.

6. Allsop, p. 293.

7. *Ibid.*, p. 255; Andrew Sinclair, *Era of Excess: A Social History of the Prohibition Movement* (New York: Harper, 1964), pp. 228–29; Pasley, p. 4.

8. Quoted in Allsop, p. 250.

9. Quoted in Sinclair, *Era of Excess*, pp. 228–29.

10. Franklin Moss, seminar paper for American Studies 402, Cornell University, March 7, 1968.

11. Jules Abels, *In the Time of Silent Cal* (New York: Putnam, 1969), pp. 100–101; John Toland, "Sad Ballad of the Real Bonnie and Clyde," *New York Times Magazine*, February 18, 1968, p. 27, and *The Dillinger Days* (New York: Random, 1963), p. 35; John Kobler, *Capone: The Life and World of Al Capone* (New York: Putnam, 1971), pp. 306–15; Allsop, pp. 291, 293; Pasley, p. 300; Edward Dean Sullivan, "I Know You, Al," *North American Review*, CCXXVIII (September 1929), 257–64.

12. Quoted in Allsop, p. 291.

13. Sullivan, p. 263.

14. Allsop, p. 56.

15. Herbert Asbury, *The Great Illusion: An Informal History of Prohibition* (Garden City, N.Y.: Doubleday, 1950), pp. 136–37; Allsop, pp. 27–28.

16. Paul A. Carter, *The Decline and Revival of the Social Gospel: Social and Political Liberalism in American Protestant Churches, 1920–1940* (Ithaca, N.Y.: Cornell U. Press, 1956), pp. 31–45. Cf. Mabel Walker Willebrandt, *The Inside of Prohibition* (Indianapolis: Bobbs-Merrill, 1929), p. 304.

17. Louis Raymond Reid, "The Small Town," in *Civilization in the United States*, p. 287.

18. Fabian Franklin, *What Prohibition Has Done to America* (New York: Harcourt, 1922), p. 73.

19. Kanhaya Lal Gauba, *Uncle Sham: The Strange Tale of a Civilization Run Amuck* (New York: Kendall, 1929), pp. 215–16.

20. Jerry R. Tompkins, ed., *D-Days at Dayton: Reflections on the Scopes Trial* (Baton Rouge, La.: Louisiana State U. Press, 1965), p. 21.

21. Sinclair, *Era of Excess*, p. 210.

22. Asbury, p. 165.

23. Allsop, p. 250.

24. *Ibid.*, p. 141.

25. Asbury, pp. 159–60.

26. Leuchtenburg, *The Perils of Prosperity*, p. 214.

27. Quoted in Allsop, pp. 85–86.

28. Edmund Wilson, "The Lexicon of Prohibition," *The American Earthquake: A Documentary of the Twenties and Thirties* (Garden City, N.Y.: Doubleday, 1964), pp. 89–91; Sinclair, *Era of Excess*, pp. 233, 236–37.

29. Willebrandt, pp. 272–73.

30. Sinclair, *Era of Excess*, p. 229. See also Abels, p. 103.

31. The principal sources used in the present account of the case are the following: *The Sacco-Vanzetti Case: Transcript of the Record of the Trial of Nicola Sacco and Bartolomeo Vanzetti in the Courts of Massachusetts and Subsequent Proceedings*, 6 vols. (New York: Holt, 1928–29); Herbert B. Ehrmann, *The Case That Will Not Die: Commonwealth vs. Sacco and Vanzetti* (Boston: Little, 1969); David Felix, *Protest: Sacco-Vanzetti and the Intellectuals* (Bloomington, Ind.: Indiana U. Press, 1965); Marion Denman Frankfurter and Gardner Jackson, eds., *The Letters of Sacco and Vanzetti* (1928; rpt. New York: Dutton, 1960); Louis Joughin and Edmund M. Morgan, *The Legacy of Sacco and Vanzetti* (Chicago: Quadrangle, 1964); Francis Russell, *Tragedy in Dedham: The Story of the Sacco-Vanzetti Case* (New York: McGraw-Hill, 1962); Robert P. Weeks, ed., *Commonwealth vs. Sacco and Vanzetti* (Englewood Cliffs, N.J.: Prentice-Hall, 1958).

32. Weeks, pp. 1–5.

33. Quoted in Joughin and Morgan, p. 216–17.

34. Quoted in Ehrmann, pp. 460–72.

35. Quoted in *ibid.*, p. 485.

36. *Ibid.*, pp. 486–92, 501–502, 529. See also Russell, pp. 380–403.

37. Quoted in Ehrmann, p. 532.

38. *The Sacco-Vanzetti Case*, p. 1875, quoted in Weeks, p. 120.

39. See above, pp. 90–91.

40. *The Sacco-Vanzetti Case*, pp. 1875–78, quoted in Weeks, pp. 119–23.

41. Russell, pp. 6, 419. Cf. *ibid.*, pp. 380, 422, 436.

42. Quoted in *ibid.*, p. 381.

43. Gauba, pp. 66–67.

44. John Moffatt Mecklin, *The Ku Klux Klan: A Study of the American Mind* (New York: Harcourt, 1924), pp. 3, 84, 90, 131; Walter White, *Rope & Faggot: A Biogra-*

phy of *Judge Lynch* (New York: Knopf, 1929), pp. 19 ff.; David M. Chalmers, *Hooded Americanism: The First Century of the Ku Klux Klan, 1865–1965* (Garden City, N.Y.: Doubleday, 1965), pp. 2–4, 33, 41, 111, 118, 291–92; Robert Moats Miller, "The Ku Klux Klan," in *Change and Continuity*, pp. 227–28, 235–36, 249–50.

45. Harold Stearns, *Liberalism in America: Its Origin, Its Temporary Collapse, Its Future* (New York: Boni & Liveright, 1919), p. viii.

46. McCoy, *Calvin Coolidge*, pp. 200, 328–29.

47. David Lowe, *Ku Klux Klan: The Invisible Empire* (New York: Norton, 1967), pp. 19–20, 65–67.

48. Moore, *A Catholic Runs for President*, pp. 157–58.

49. James Weldon Johnson, "Harlem: The Culture Capital," in *The New Negro*, ed. Alain Locke (1925; rpt. New York: Atheneum, 1968), p. 310.

50. Harold Cruse, *The Crisis of the Negro Intellectual* (New York: Morrow, 1967), p. 47. See also Garvey, pp. 1–15; Theodore Draper, "The Fantasy of Black Nationalism," *Commentary*, XLVIII (September 1969), 31–32.

51. James Weldon Johnson, *Black Manhattan* (1930; rpt. New York: Atheneum, 1968), p. 144.

52. *Ibid.*, pp. 147–58.

53. Garvey, p. 21.

54. Quoted in *ibid.*, p. 29; Johnson, *Black Manhattan*, pp. 251–56.

55. Johnson, *Black Manhattan*, pp. 254–55.

56. *Ibid.*, p. 257.

57. Quoted in Garvey, pp. 23, 29, 33.

58. Langston Hughes, *The Big Sea: An Autobiography* (1940; rpt. New York: Hill, 1963), pp. 102–103, 325; Johnson, *Black Manhattan*, pp. 258–59; Garvey, pp. 54–55; Edmund David Cronon, *Black Moses: The Story of Marcus Garvey and the Universal Negro Improvement Association* (Madison, Wisc.: U. of Wisconsin Press, 1968), pp. 220–22; Cruse, pp. 124–25; Draper, pp. 32–33.

59. Quoted in Draper, p. 31. See also Elliott M. Rudwick, "DuBois versus Garvey: Race Propagandists at War," *Journal of Negro Education*, XXVIII (Fall 1959), 421–29.

60. Robert H. Kinzer and Edward Sagarin, *The Negro in American Business: The Conflict between Separatism and Integration* (New York: Greenberg, 1950), pp. 68–69.

61. Sterling D. Spero and Abram L. Harris, *The Black Worker: The Negro and the Labor Movement* (New York: Columbia U. Press, 1931), pp. 136–38, 385–88; Leonard Broom and Norval D. Glenn, *Transformation of the Negro American* (New York: Harper, 1965), p. 49.

62. E. Franklin Frazier, *Black Bourgeoisie: The Rise of a New Middle Class in the United States* (1957; rpt. New York: Collier, 1962), p. 76.

63. *The Blacker the Berry . . .: A Novel of Negro Life* (1929; rpt. New York: Collier, 1970), p. 3.

64. Frazier, pp. 184–88.

65. Cruse, p. 81.

66. Claude McKay, *A Long Way from Home* (1957; rpt. New York: Arno Press and *New York Times*, 1969), p. 340.

67. *Ibid.*, p. 244.

68. *Ibid.*, pp. 260, 321.

69. *Ibid.*, p. 270.

70. *Ibid.*, p. 148.

71. Cruse, pp. 34–39, 48, 80–85.

72. Johnson, *Black Manhattan*, pp. 160–68.

73. Rudolph Fisher, *The Walls of Jericho* (1928; rpt. New York: Arno Press and *New York Times*, 1969), pp. 78–79.

74. *The Blacker the Berry*, p. 192.

75. Author's recollection. See also Malcolm Cowley, *Exile's Return: A Narrative of Ideas* (New York: Norton, 1934), p. 230.

76. Cruse, pp. 71–80; Chadwick Hansen, "Social Influences on Jazz Style: Chicago, 1920–30," *American Quarterly*, XII (Winter 1960), 493–507.

77. Saunders Redding, "The Negro Writer and American Literature," in *Anger, and Beyond: The Negro Writer in the United States*, ed. Herbert Hill, Perennial Library (New York: Harper, 1968), pp. 15–16.

78. Quoted from New York *Evening Bulletin*, August 2, 1924, in Garvey, p. 160.

79. Quoted in Garvey, p. 91.

80. Johnson, *Black Manhattan*, pp. 202–80; Redding, pp. 11–16; Arthur P. Davis, "Growing Up in the New Negro Renaissance: 1920–1935," *Negro American Literature Forum*, II (Fall 1968), 53–59; James A. Emanuel and Theodore L. Gross, eds., *Dark Symphony: Negro Literature in America* (New York: Free Press, 1968), pp. 62–68; Cruse, pp. 11–63; S. P. Fullinwider, *The Mind and Mood of Black Ameri-*

ca: *20th Century Thought* (Homewood, Ill.: Dorsey, 1969), pp 123–71.

81. Locke, Foreword, *The New Negro*, p. xvii. See also Johnson, *Black Manhattan*, pp. 276–77.

82. John Heintz, "Alienation and Black Culture: The 1920s," seminar paper for English 480, Cornell University, April 30, 1970.

83. Ellen Glanz, "The Poets of the Harlem Renaissance: Themes of Identity," seminar paper for English 480, Cornell University, April 23, 1970.

84. Stephen H. Bronz, *Roots of Negro Racial Consciousness: The 1920's: Three Harlem Renaissance Writers* (New York: Libra, 1964), p. 72.

85. Claude McKay, "The Tropics in New York," in *The New Negro*, p. 135, and *Selected Poems of Claude McKay* (New York: Bookman Associates, 1953), p. 31.

86. "Harlem Dancer," *Selected Poems*, p. 61.

87. "Harlem Shadows," *ibid.*, p. 60.

88. "White Houses," *ibid.*, p. 78, and in *The New Negro*, p. 134.

89. "Baptism," in *The New Negro*, p. 133, and *Selected Poems*, p. 35.

90. "If We Must Die," *Selected Poems*, p. 36.

91. "America," *ibid*, p. 59.

92. McKay, *A Long Way from Home*, pp. 133, 135.

93. This view coincides with the one set forth by Bronz, pp. 70–75.

94. *Caroling Dusk* (New York: Harper, 1927), p. xi.

95. *Ibid.*, p. xii.

96. Quoted in Bronz, p. 57.

97. Countee Cullen, *Color* (New York: Harper, 1925), pp. 22, 23, 79, 106 and *On These I Stand: An Anthology of the Best Poems of Countee Cullen* (New York: Harper, 1947), pp. 65, 71.

98. Blanche E. Ferguson, *Countee Cullen and the Negro Renaissance* (New York: Dodd, 1966), pp. 30–31.

99. Quoted in Bronz, p. 58.

100. *Color*, pp. 36–41.

101. *Ibid.*, p. 3.

102. *Ibid.*, pp. 26–35. See also Bronz, pp. 52–53.

103. *On These I Stand*, pp. 104–37.

104. Langston Hughes, "The Negro Artist and the Racial Mountain," *Nation*, CXXII (June 23, 1926), rpt. in *Black Expression: Essays by and About Black Americans in the Creative Arts*, ed. Addison Gayle, Jr. (New York: Weybright, 1969), p. 263.

105. *The Weary Blues*, intro. Carl Van Vechten (New York: Knopf, 1926), p. 19.

106. *Ibid.*, p. 30.

107. *Ibid.*, p. 43.

108. *Ibid.*, p. 99.

109. *Ibid.*, p. 51.

110. Hughes, "The Negro Artist," p. 262.

111. Quoted in James A. Emanuel, *Langston Hughes* (New York: Twayne, 1967), pp. 31–32, 137–40.

112. *The Weary Blues*, p. 39.

113. *Ibid.*, pp. 23–24; Emanuel, pp. 138–39.

114. *The Weary Blues*, p. 107.

115. Langston Hughes, *Selected Poems* (New York: Knopf, 1959), pp. 160–61.

116. *The Weary Blues*, p. 109.

117. *The New Negro*, pp. 113–14.

118. *Ibid.*, pp. 115–26.

119. *Ibid.*, p. 118.

120. *Ibid.*, pp. 105–12.

121. *Ibid.*, pp. 85–95.

122. "The City of Refuge" and "Vestiges," in *ibid.*, pp. 57–84.

123. "Carma" and "Fern," in *ibid.*, pp. 96–104.

124. *The Blacker the Berry*, p. 3.

125. *Ibid.*, pp. 226–27.

126. Jean Toomer, *Cane*, intro. Arna Bontemps, Perennial Classic (1923; rpt. New York: Harper, 1969); Bontemps, in *ibid.*, p. xii; Robert Bone, review of *Cane*, *New York Times Book Review*, January 19, 1969, p. 3; Todd Lieber, "Design and Movement in *Cane*," *CLA Journal*, XIII (September 1969), 37–38.

127. Quoted in Bontemps, intro. to *Cane*, p. ix, and Lieber, pp. 36–37.

128. Fullinwider, pp. 136–44; Bontemps, pp. viii–ix, xiii–xv.

129. *Cane*, p. 211.

130. *Ibid.*, p. 217.

131. *Ibid.*, p. 212.

132. *Ibid.*, p. 237.

133. *Ibid.*, p. 239.

134. Hughes, *The Big Sea*, p. 303.

135. *Ibid.*, pp. 303–304.

136. *Not Without Laughter* (1930; rpt. New York: Collier, 1969), p. 303.

137. *Ibid.*, p. 304.

138. Fullinwider, pp. 168–69.

139. Alain Locke, "The New Negro," in *The New Negro*, p. 6.

140. *Ibid.*, p. 7.

141. *Ibid.*, p. 12.

142. Arthur A. Schomburg, "The Negro Digs up His Past," in *The New Negro*, p. 231.

143. Arthur Huff Fauset, "American Negro Folk Literature," in *ibid.*, p. 242.

144. Alain Locke, "The Legacy of the

Ancestral Arts," in *ibid.*, pp. 254–67; James Porter, *Modern Negro Art* (New York: Dryden, 1943), chs. 5, 6. Cf. Meyer Schapiro, "Race, Nationality and Art," *Art Front*, I (March 1936), 10–12.

145. Cruse, pp. 22–28; Bruce Kellner, *Carl Van Vechten and the Irrever-*
ent Decades (Norman, Okla.: U. of Oklahoma Press, 1968), pp. 195–223; Carl Van Vechten, *Nigger Heaven* (New York: Knopf, 1926); McKay, *A Long Way from Home*, pp. 318–20; Hughes, *The Big Sea*, pp. 268–72.

6. The Individual and His Protagonists

1. Ernest Hemingway, *A Farewell to Arms*, intro. Robert Penn Warren, Modern Standard Authors (1929; rpt. New York: Scribner, 1949), p. 252.
2. Quoted in McCoy, *Calvin Coolidge*, p. 22.
3. White, *A Puritan*, p. 346.
4. John W. Ward, "The Meaning of Lindbergh's Flight," *American Quarterly*, X (Spring 1958), 13–15.
5. Quoted in *ibid.*, p. 9. Cf. Abels, *In the Time of Silent Cal*, p. 135.
6. Quoted in Ward, p. 11.
7. *We* (New York: Putnam, 1927), pp. 217–18.
8. Author's recollections; Leuchtenburg, *The Perils of Prosperity*, p. 195.
9. Arthur Mizener, "The 'Lost Generation,'" in *A Time of Harvest: American Literature, 1910–1960*, ed. Robert E Spiller (New York: Hill, 1962), p. 79.
10. Ring W. Lardner. "Sport and Play," in *Civilization in the United States*, p. 461. See also Gregory P. Stone, "American Sports: Play and Dis-Play," *Chicago Review*, IX (Fall 1955), 83–100.
11. Lynd and Lynd, *Middletown*, pp. 244–47.
12. H. L. Mencken, *Prejudices: Fifth Series* (New York: Knopf, 1926), p. 304.
13. *Main Street* (New York: Harcourt, 1920), p. 138.
14. *Ibid.*, p. 141.
15. *Ibid.*, p. 186.
16. *Ibid.*, pp. 209–12, 217–23.
17. *Ibid.*, pp. 120–21.
18. *Ibid.*, pp. 186–92.
19. *Ibid.*, p. 422.
20. *Ibid.*, p. 451.
21. For this suggestion I am indebted to a seminar discussion led by Rosalind Kenworthy, Cornell University, Spring 1969. See also Mark Schorer, Afterword, in Sinclair Lewis, *Main Street*, Signet Classics (1920; rpt. New York: New American Library, 1961), pp. 433–34.
22. *Main Street* (1920), pp. 54–58.
23. *Ibid.*, p. 423.
24. Lippmann, *Men of Destiny*, p. 78.
25. *Main Street*, p. 430.
26. *Babbitt* (New York: Harcourt, 1922), p. 2.
27. *Ibid.*, p. 85.
28. *Ibid.*, pp. 127–28, 188–89.
29. *Ibid.*, p. 149.
30. *Ibid.*, p. 300.
31. Cf. Mark Schorer, Afterword, in Sinclair Lewis, *Babbitt*, Signet Classics (1922; rpt. New York: New American Library, 1961), pp. 322–23.
32. *Babbitt* (1922), p. 401.
33. *Arrowsmith* (New York: Harcourt, 1925), pp. 222–28, 248 ff.
34. *Ibid.*, p. 44.
35. *Ibid.*, p. 228.
36. *Ibid.*, p. 275.
37. *Ibid.*, pp. 279–80.
38. *Ibid.*, pp. 280–81.
39. *Ibid.*, p. 448.
40. My views concur with those found in Mark Schorer, Afterword, in Sinclair Lewis, *Arrowsmith*, Signet Classics (1925; rpt. New York: New American Library, 1961), pp. 434–35, and Charles E. Rosenberg, "Martin Arrowsmith: The Scientist as Hero." *American Quarterly*, XV (Fall 1963), 447–58.
41. *One Man's Initiation: 1917* (1920; unexpurgated ed., Ithaca, N.Y.: Cornell U. Press, 1969), pp. 46, 50, 55.
42. *Ibid.*, pp. 157–58.
43. *Ibid.*, pp. 159, 166.
44. *Ibid.*, pp. 9–10.
45. *Ibid.*, pp. 13, 23.
46. *Ibid.*, pp. 25–26.
47. *Three Soldiers* (1921; rpt. New York: Modern Library, 1932), p. 17.
48. *Ibid.*, p. 51.
49. *Ibid.*, pp. 163–65.
50. *Ibid.*, pp. 211–12.
51. *Ibid.*, pp. 220–21.
52. *Ibid..* pp. 225–26.
53. *Ibid.*, pp. 251, 255.
54. *Ibid.*, p. 287.
55. *Ibid.*, pp. 427–28.
56. *Ibid.*, p. 448.

57. *Ibid.*, pp. 455, 462.
58. *Ibid.*, pp. 460 ff.
59. *Ibid.*, p. 458.
60. Cf. John H. Wrenn, *John Dos Passos* (New York: Twayne, 1961), pp. 110–12.
61. John Dos Passos, seminar discussion, Cornell University, April 1959.
62. *Manhattan Transfer* (New York: Harper, 1925), p. 3.
63. *Ibid.*, p. 283.
64. *Ibid.*, p. 12.
65. *Ibid.*, p. 345.
66. *Ibid.*, pp. 353, 404.
67. Wrenn, pp. 123–25.
68. *Manhattan Transfer*, p. 227.
69. F. Scott Fitzgerald, *The Great Gatsby* (1925; rpt. New York: Modern Library, 1934), p. 216.
70. *Ibid.*, p. 185.
71. *Ibid.*, pp. 156–62.
72. *Ibid.*, p. 182.
73. *Ibid.*, pp. 160, 185.
74. *Ibid.*, p. 218.
75. *Ibid.*, p. 212.
76. *Ibid.*, p. 218.
77. My conclusions about the novel have been partially shaped by a seminar discussion led by Leo Marx, Cornell University, April 1962.
78. *A Farewell to Arms*, p. 191.
79. *Ibid.*, pp. 252, 258.
80. *Ibid.*, p. 338.
81. *Ibid.*, p. 342.
82. *Ibid.*, p. 343.
83. Ralph Ellison, *Shadow and Act* (New York: Random, 1964), p. 38.
84. *The Sun Also Rises* (1926; rpt. New York: Scribner, 1953), p. 215.
85. *Ibid.*, pp. 216–17.
86. *Ibid.*, p. 245.
87. I am again indebted to Leo Marx's discussion (see note 77 above).
88. *The Sun Also Rises*, p. 247.
89. Cf. Carlos Baker, *Hemingway: The Writer as Artist* (Princeton, N.J.: Princeton U. Press, 1952), pp. 79–93; Arthur Mizener, "*The Sun Also Rises*," *Twelve Great American Novels* (New York: World, 1967), pp. 120–41; Mark Spilka, "The Death of Love in *The Sun Also Rises*." in *Twelve Original Essays on Great American Novels*, ed. Charles Shapiro (Detroit: Wayne State U. Press, 1958), rpt. in *Studies in "The Sun Also Rises*," comp. William White (Columbus, O.: Merrill, 1969), pp. 73–85. See also Frederick J. Hoffman, "Fiction of the Jazz Age," in *Change and Continuity*, pp. 310–18; Robert L. Lair, "Hemingway and Cezanne,"

Modern Fiction Studies, VI (Summer 1960), 165–68.
90. *The Enormous Room* (1922; rpt. New York: Modern Library, 1934), titles of chs. 1, 3, and 7, for example, and p. 113.
91. A detailed analysis of the parallels may be found in David E. Smith, "*The Enormous Room* and *The Pilgrim's Progress*," *Twentieth Century Literature*, XI (July 1965), 67–75.
92. I am indebted for some of my analysis, especially in this paragraph about language, to Marilyn Gaull, "Language and Identity: A Study of E. E. Cummings' *The Enormous Room*," *American Quarterly*, XIX (Winter 1967), 645–62. Although my own approach and orientation differ from hers, and my general interpretation was developed before I read her article, she has provided valuable support for my argument and thus enabled me to expand and refine it. In four instances I have used in behalf of my purposes illustrations that she has used in behalf of hers.
93. *The Enormous Room*, pp. 3, 169, 167, 201.
94. *Ibid.*, p. 19.
95. *Ibid.*, p. 116.
96. *Ibid.*, p. 23.
97. *Ibid.*, p. 111.
98. *Ibid.*, p. 72.
99. *Ibid.*, p. 255.
100. *Ibid.*, p. 226.
101. *Ibid.*, p. 257.
102. *Ibid.*, p. 125.
103. *Ibid.*, p. 97.
104. *Ibid.*, p. 122.
105. *Ibid.*, p. 239.
106. *Ibid.*, p. 271.
107. I generally concur with the structural analysis set forth in Norman Friedman, *e. e. cummings: The Growth of a Writer* (Carbondale, Ill.: Southern Illinois U. Press, 1964), pp. 25–32; but my concerns and interpretation differ from Friedman's.
108. *The Enormous Room*, p. 139.
109. *Ibid.*, p. 239.
110. Cowley, *Exile's Return*, p. 50.
111. *The Enormous Room*, p. ix.
112. Cowley, pp. 69 ff.
113. Daniel Aaron, *Writers on the Left: Episodes in American Literary Communism* (New York: Harcourt, 1961), pp. 10 ff.
114. Caroline F. Ware, *Greenwich Village 1920–1930* (Boston: Houghton, 1935), pp. 4–6. 404–21.
115. Edmund Wilson, *The Shores of Light: A Literary Chronicle of the*

Twenties and Thirties (New York: Farrar, 1952), p. x.

116. Quoted in Aaron, p. 107n. See also Susan J. Turner, *A History of "The Freeman": Literary Landmark of the Early Twenties* (New York: Columbia U. Press, 1963), pp. 33–55; William L. O'Neill, ed., *Echoes of Revolt: THE MASSES, 1911–1917* (Chicago: Quadrangle, 1966), pp. 18–19, 22–23.

117. Alan Solomon, "The Crisis of the Object in the 20th Century," lecture, Cornell University, April 25, 1961; Meyer Schapiro, "Rebellion in Art," in *America in Crisis*, ed. Daniel Aaron (New York: Knopf, 1952), pp. 202–42. See also Erich Kahler, *Man the Measure: A New Approach to History* (New York: Pantheon, 1943), *passim*, and *The Tower and the Abyss: An Inquiry into the Transformation of Man* (New York: Viking, 1957), *passim*.

118. E. H. Gombrich, *Art and Illusion: A Study in the Psychology of Pictorial Representation* (New York: Pantheon, 1960), p. 281.

119. See also *ibid.*, ch. 8.

120. Stephen Kaplan, seminar report for American Studies 402, Cornell University, April 18, 1962.

121. José Ortega y Gasset, *The Dehumanization of Art and Other Writings on Art and Culture* (Garden City, N.Y.: Doubleday Anchor, 1956), p. 8.

122. *Ibid.*, p. 13.

123. *Ibid.*, pp. 20–21.

124. *Ibid.*, pp. 35–36.

125. Kenneth Clark, *The Nude: A Study in Ideal Form* (New York: Pantheon, 1956), p. 370. Cf. Lionel Trilling, "The Nude Renewed," *Griffin*, VI (July 1957), pp. 4–12.

126. Robert E. Knoll, *Robert McAlmon, Expatriate Publisher and Writer*, U. of Nebraska Studies, n.s. 18 (Lincoln, Neb.: U. of Nebraska, August 1957), pp. 11–12.

127. Harold Loeb, seminar discussion, Cornell University, May 16. 1962.

128. Daniel Bell, *The Reforming of General Education: The Columbia College Experience in Its National Setting* (New York: Columbia U. Press, 1966), p. 233.

129. André Breton, *Manifestes du surréalisme* (Paris: Gallimard, 1963), pp. 12–13.

130. *Surrealism & Revolution*, documents in translation, first published by Ztangi (Chicago) and distributed by Solidarity Bookshop [1966?]; reissued by the "Wooden Shoe" (London) and distributed by Coptic Press [1967], mimeographed, p. 9.

131. *Ibid.*, p. 5.

132. Quoted in Cowley, p. 158.

133. John I. H. Baur, *Revolution and Tradition in Modern American Art* (Cambridge, Mass.: Harvard U. Press, 1951), p. 3; Robert Rosenblum, *Cubism and Twentieth-Century Art*, rev. ed. (New York: Abrams, [1966]), p. 222. See also Sam Hunter, *Modern American Painting and Sculpture* (New York: Dell, 1959); Milton W. Brown, *American Painting from the Armory Show to the Depression* (Princeton, N.J.: Princeton U. Press, 1955).

134. John I. H. Baur, *Nature in Abstraction: The Relation of Abstract Painting and Sculpture to Nature in Twentieth-Century American Art* (New York: Macmillan, for Whitney Museum of American Art, 1958), p. 7.

135. Quoted in Hunter, p. 92.

136. See also Carolyn Wynne, "Aspects of Space: John Marin and William Faulkner," *American Quarterly*, XVI (Spring 1964), 59–71; Felix Marti Ibañez, "The Psychological Impact of Atomic Science on Modern Art: An Experiment in Correlation," *Journal of Clinical and Experimental Psychotherapy*, XIII (1952), rpt. "An Experiment in Correlation: The Psychological Impact of Atomic Science on Modern Art," *Art and Architecture*, LXX (January 1953), 16–17, 30–31, 33; (February 1953), 18–19, 36–38; (March 1953), 22–23, 33–35.

137. Robert H. Elias, "Letters," *Story*, X (January 1937), 108–109; George Haines IV, "Forms of Imaginative Prose, 1900–1940," *Southern Review*, VII (Spring 1942), 755–75; Michael J. Hoffman, *The Development of Abstractionism in the Writings of Gertrude Stein* (Philadelphia: U. of Pennsylvania Press, 1965), pp. 54, 162; Allegra Stewart, *Gertrude Stein and the Present* (Cambridge, Mass.: Harvard U. Press, 1967), pp. 36–37, 85, 141; Edwin E. Slosson, *Major Prophets of To-day* (Boston: Little, 1914), pp. 44–103; Georges Poulet, *Studies in Human Time*, trans. Elliott Coleman (Baltimore: Johns Hopkins Press, 1956), pp. 22–35.

138. See also Graham Hough, *Image and Experience: Studies in a Literary Revolution* (London: Duckworth, 1960).

7. The Individual and Himself

1. *The World in Falseface* (New York: Knopf, 1923), p. xxix.
2. *Human Nature and Conduct: An Introduction to Social Psychology* (1922; rpt. New York: Modern Library, 1930), p. 12.
3. *Ibid.*, p. 19.
4. Arthur E. Murphy, "John Dewey and American Liberalism," *Journal of Philosophy*, LVII (June 23, 1960), 420. See also Cushing Strout, "Pragmatism in Retrospect: The Legacy of James and Dewey," *Virginia Quarterly Review*, XLIII (Winter 1967), 123–34.
5. Dewey, *Human Nature*, p. 34.
6. Stearns, *Liberalism in America*, p. 183.
7. Murphy, p. 428.
8. *The Modern Temper: A Study and a Confession*, Harvest Books (1929; rpt. New York: Harcourt, 1956), p. 74.
9. *Ibid.*, pp. 160–61.
10. *Ibid.*, p. 169.
11. *A Preface to Morals* (New York: Macmillan, 1929), p. 175.
12. *Ibid.*, p. 180.
13. *Ibid.*, p. 184.
14. *Ibid.*, p. 209.
15. *Ibid.*, p. 220.
16. *Ibid.*, p. 323.
17. *Ibid.*, pp. 329–30.
18. *The World in Falseface*, p. x.
19. *Ibid.*, p. xxix.
20. Edna St. Vincent Millay, "First Fig," *A Few Figs from Thistles: Poems and Sonnets* (New York: Shay, 1922), p. 9.

Index